WITH
STER
GIRLS

Volume 6

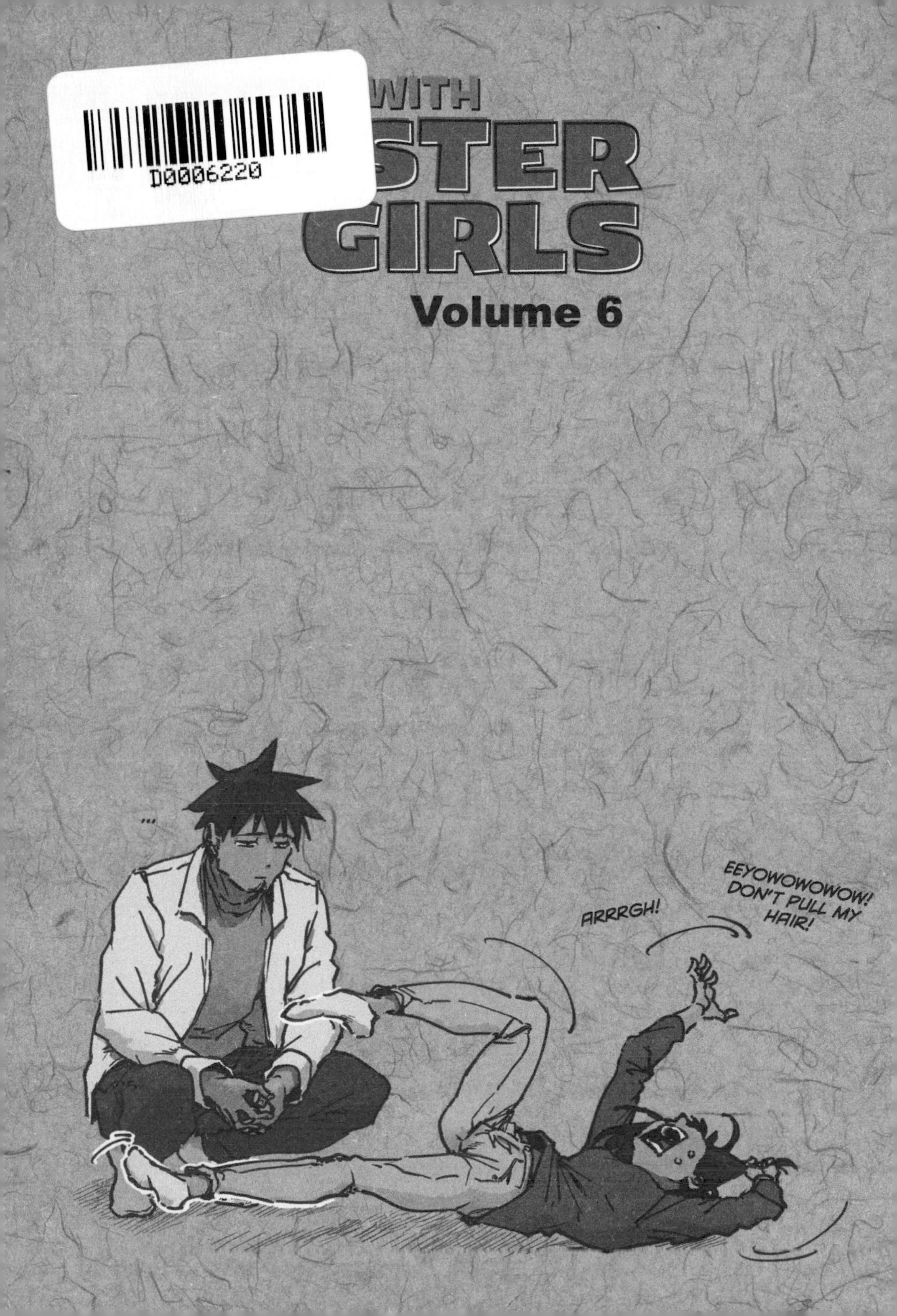
EEYOWOWOWOW! DON'T PULL MY HAIR!
ARRRGH!
...

INTERVIEWS WITH
MONSTER GIRLS

Characters

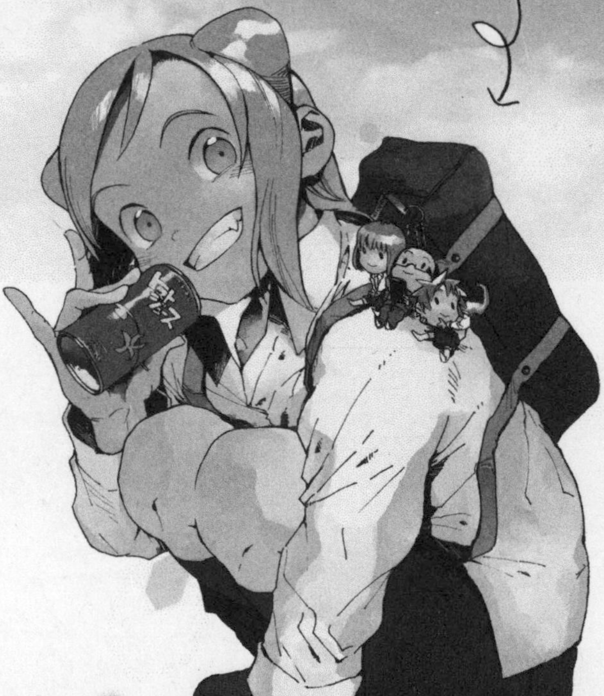

Vampire
Hikari Takanashi
Class 1-B

- Likes liver, tomato juice.
- Receives blood from the government once a month.
- Opinions on romance: plenty; actual experience: none.

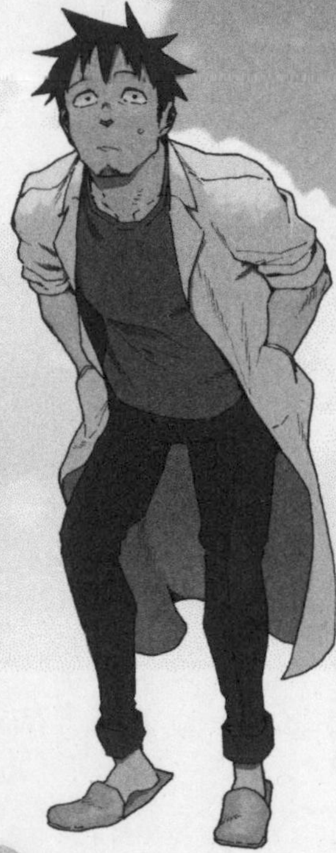

Tetsuo Takahashi

- Biology teacher.
- Fascinated by demi studies since college.
- Tries his best to understand demis.

**"Demi-humans" are just a little different from us—
these days, they go by "Demis."
Their problems are as adorable as they are.**

Can: Tomato juice

*DEMIS: SHORT FOR "DEMI-HUMANS."

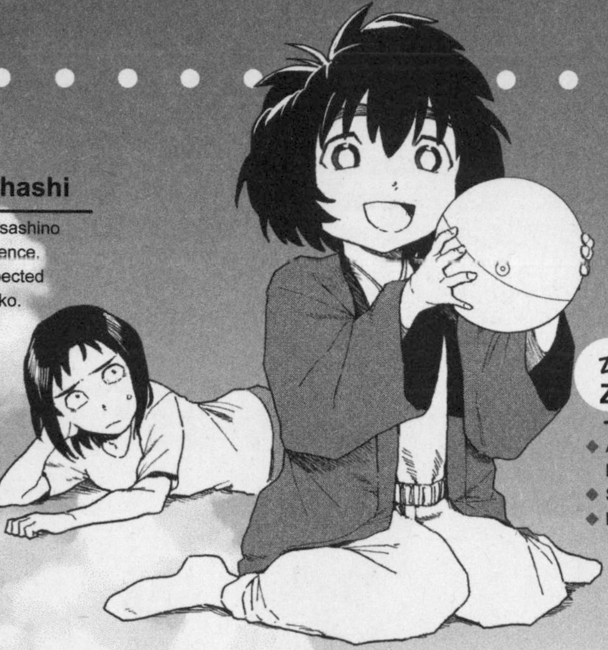

Yoko Takahashi

- Freshman at Musashino University of Science.
- Lives with unexpected roommate Zashiko.
- Only Yoko can see Zashiko.
- Same eyes as Takahashi-sensei.

Zashiki-warashi
Zashiko

- A spirit from Tohoku-region legends.
- Said to bring happiness.
- Likes: eating and sleeping.

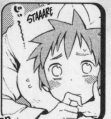

Dullahan
Kyoko Machi Class 1-B

- A demi of Irish legend whose head and body are separate.
- Likes her head to be held.
- In love with Takahashi-sensei.
- Top grades—has even been No. 1 in her class.

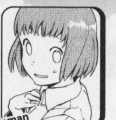
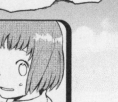

Snow Woman
Yuki Kusakabe Class 1-A

- Exudes cold air and weeps ice under stress.
- Sometimes wishes she could control her powers.
- Embarrassed to admit she likes gag manga; tries to hide it.

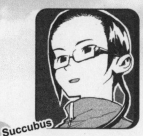

Succubus
Sakie Sato

- Math teacher.
- Lives in an isolated, dilapidated house so as not to unintentionally arouse anyone.
- Has a crush on Takahashi-sensei; has tried to arouse him.
- Romantic history: zilch.

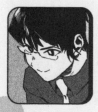

Soma

- Assistant Professor at Musashino University of Science.
- Physicist.
- Takahashi-sensei's college classmate.

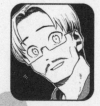

Koji Takanashi

- Father of Hikari and Himari; stay-at-home dad.
- On good terms with Kyoko's parents.
- Trying to learn not to shake too much while carrying Kyoko's head.

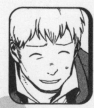

Ugaki

- Detective with the Demi Affairs Dept.
- Father figure to Sato-sensei, a succubus on his beat.
- Encourages Sato-sensei's love for Takahashi-sensei.

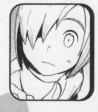

Kurtz

- Ugaki's junior detective.
- Apparently the ultimate anti-succubus weapon.
- Easy-going.

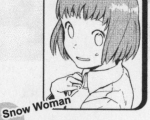

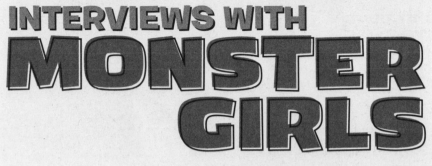

INTERVIEWS WITH MONSTER GIRLS

CONTENTS

6

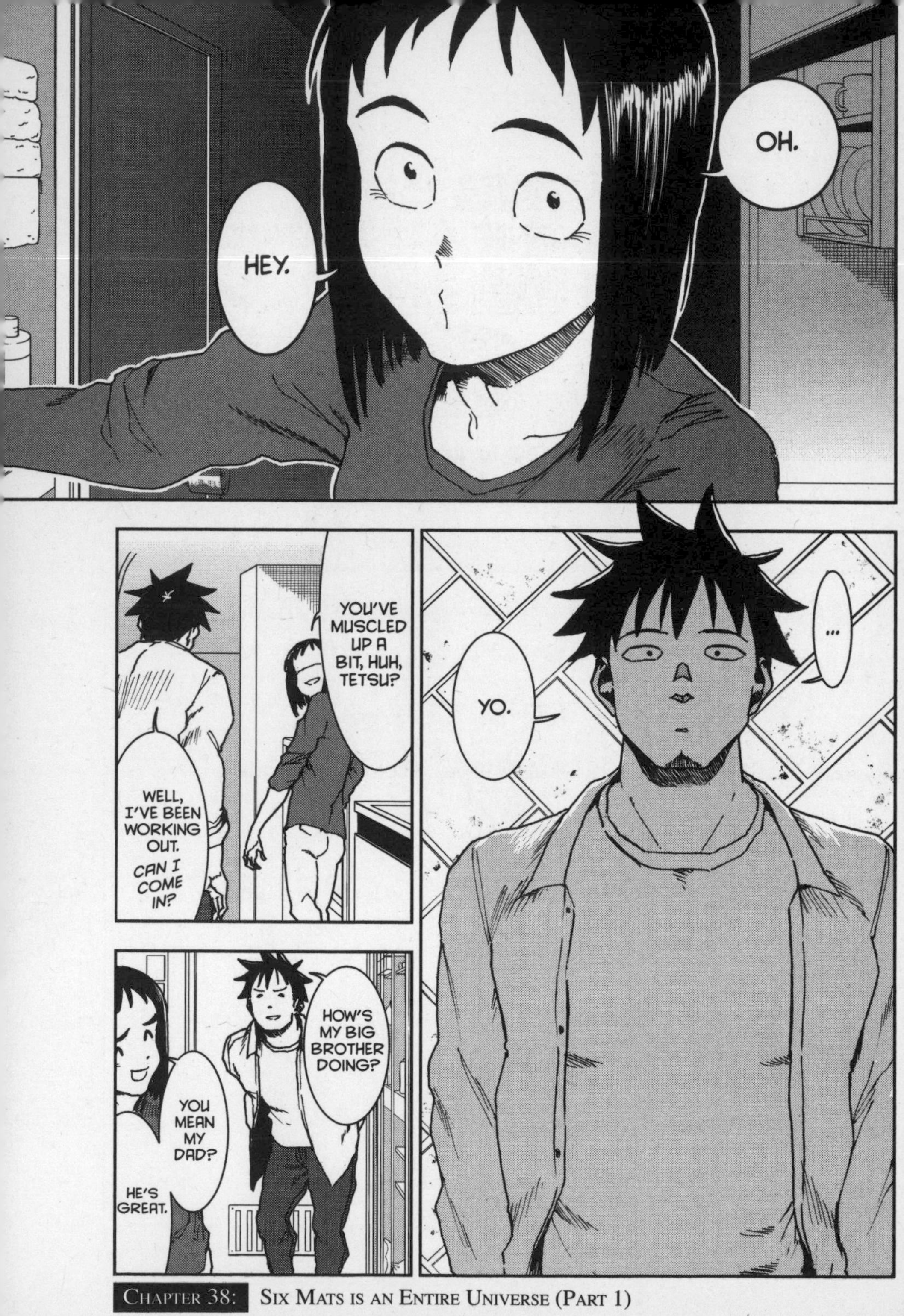
OH.
HEY.
...
YO.
YOU'VE MUSCLED UP A BIT, HUH, TETSU?
WELL, I'VE BEEN WORKING OUT.
CAN I COME IN?
HOW'S MY BIG BROTHER DOING?
YOU MEAN MY DAD?
HE'S GREAT.

Chapter 38: Six Mats is an Entire Universe (Part 1)

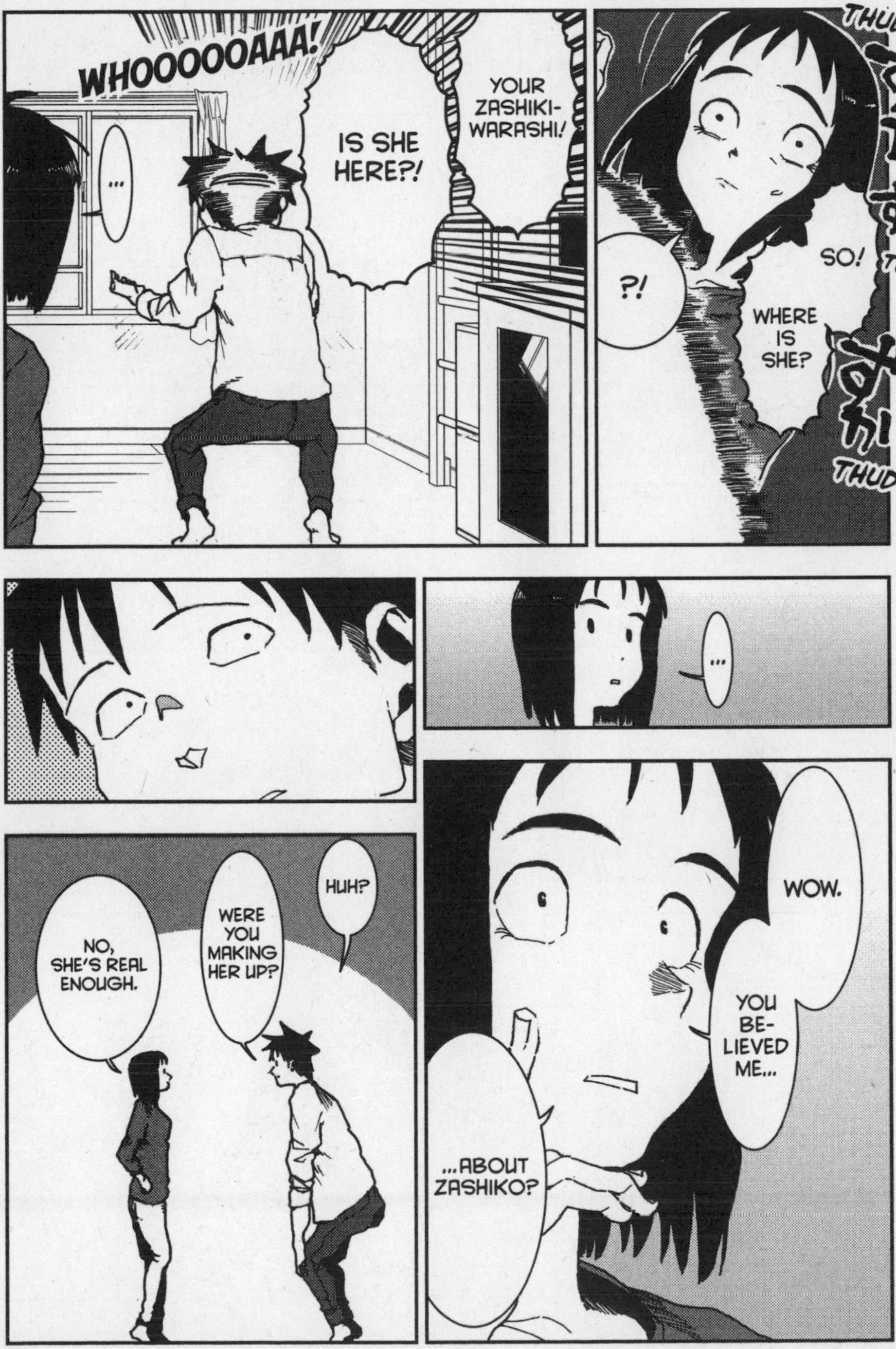
THUD
ずか
ずか
THUD
SO!
WHERE IS SHE?
ずか
THUD
?!
WHOOOOOAAA!
YOUR ZASHIKI-WARASHI!
IS SHE HERE?!
...
...
WOW.
YOU BE-LIEVED ME...
...ABOUT ZASHIKO?
HUH?
WERE YOU MAKING HER UP?
NO, SHE'S REAL ENOUGH.

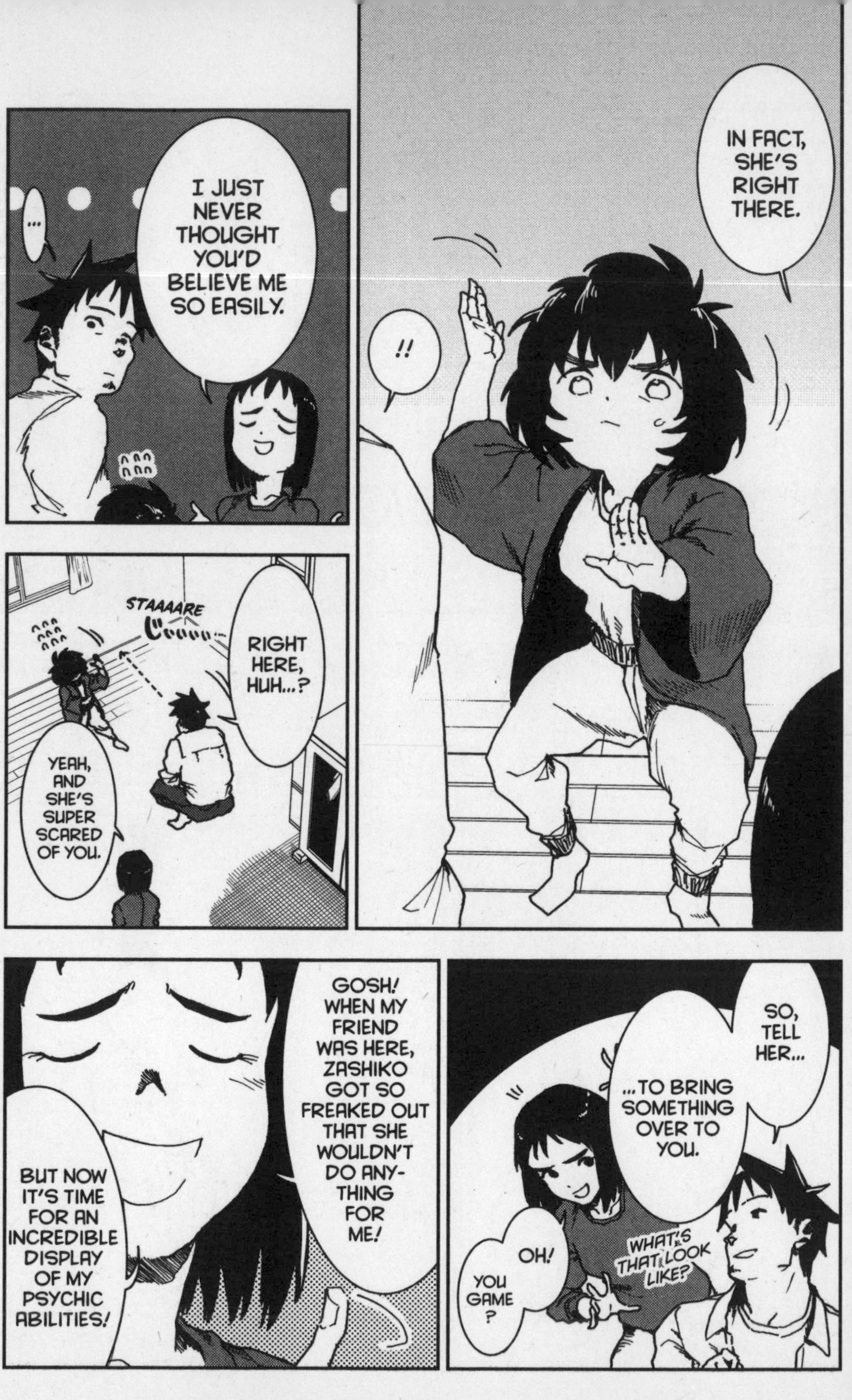
IN FACT, SHE'S RIGHT THERE.
!!
I JUST NEVER THOUGHT YOU'D BELIEVE ME SO EASILY.
...
RIGHT HERE, HUH...?
STAAAARE
YEAH, AND SHE'S SUPER SCARED OF YOU.
SO, TELL HER...
...TO BRING SOMETHING OVER TO YOU.
WHAT'S THAT LOOK LIKE?
OH!
YOU GAME?
GOSH! WHEN MY FRIEND WAS HERE, ZASHIKO GOT SO FREAKED OUT THAT SHE WOULDN'T DO ANY-THING FOR ME!
BUT NOW IT'S TIME FOR AN INCREDIBLE DISPLAY OF MY PSYCHIC ABILITIES!

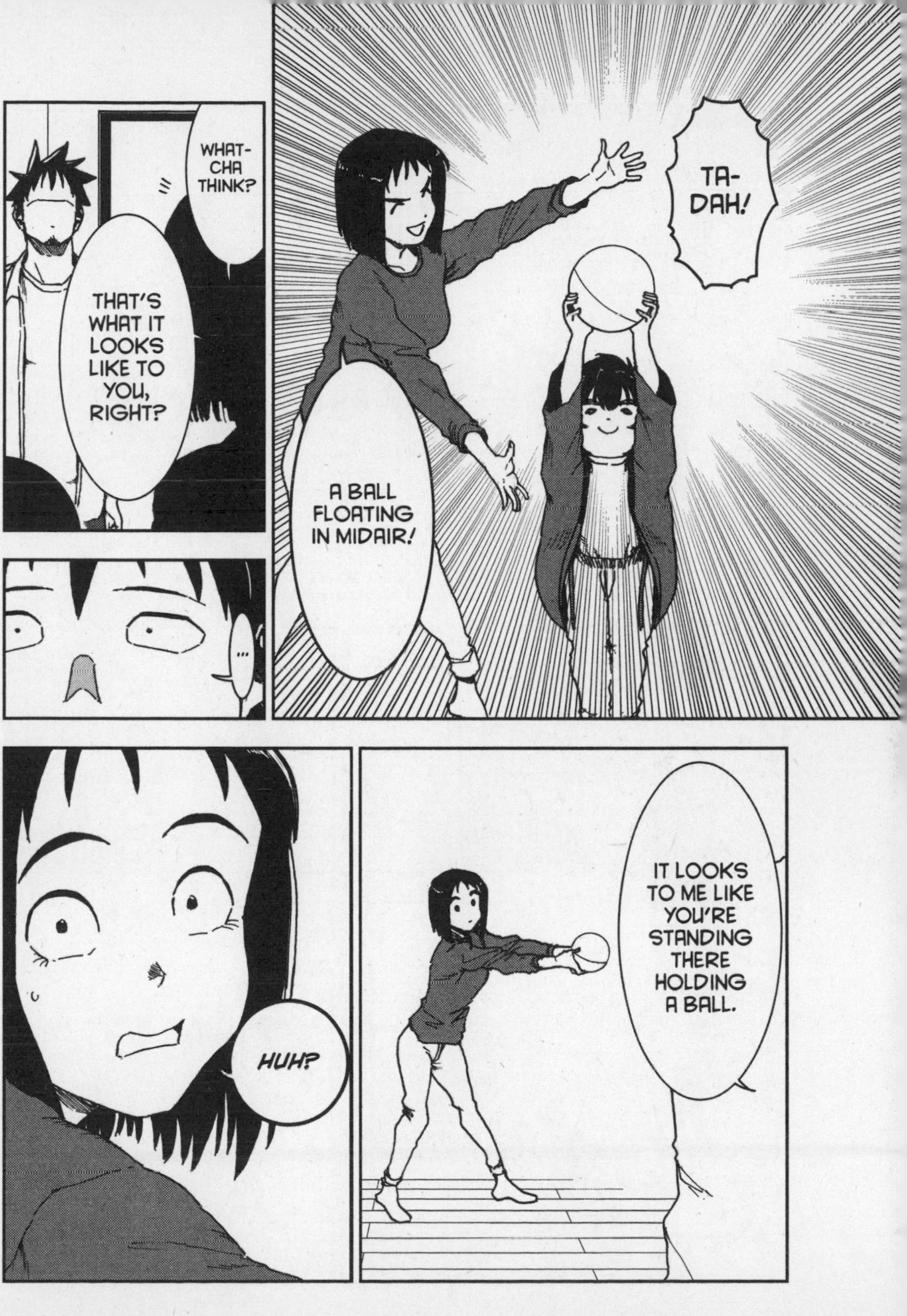
TA-DAH!
A BALL FLOATING IN MIDAIR!
WHAT-CHA THINK?
THAT'S WHAT IT LOOKS LIKE TO YOU, RIGHT?
...
IT LOOKS TO ME LIKE YOU'RE STANDING THERE HOLDING A BALL.
HUH?

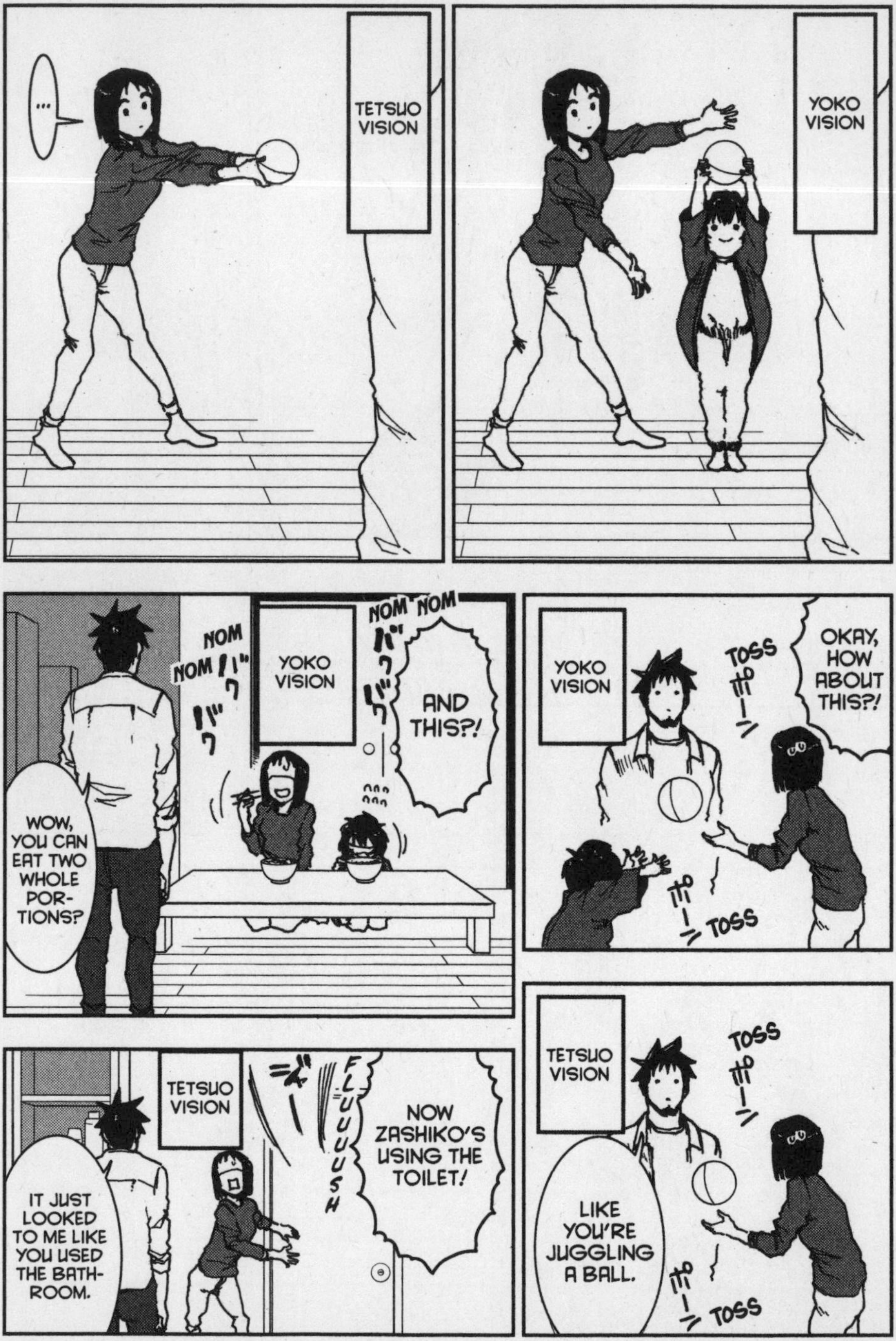
YOKO VISION
TETSUO VISION
...
YOKO VISION
TOSS
OKAY, HOW ABOUT THIS?!
TOSS
NOM NOM
NOM NOM
YOKO VISION
AND THIS?!
WOW, YOU CAN EAT TWO WHOLE PORTIONS?
TETSUO VISION
TOSS
LIKE YOU'RE JUGGLING A BALL.
TOSS
TETSUO VISION
FLUUUUSH
NOW ZASHIKO'S USING THE TOILET!
IT JUST LOOKED TO ME LIKE YOU USED THE BATHROOM.

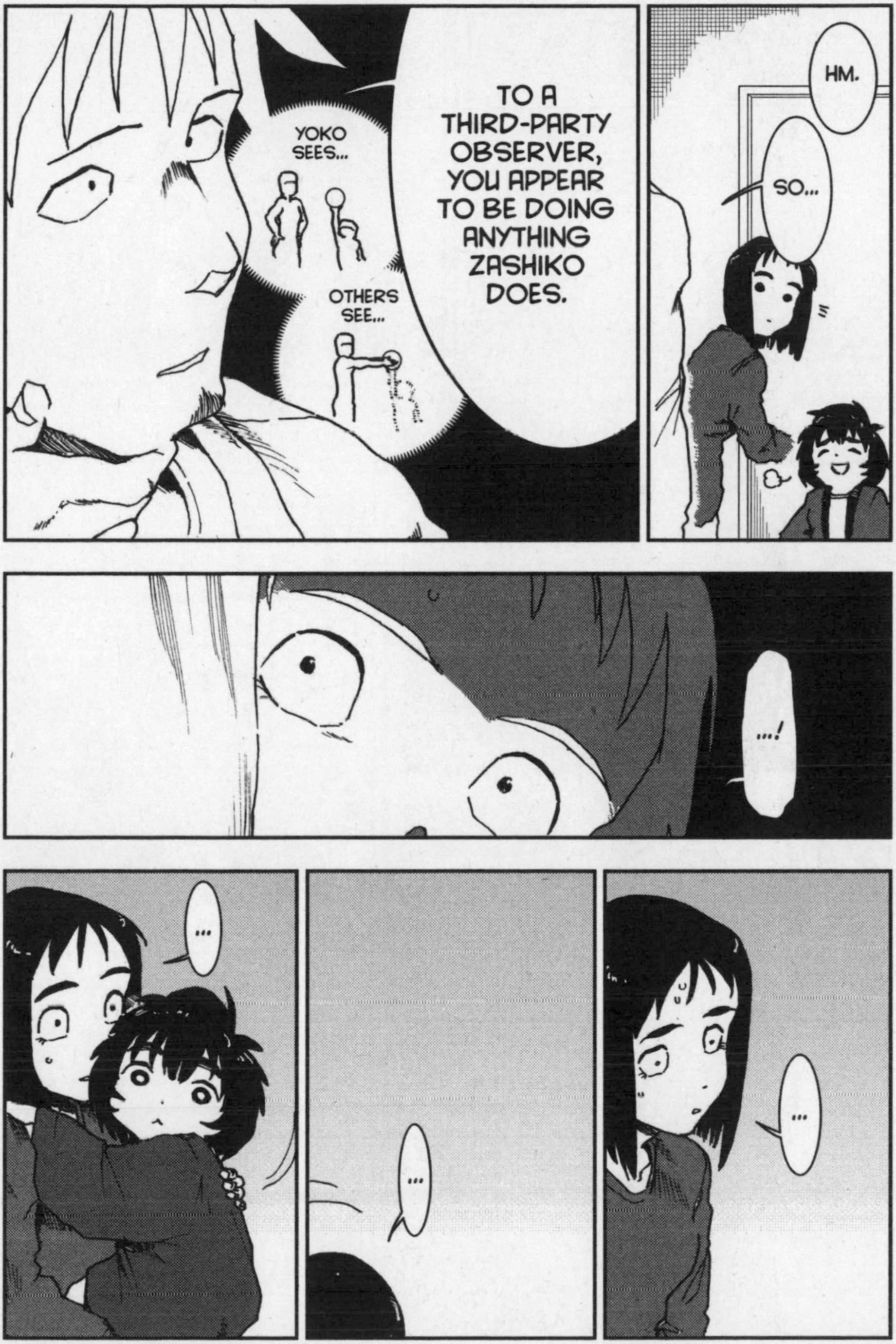
HM.
SO...
TO A THIRD-PARTY OBSERVER, YOU APPEAR TO BE DOING ANYTHING ZASHIKO DOES.
YOKO SEES...
OTHERS SEE...
...!
...
...
...

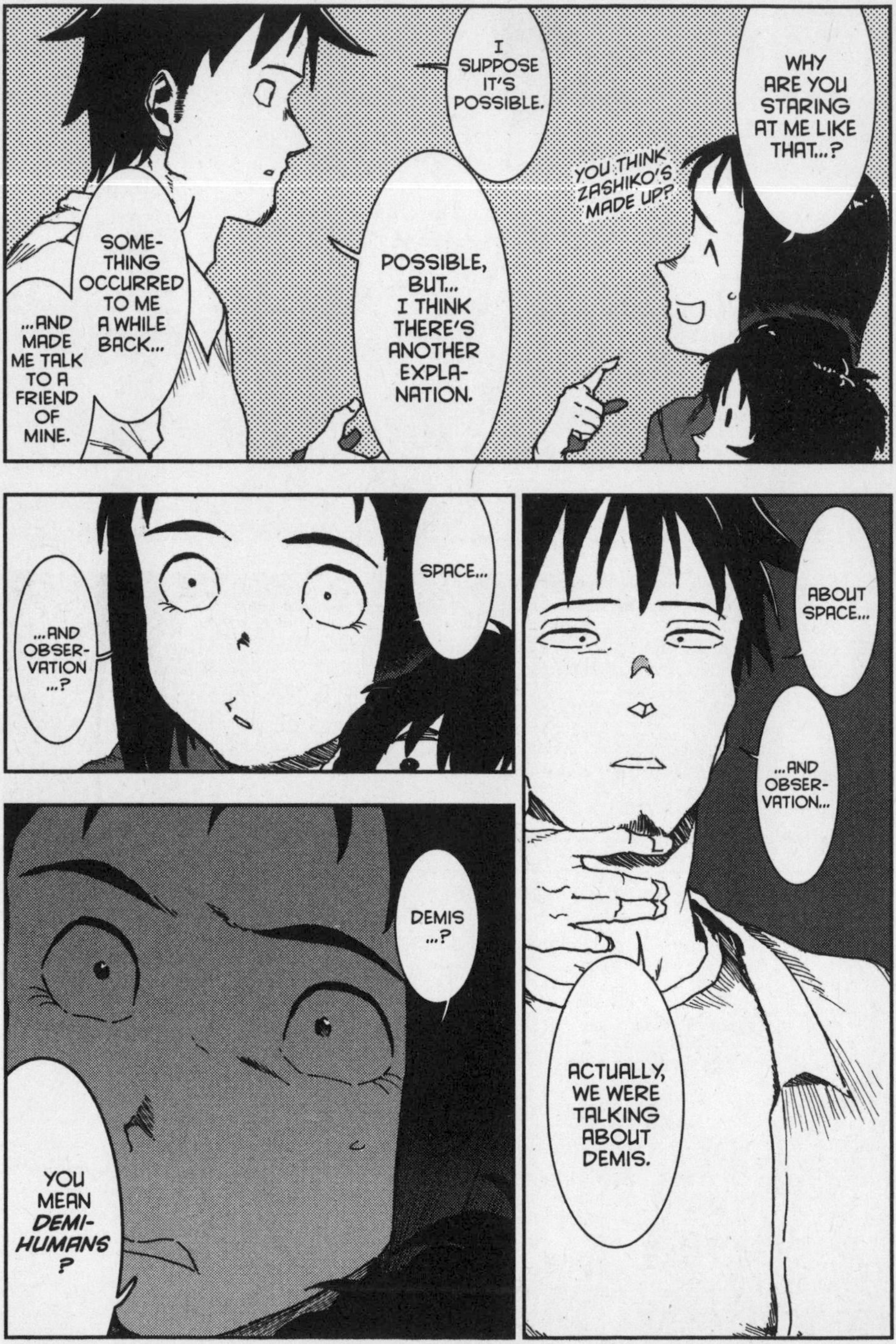
WHY ARE YOU STARING AT ME LIKE THAT...?
YOU THINK ZASHIKO'S MADE UP?
I SUPPOSE IT'S POSSIBLE.
POSSIBLE, BUT... I THINK THERE'S ANOTHER EXPLA-NATION.
SOME-THING OCCURRED TO ME A WHILE BACK...
...AND MADE ME TALK TO A FRIEND OF MINE.
ABOUT SPACE...
...AND OBSER-VATION...
ACTUALLY, WE WERE TALKING ABOUT DEMIS.
SPACE...
...AND OBSER-VATION ...?
DEMIS ...?
YOU MEAN *DEMI-HUMANS* ?

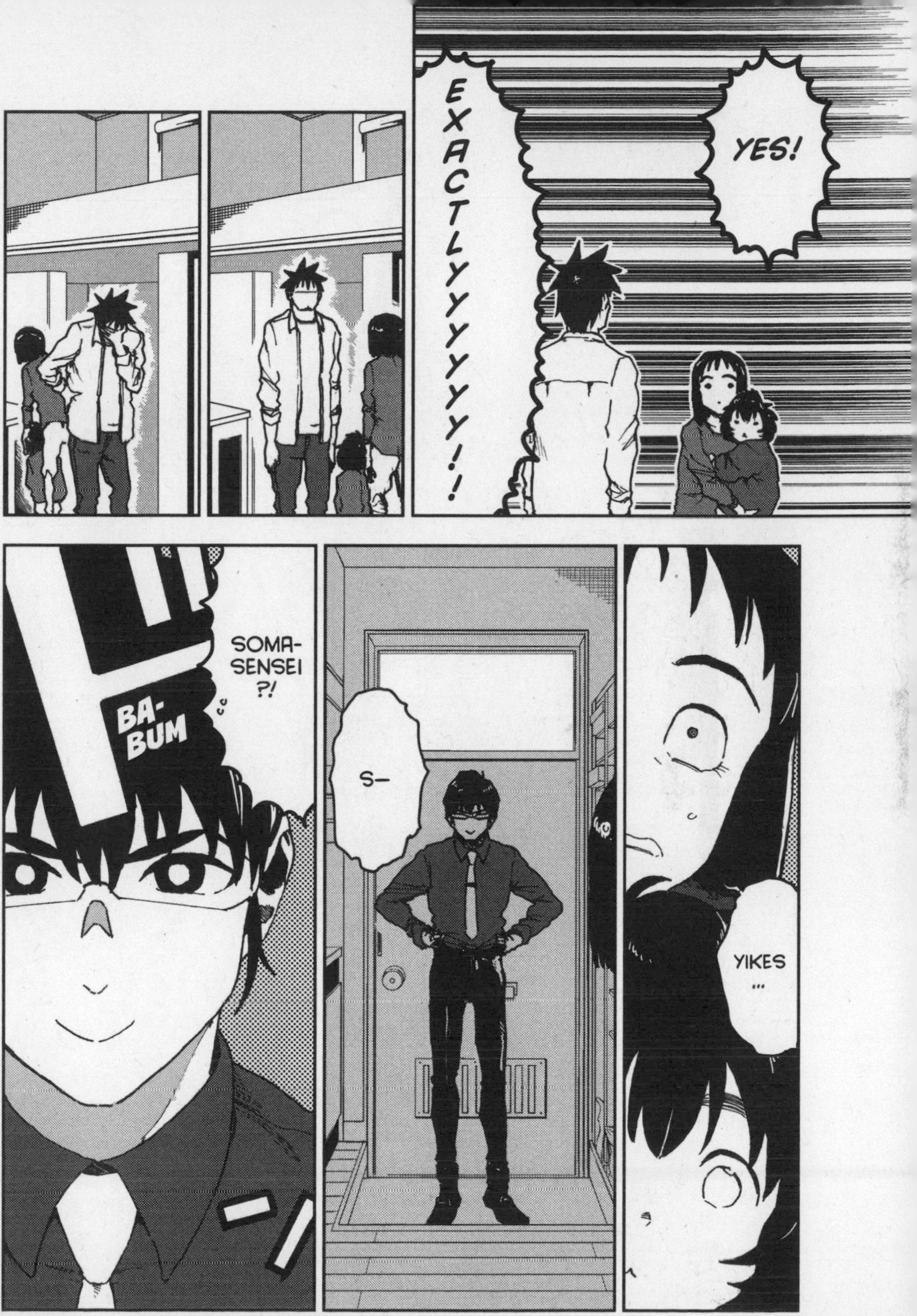
YES!
EXACTLYYYYYYY!!
YIKES ...
S—
SOMA-SENSEI ?!
BA-BUM

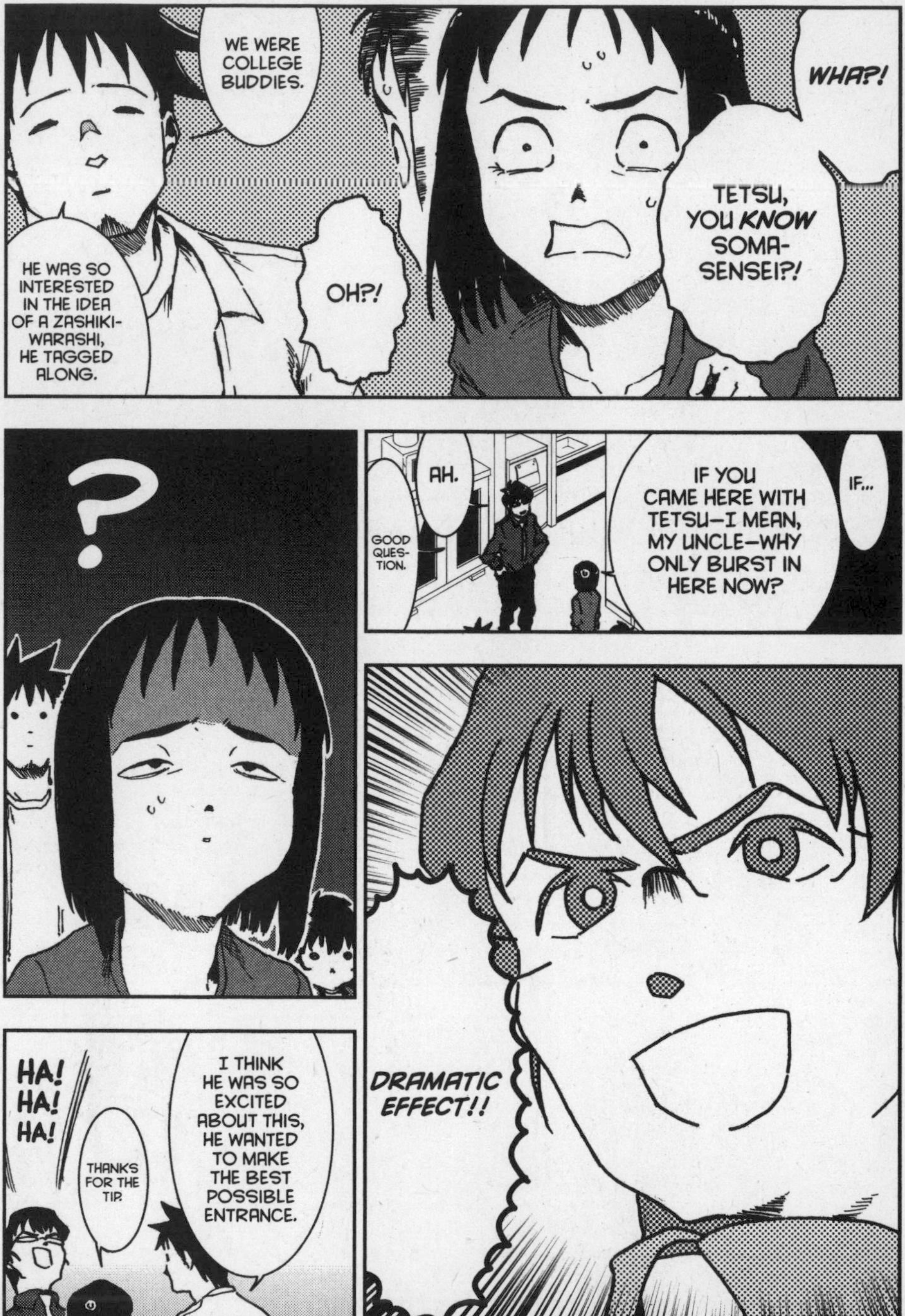
WHA?!
TETSU, YOU KNOW SOMA-SENSEI?!
WE WERE COLLEGE BUDDIES.
OH?!
HE WAS SO INTERESTED IN THE IDEA OF A ZASHIKI-WARASHI, HE TAGGED ALONG.
IF...
IF YOU CAME HERE WITH TETSU—I MEAN, MY UNCLE—WHY ONLY BURST IN HERE NOW?
AH.
GOOD QUES-TION.
DRAMATIC EFFECT!!
?
I THINK HE WAS SO EXCITED ABOUT THIS, HE WANTED TO MAKE THE BEST POSSIBLE ENTRANCE.
THANKS FOR THE TIP.
HA! HA! HA!

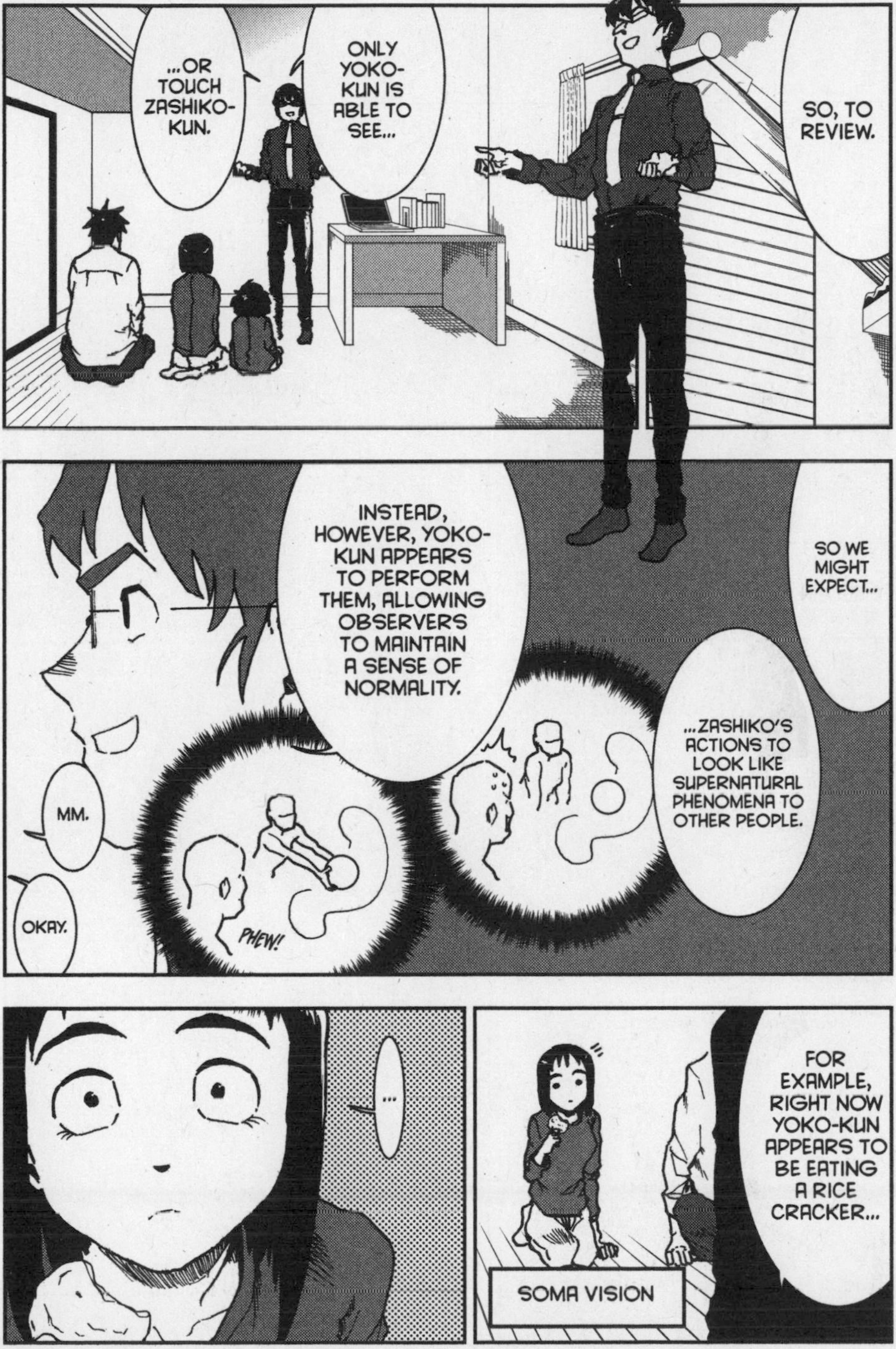
SO, TO REVIEW.
ONLY YOKO-KUN IS ABLE TO SEE...
...OR TOUCH ZASHIKO-KUN.
SO WE MIGHT EXPECT...
...ZASHIKO'S ACTIONS TO LOOK LIKE SUPERNATURAL PHENOMENA TO OTHER PEOPLE.
INSTEAD, HOWEVER, YOKO-KUN APPEARS TO PERFORM THEM, ALLOWING OBSERVERS TO MAINTAIN A SENSE OF NORMALITY.
PHEW!
MM.
OKAY.
FOR EXAMPLE, RIGHT NOW YOKO-KUN APPEARS TO BE EATING A RICE CRACKER...
SOMA VISION
...

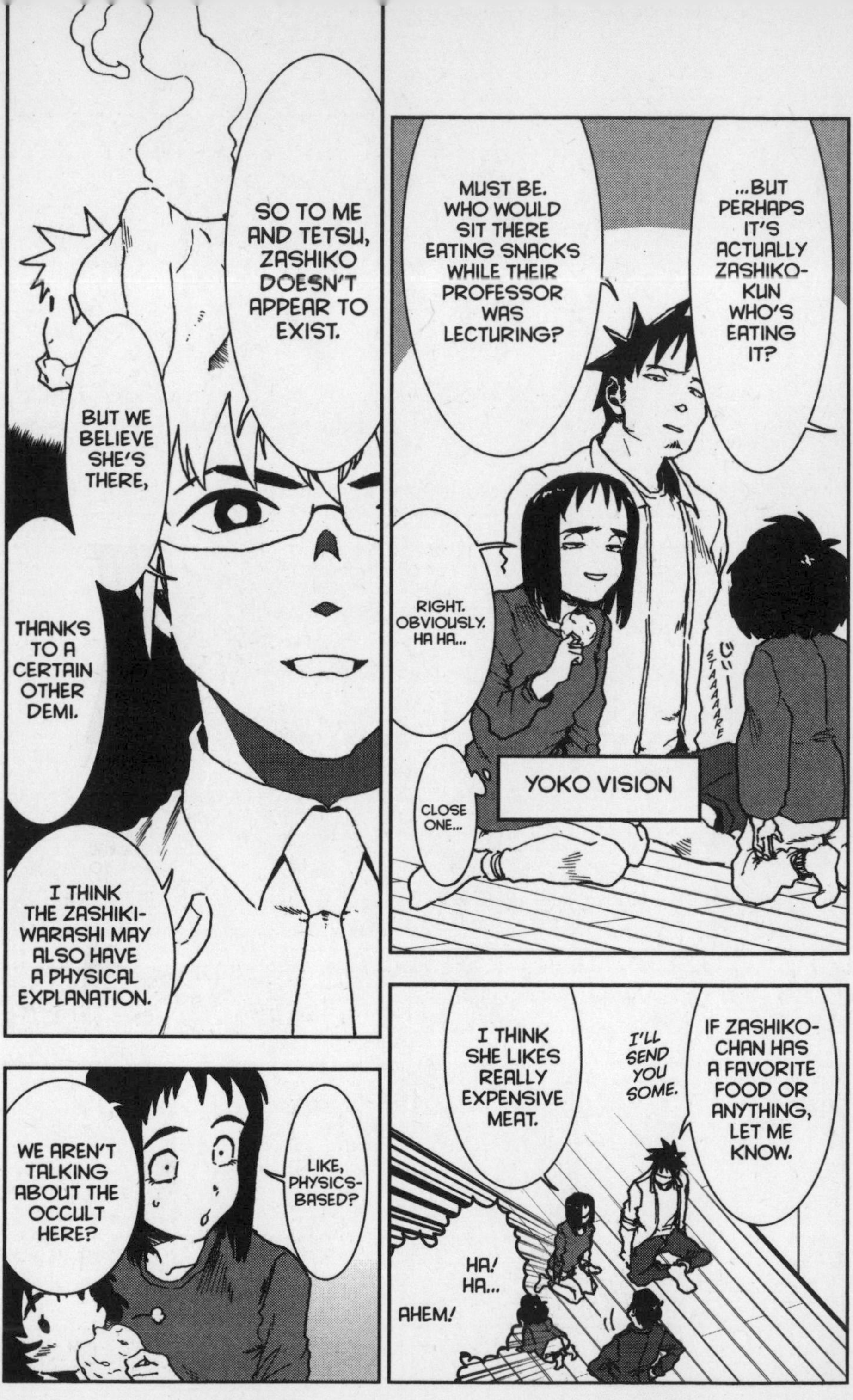
...BUT PERHAPS IT'S ACTUALLY ZASHIKO-KUN WHO'S EATING IT?
MUST BE. WHO WOULD SIT THERE EATING SNACKS WHILE THEIR PROFESSOR WAS LECTURING?
RIGHT. OBVIOUSLY. HA HA...
STAAAAARE
YOKO VISION
CLOSE ONE...
SO TO ME AND TETSU, ZASHIKO DOESN'T APPEAR TO EXIST.
BUT WE BELIEVE SHE'S THERE,
THANKS TO A CERTAIN OTHER DEMI.
I THINK THE ZASHIKI-WARASHI MAY ALSO HAVE A PHYSICAL EXPLANATION.
IF ZASHIKO-CHAN HAS A FAVORITE FOOD OR ANYTHING, LET ME KNOW.
I'LL SEND YOU SOME.
I THINK SHE LIKES REALLY EXPENSIVE MEAT.
HA! HA...
AHEM!
LIKE, PHYSICS-BASED?
WE AREN'T TALKING ABOUT THE OCCULT HERE?

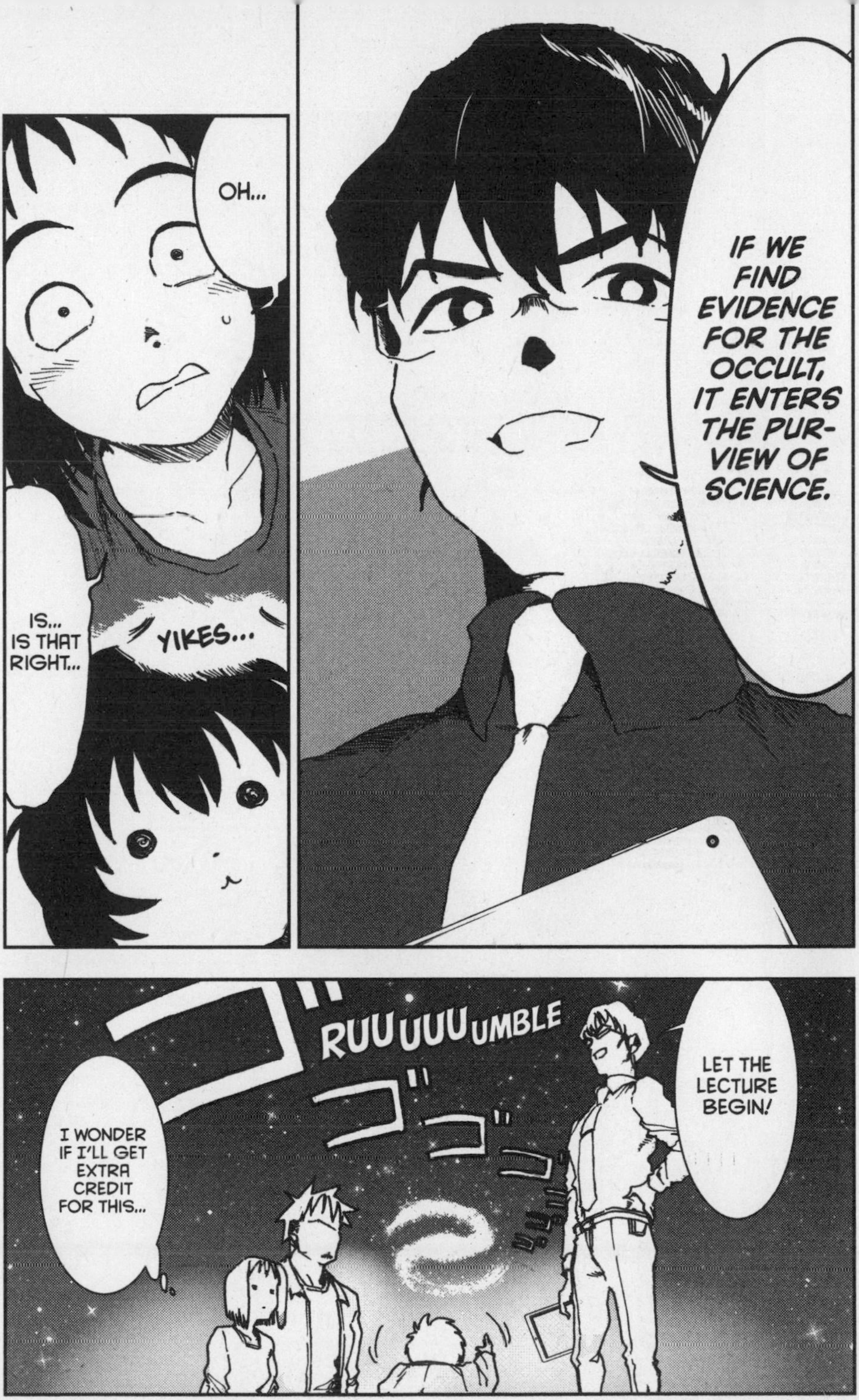
IF WE FIND EVIDENCE FOR THE OCCULT, IT ENTERS THE PUR-VIEW OF SCIENCE.
OH...
IS... IS THAT RIGHT...
YIKES...
LET THE LECTURE BEGIN!
RUUUUUUMBLE
I WONDER IF I'LL GET EXTRA CREDIT FOR THIS...

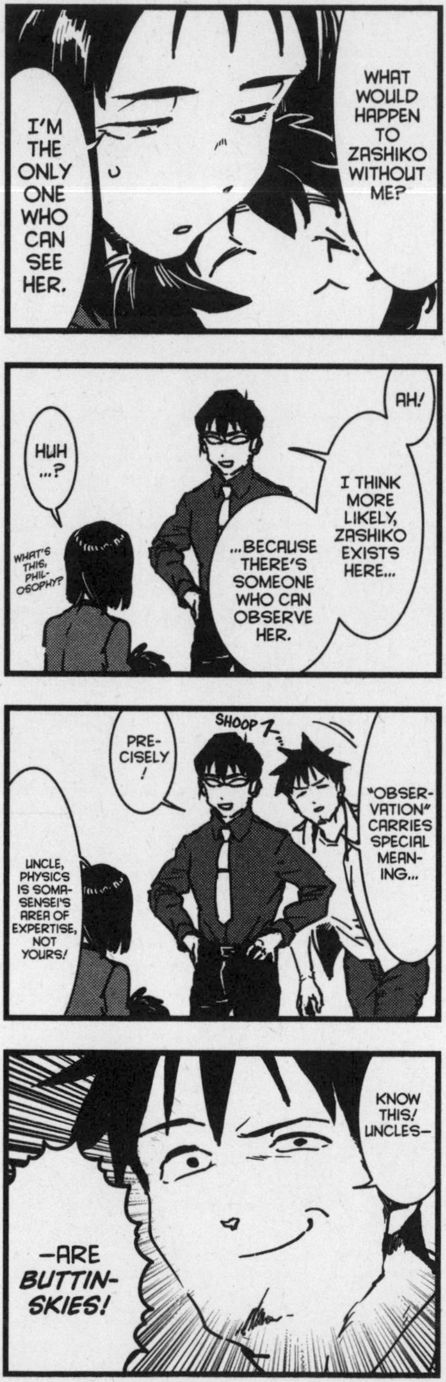
WHAT WOULD HAPPEN TO ZASHIKO WITHOUT ME?
I'M THE ONLY ONE WHO CAN SEE HER.
AH!
I THINK MORE LIKELY, ZASHIKO EXISTS HERE...
...BECAUSE THERE'S SOMEONE WHO CAN OBSERVE HER.
HUH ...?
WHAT'S THIS, PHILOSOPHY?
"OBSERVATION" CARRIES SPECIAL MEANING...
SHOOP
PRECISELY!
UNCLE, PHYSICS IS SOMA-SENSEI'S AREA OF EXPERTISE, NOT YOURS!
KNOW THIS! UNCLES—
—ARE *BUTTINSKIES!*

INTERVIEWS WITH MONSTER GIRLS

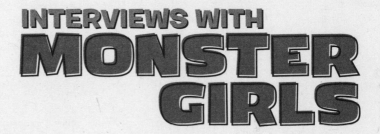

Chapter 39: Six Mats is an Entire Universe (Part 2)

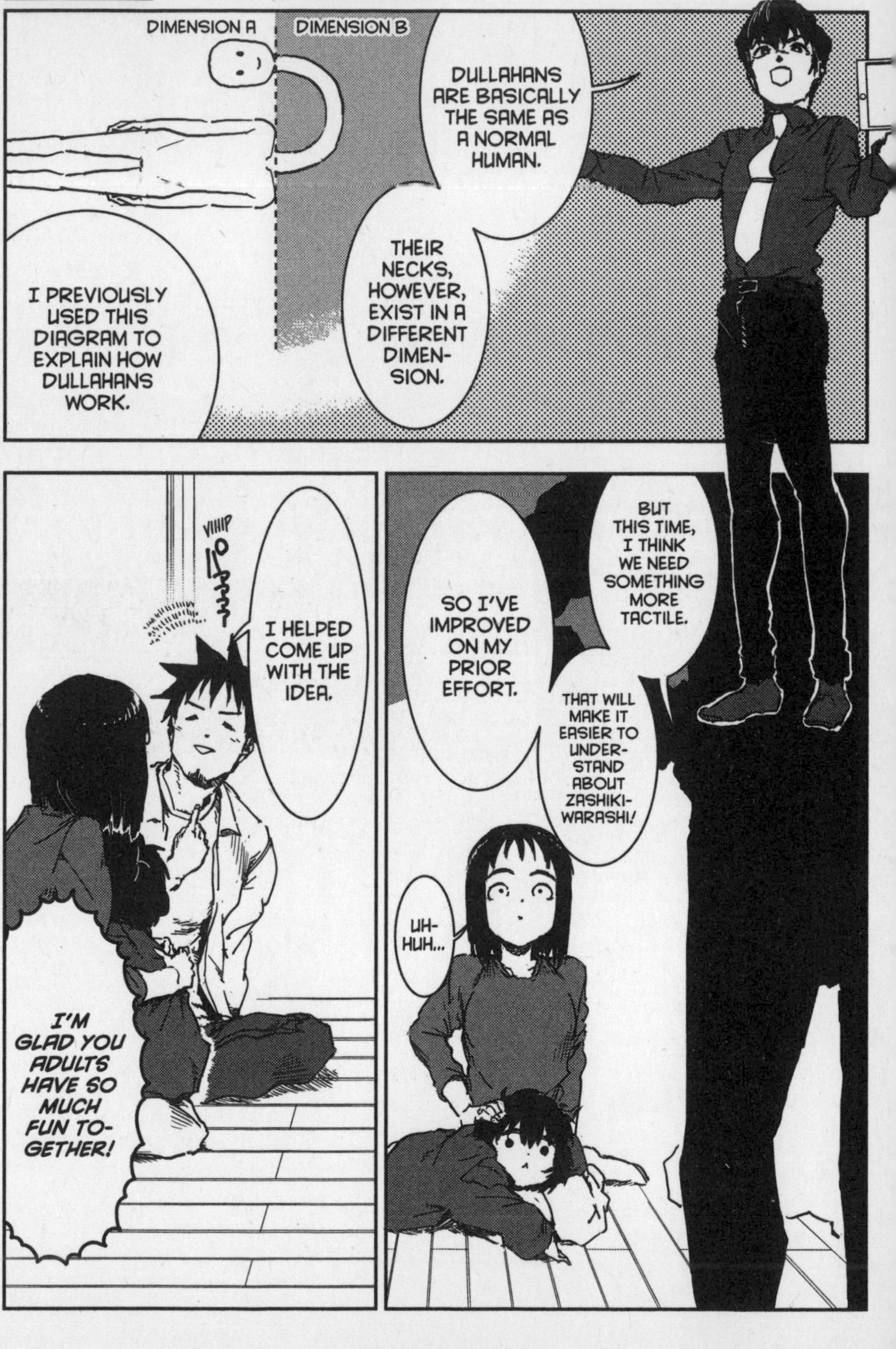
DULLAHANS ARE BASICALLY THE SAME AS A NORMAL HUMAN.
THEIR NECKS, HOWEVER, EXIST IN A DIFFERENT DIMEN-SION.
DIMENSION A
DIMENSION B
I PREVIOUSLY USED THIS DIAGRAM TO EXPLAIN HOW DULLAHANS WORK.
BUT THIS TIME, I THINK WE NEED SOMETHING MORE TACTILE.
SO I'VE IMPROVED ON MY PRIOR EFFORT.
THAT WILL MAKE IT EASIER TO UNDER-STAND ABOUT ZASHIKI-WARASHI!
UH-HUH...
VIIIP
I HELPED COME UP WITH THE IDEA.
I'M GLAD YOU ADULTS HAVE SO MUCH FUN TO-GETHER!

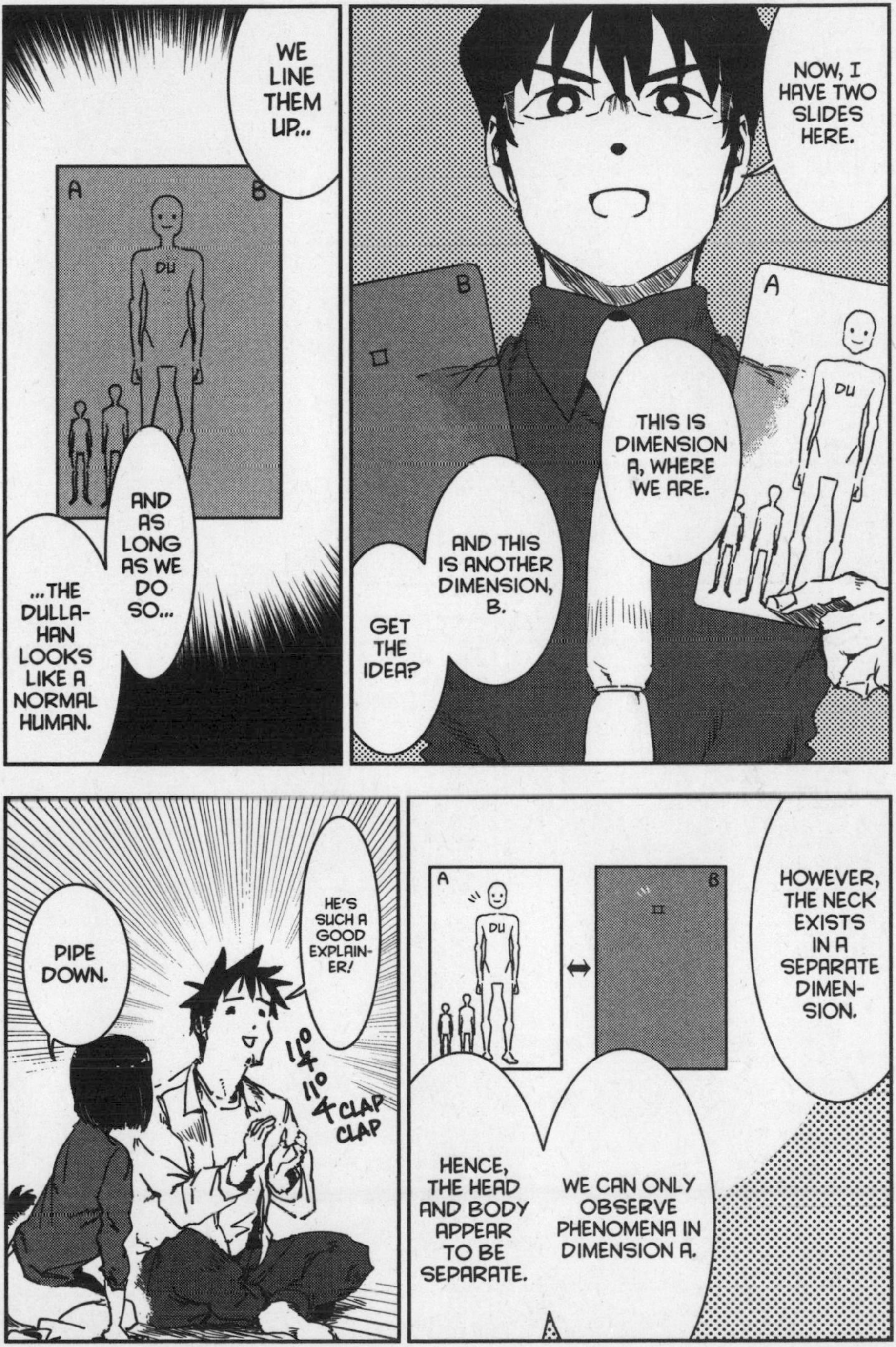
NOW, I HAVE TWO SLIDES HERE.
THIS IS DIMENSION A, WHERE WE ARE.
AND THIS IS ANOTHER DIMENSION, B.
GET THE IDEA?
WE LINE THEM UP...
AND AS LONG AS WE DO SO...
...THE DULLA-HAN LOOKS LIKE A NORMAL HUMAN.
HOWEVER, THE NECK EXISTS IN A SEPARATE DIMEN-SION.
WE CAN ONLY OBSERVE PHENOMENA IN DIMENSION A.
HENCE, THE HEAD AND BODY APPEAR TO BE SEPARATE.
HE'S SUCH A GOOD EXPLAIN-ER!
CLAP CLAP
PIPE DOWN.

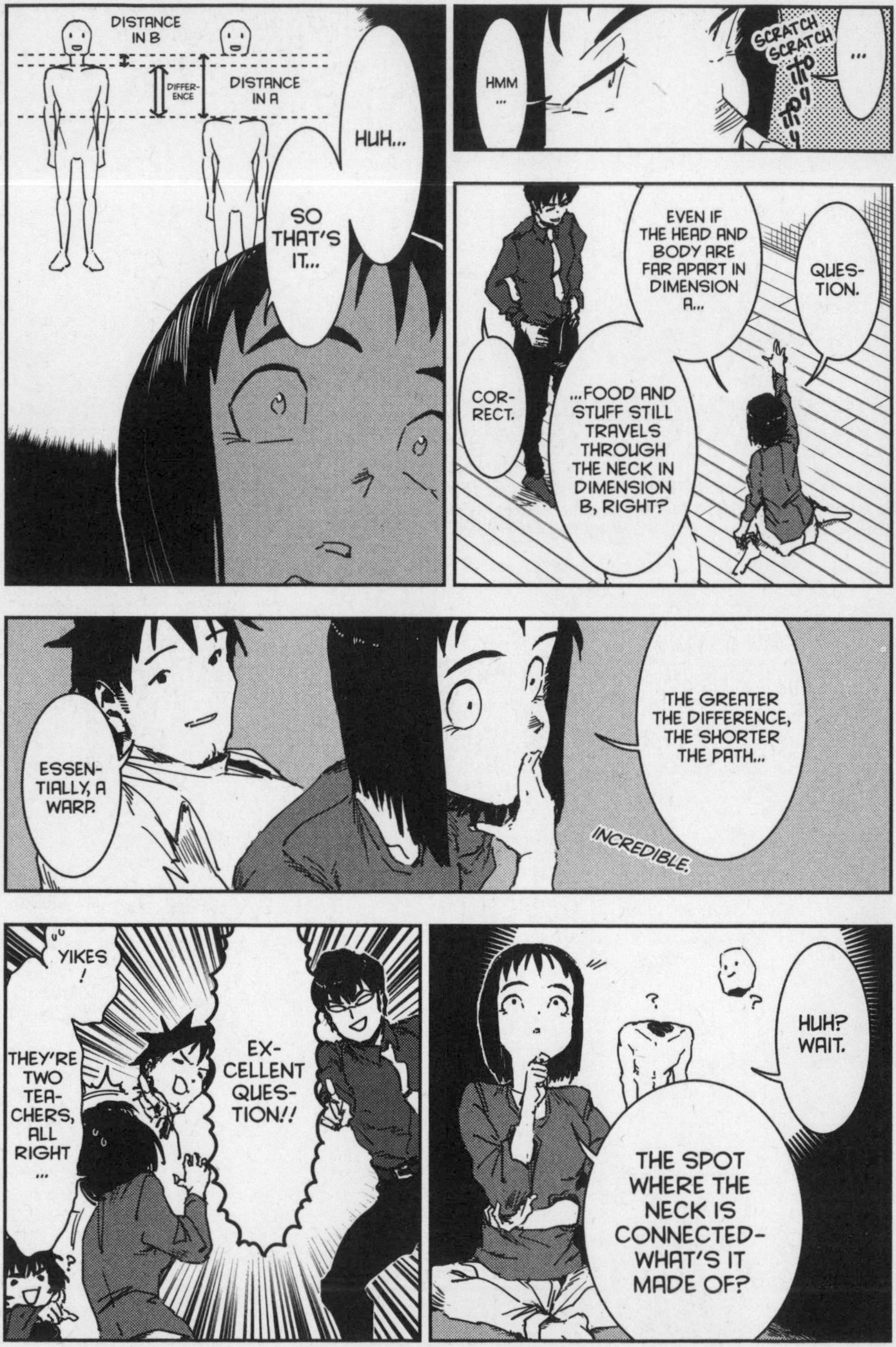
...
SCRATCH SCRATCH
HMM...
QUES-TION.
EVEN IF THE HEAD AND BODY ARE FAR APART IN DIMENSION A...
...FOOD AND STUFF STILL TRAVELS THROUGH THE NECK IN DIMENSION B, RIGHT?
COR-RECT.
DISTANCE IN B
DIFFER-ENCE
DISTANCE IN A
HUH...
SO THAT'S IT...
THE GREATER THE DIFFERENCE, THE SHORTER THE PATH...
INCREDIBLE.
ESSEN-TIALLY, A WARP.
HUH? WAIT.
THE SPOT WHERE THE NECK IS CONNECTED- WHAT'S IT MADE OF?
EX-CELLENT QUES-TION!!
YIKES!
THEY'RE TWO TEA-CHERS, ALL RIGHT...

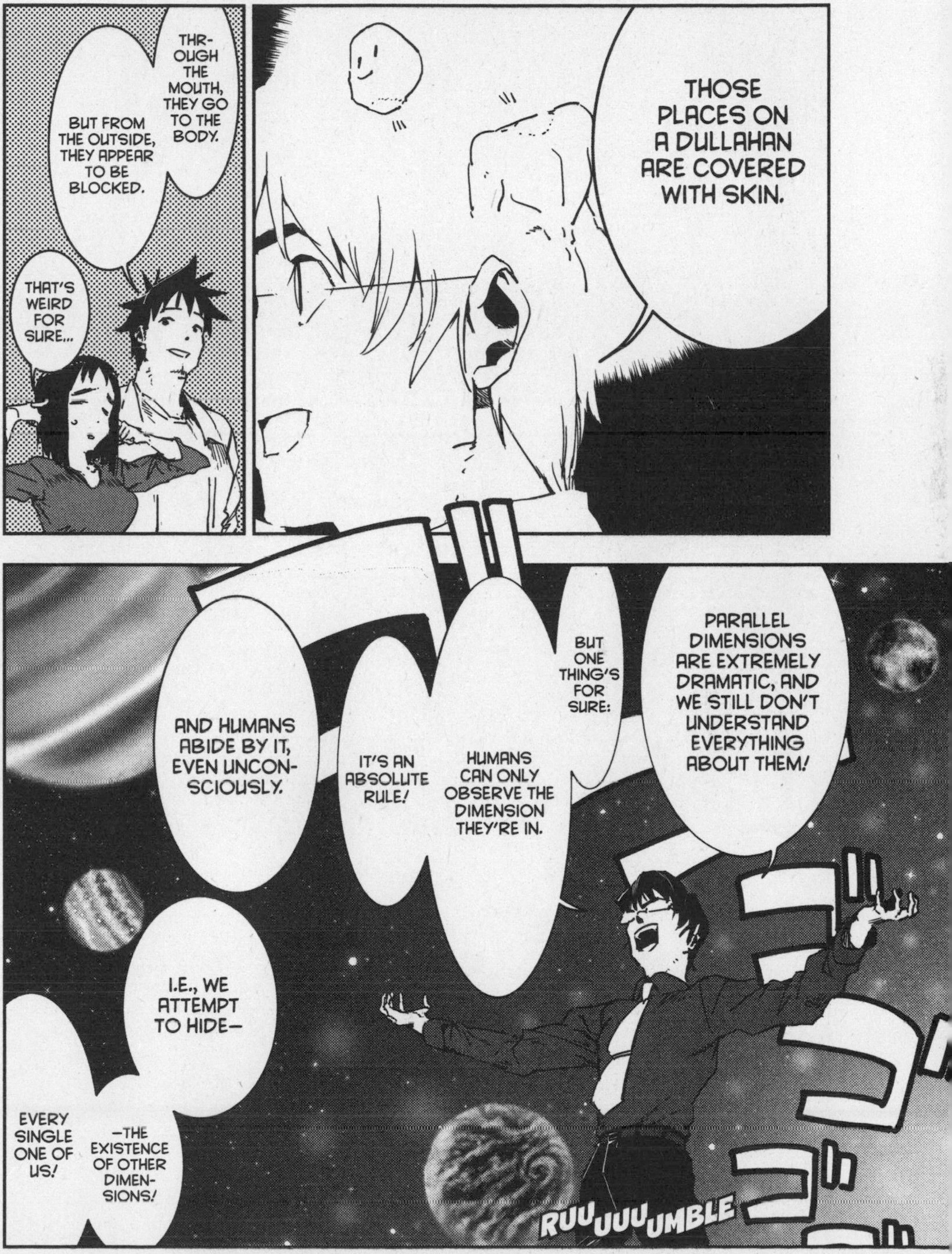
THOSE PLACES ON A DULLAHAN ARE COVERED WITH SKIN.
THROUGH THE MOUTH, THEY GO TO THE BODY.
BUT FROM THE OUTSIDE, THEY APPEAR TO BE BLOCKED.
THAT'S WEIRD FOR SURE...
PARALLEL DIMENSIONS ARE EXTREMELY DRAMATIC, AND WE STILL DON'T UNDERSTAND EVERYTHING ABOUT THEM!
BUT ONE THING'S FOR SURE:
HUMANS CAN ONLY OBSERVE THE DIMENSION THEY'RE IN.
IT'S AN ABSOLUTE RULE!
AND HUMANS ABIDE BY IT, EVEN UNCONSCIOUSLY.
I.E., WE ATTEMPT TO HIDE—
—THE EXISTENCE OF OTHER DIMENSIONS!
EVERY SINGLE ONE OF US!
RUUUUUUMBLE

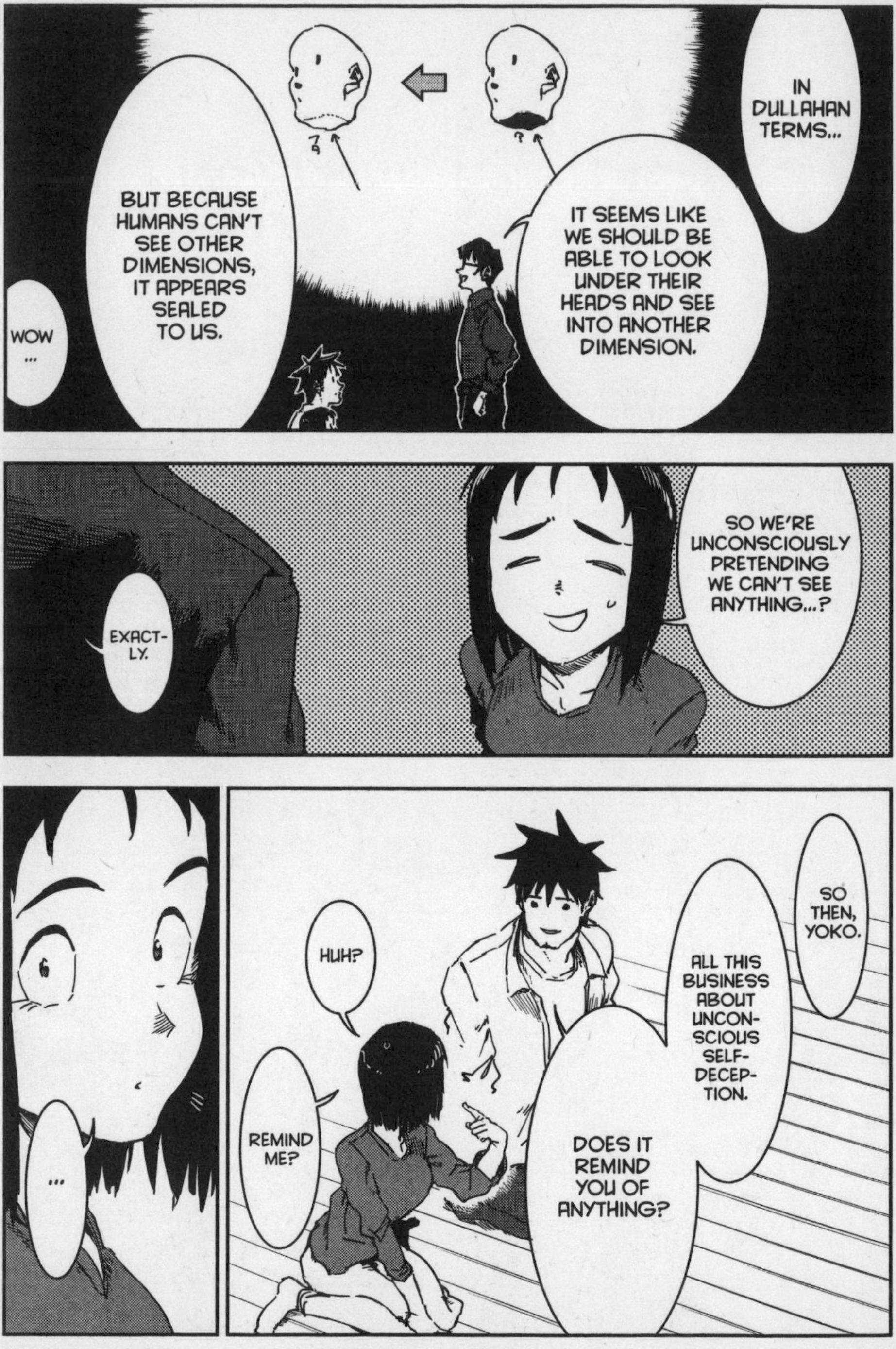
IN DULLAHAN TERMS...
IT SEEMS LIKE WE SHOULD BE ABLE TO LOOK UNDER THEIR HEADS AND SEE INTO ANOTHER DIMENSION.
BUT BECAUSE HUMANS CAN'T SEE OTHER DIMENSIONS, IT APPEARS SEALED TO US.
WOW ...
SO WE'RE UNCONSCIOUSLY PRETENDING WE CAN'T SEE ANYTHING...?
EXACT-LY.
SO THEN, YOKO.
ALL THIS BUSINESS ABOUT UNCON-SCIOUS SELF-DECEP-TION.
DOES IT REMIND YOU OF ANYTHING?
HUH?
REMIND ME?
...

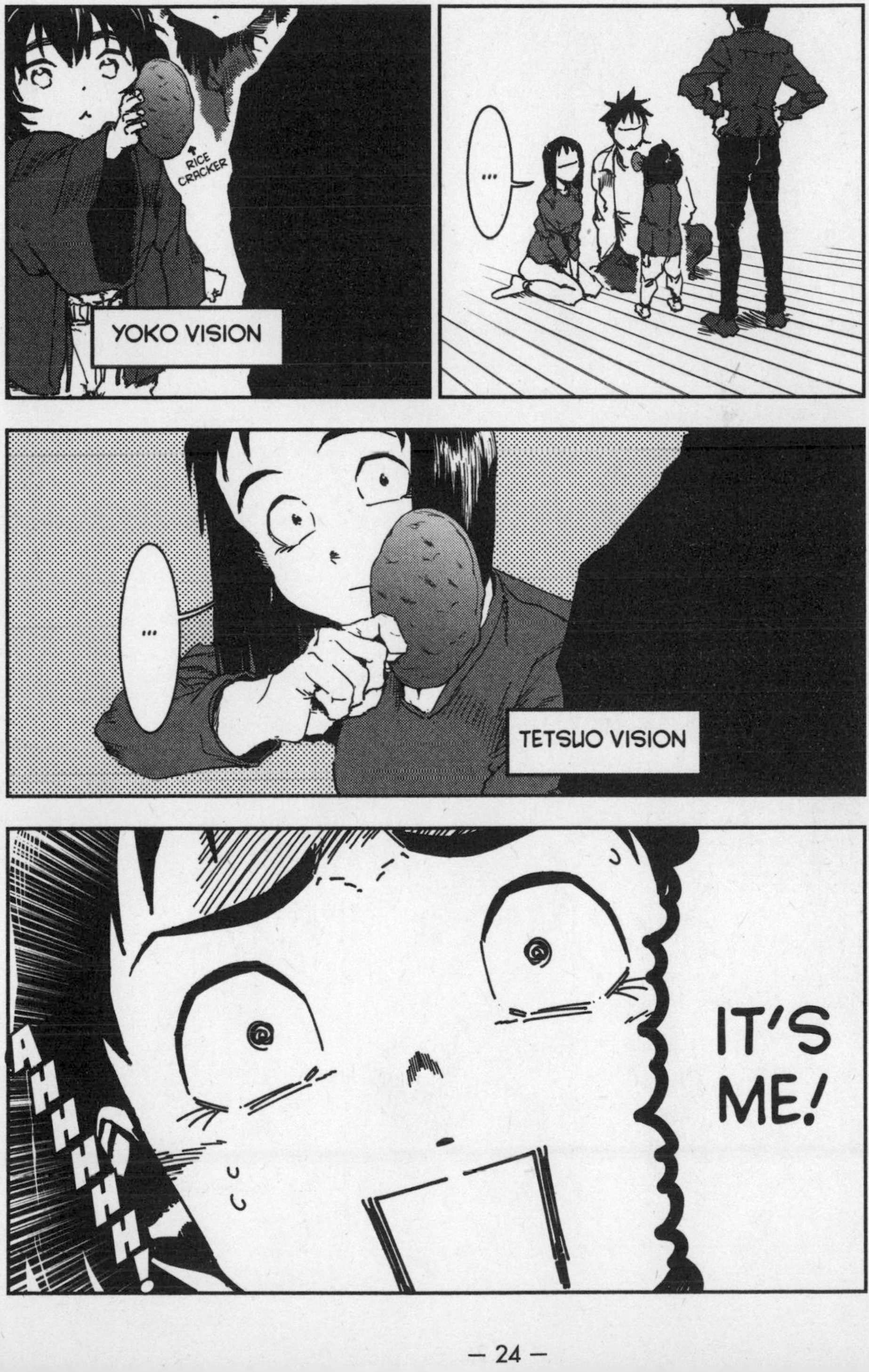
...
RICE CRACKER
YOKO VISION
...
TETSUO VISION
IT'S ME!
AHHHHHH!

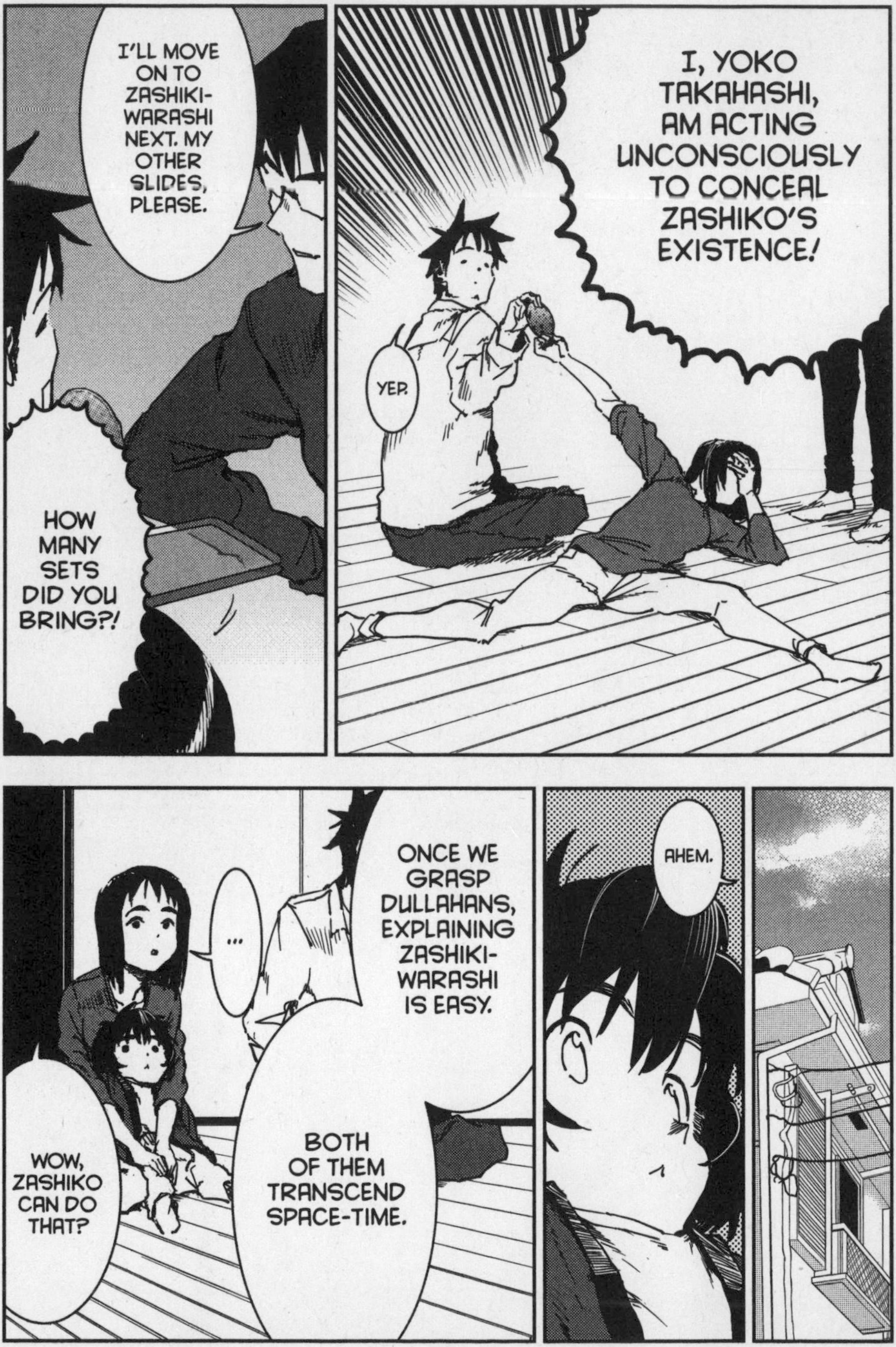
I, YOKO TAKAHASHI, AM ACTING UNCONSCIOUSLY TO CONCEAL ZASHIKO'S EXISTENCE!
YEP.
I'LL MOVE ON TO ZASHIKI-WARASHI NEXT. MY OTHER SLIDES, PLEASE.
HOW MANY SETS DID YOU BRING?!
AHEM.
ONCE WE GRASP DULLAHANS, EXPLAINING ZASHIKI-WARASHI IS EASY.
...
BOTH OF THEM TRANSCEND SPACE-TIME.
WOW, ZASHIKO CAN DO THAT?

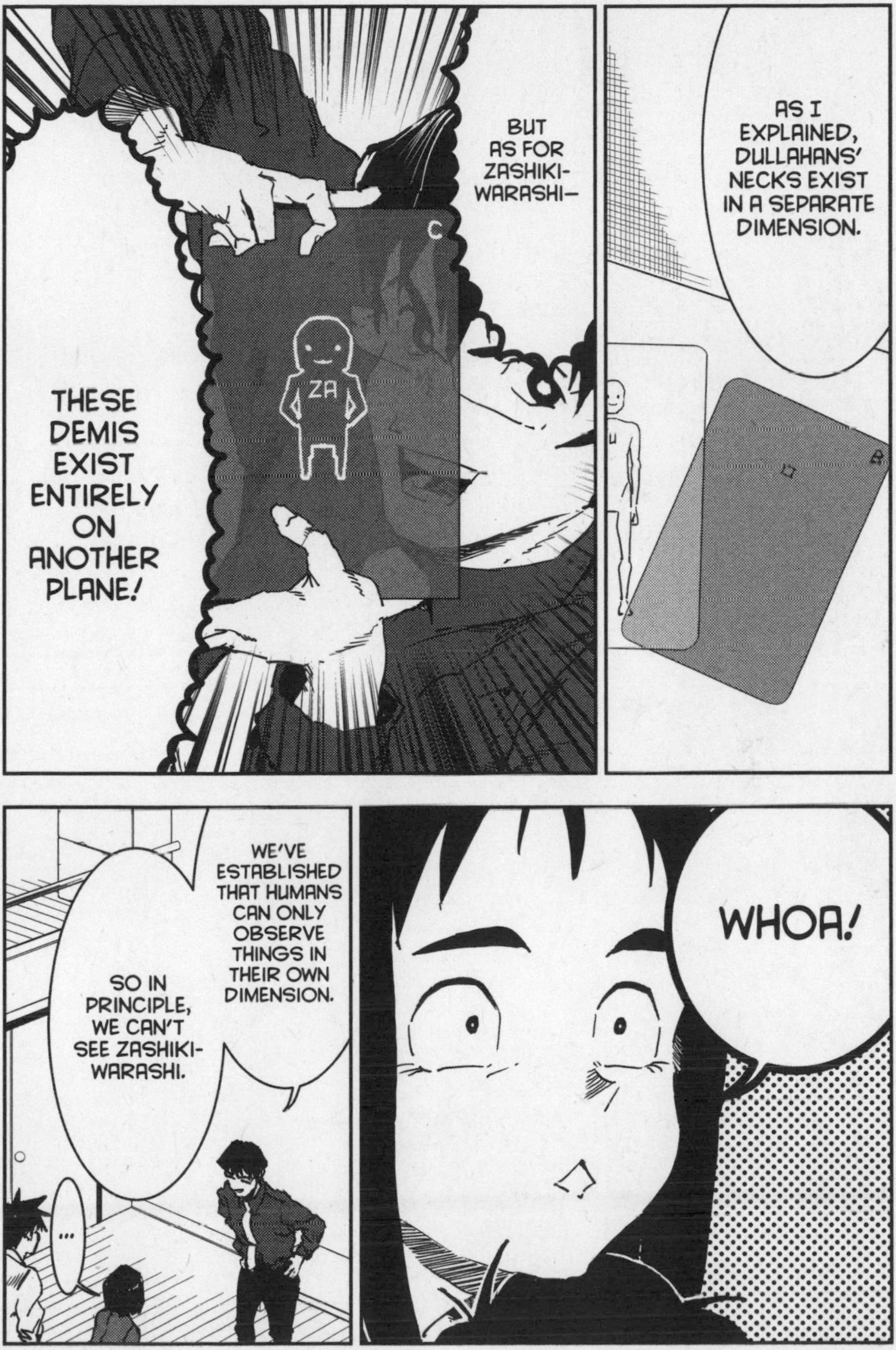
AS I EXPLAINED, DULLAHANS' NECKS EXIST IN A SEPARATE DIMENSION.
BUT AS FOR ZASHIKI-WARASHI—
C
ZA
THESE DEMIS EXIST ENTIRELY ON ANOTHER PLANE!
WHOA!
WE'VE ESTABLISHED THAT HUMANS CAN ONLY OBSERVE THINGS IN THEIR OWN DIMENSION.
SO IN PRINCIPLE, WE CAN'T SEE ZASHIKI-WARASHI.
...

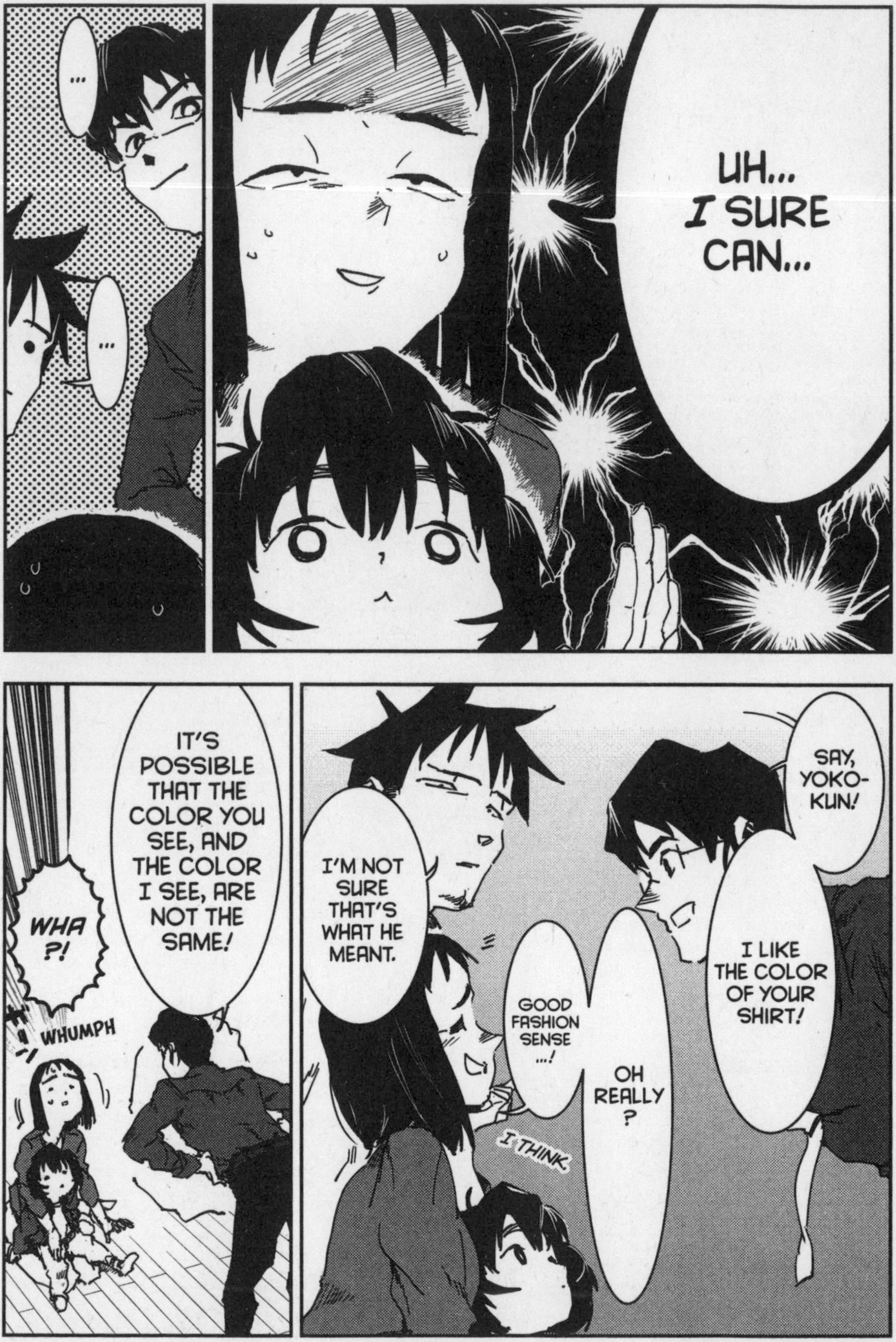
UH... I SURE CAN...
...
...
SAY, YOKO-KUN!
I LIKE THE COLOR OF YOUR SHIRT!
OH REALLY?
GOOD FASHION SENSE ...!
I THINK.
I'M NOT SURE THAT'S WHAT HE MEANT.
IT'S POSSIBLE THAT THE COLOR YOU SEE, AND THE COLOR I SEE, ARE NOT THE SAME!
WHA?!
WHUMPH

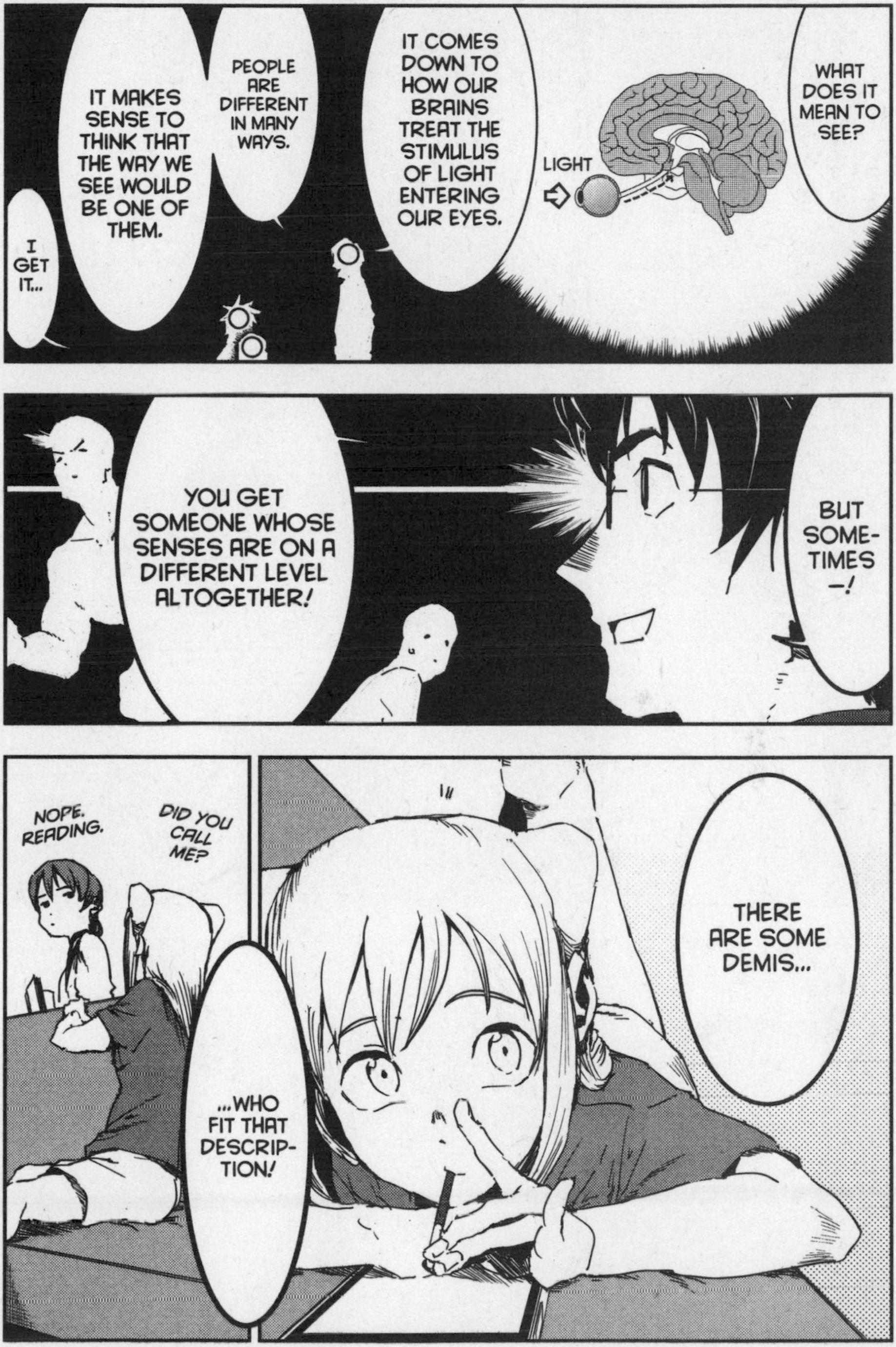
WHAT DOES IT MEAN TO SEE?
LIGHT
IT COMES DOWN TO HOW OUR BRAINS TREAT THE STIMULUS OF LIGHT ENTERING OUR EYES.
PEOPLE ARE DIFFERENT IN MANY WAYS.
IT MAKES SENSE TO THINK THAT THE WAY WE SEE WOULD BE ONE OF THEM.
I GET IT...
BUT SOME-TIMES —!
YOU GET SOMEONE WHOSE SENSES ARE ON A DIFFERENT LEVEL ALTOGETHER!
THERE ARE SOME DEMIS...
...WHO FIT THAT DESCRIP-TION!
DID YOU CALL ME?
NOPE. READING.

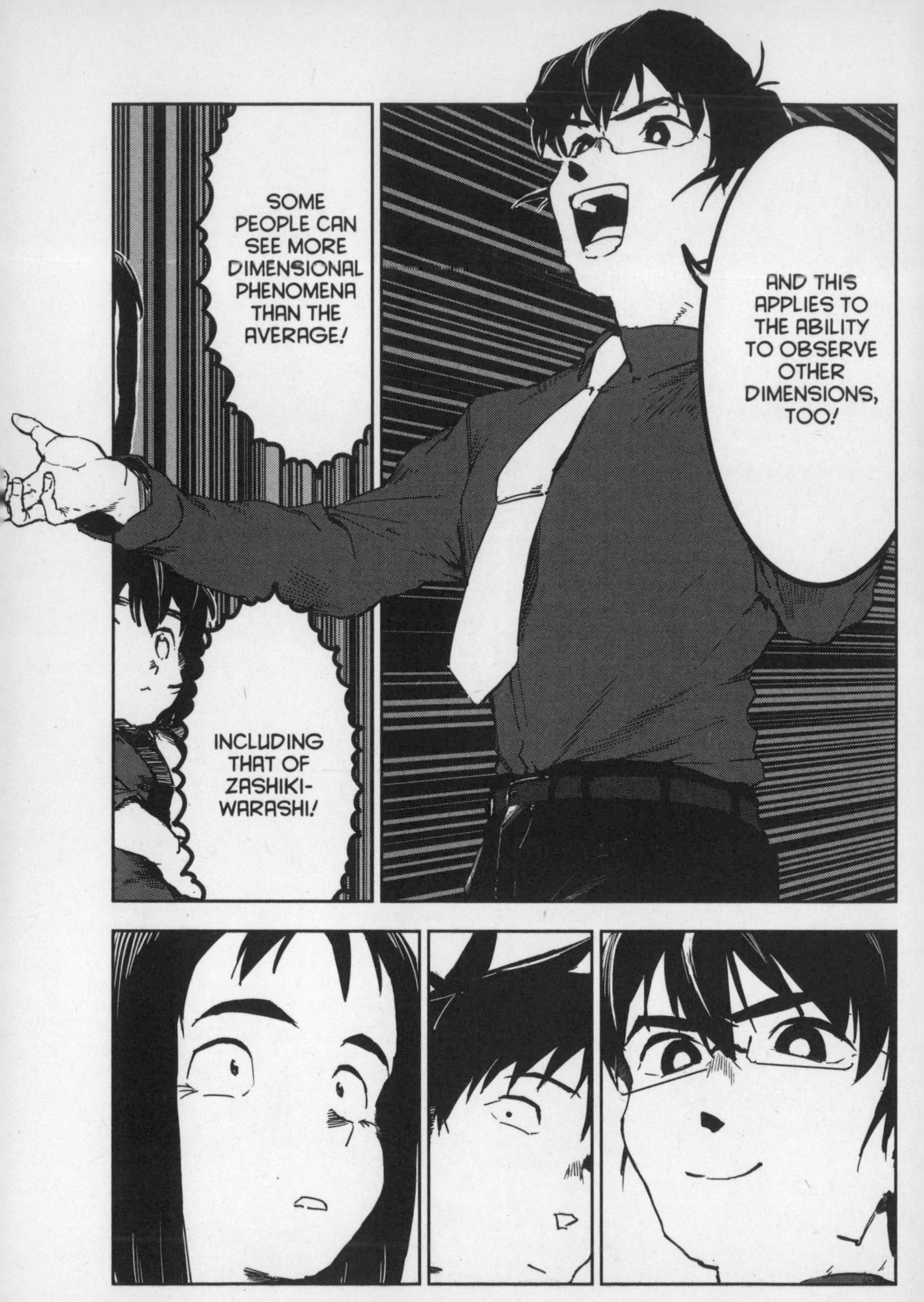
AND THIS APPLIES TO THE ABILITY TO OBSERVE OTHER DIMENSIONS, TOO!
SOME PEOPLE CAN SEE MORE DIMENSIONAL PHENOMENA THAN THE AVERAGE!
INCLUDING THAT OF ZASHIKI-WARASHI!

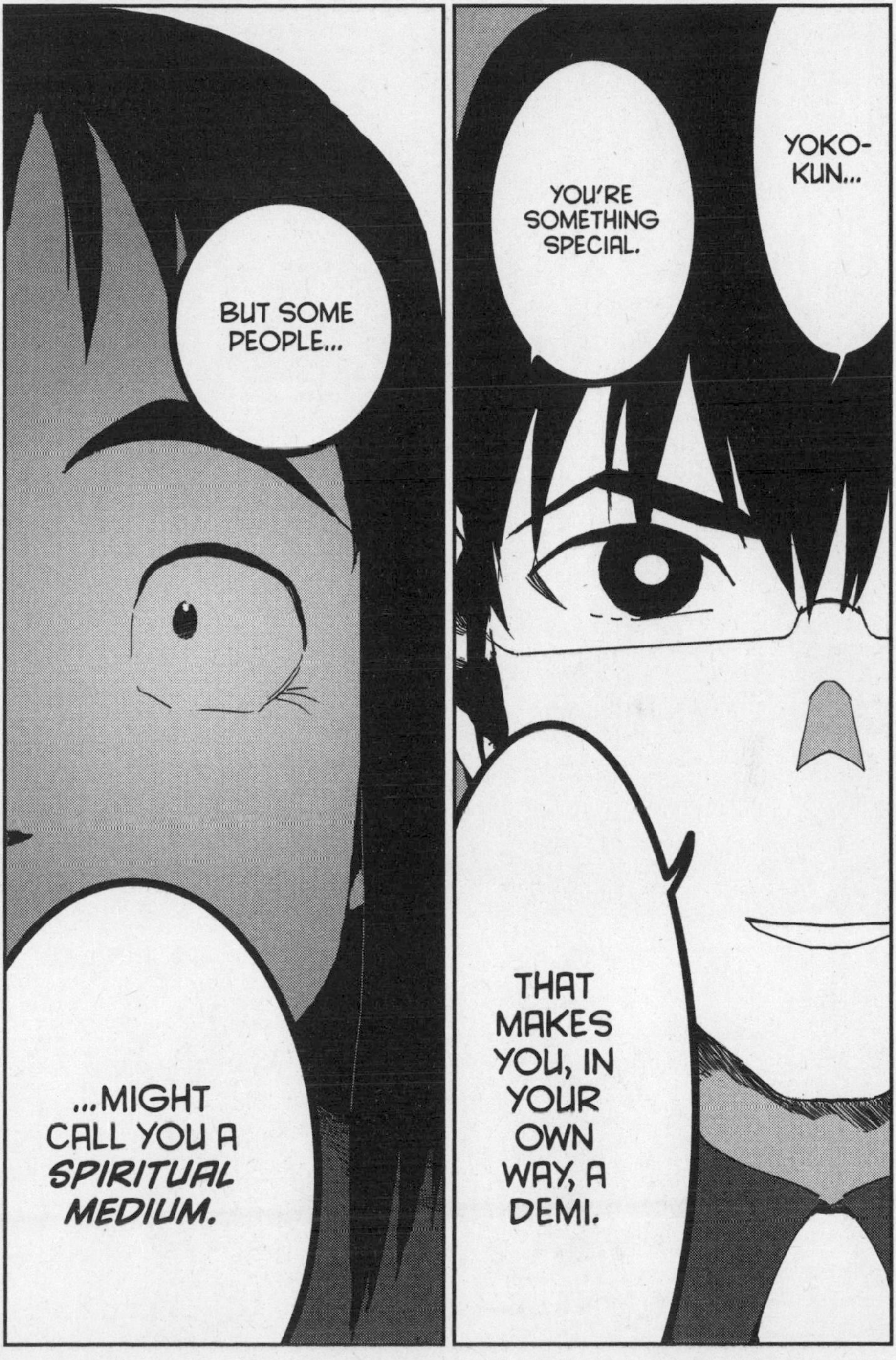
YOKO-KUN...
YOU'RE SOMETHING SPECIAL.
THAT MAKES YOU, IN YOUR OWN WAY, A DEMI.
BUT SOME PEOPLE...
...MIGHT CALL YOU A *SPIRITUAL MEDIUM.*

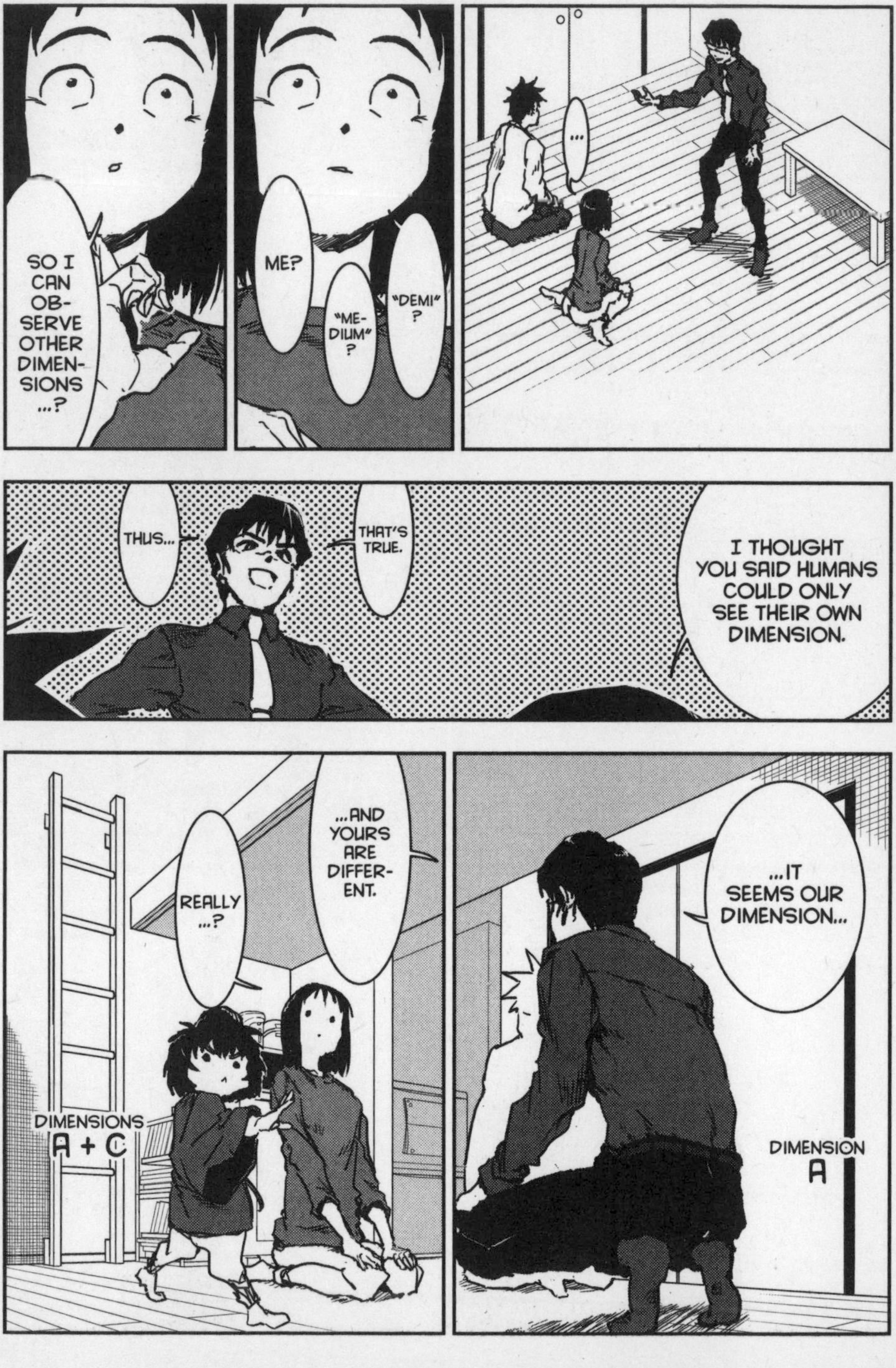
...
ME?
"DEMI"?
"MEDIUM"?
SO I CAN OBSERVE OTHER DIMENSIONS...?
I THOUGHT YOU SAID HUMANS COULD ONLY SEE THEIR OWN DIMENSION.
THAT'S TRUE.
THUS...
...IT SEEMS OUR DIMENSION...
DIMENSION A
...AND YOURS ARE DIFFERENT.
REALLY...?
DIMENSIONS A + C

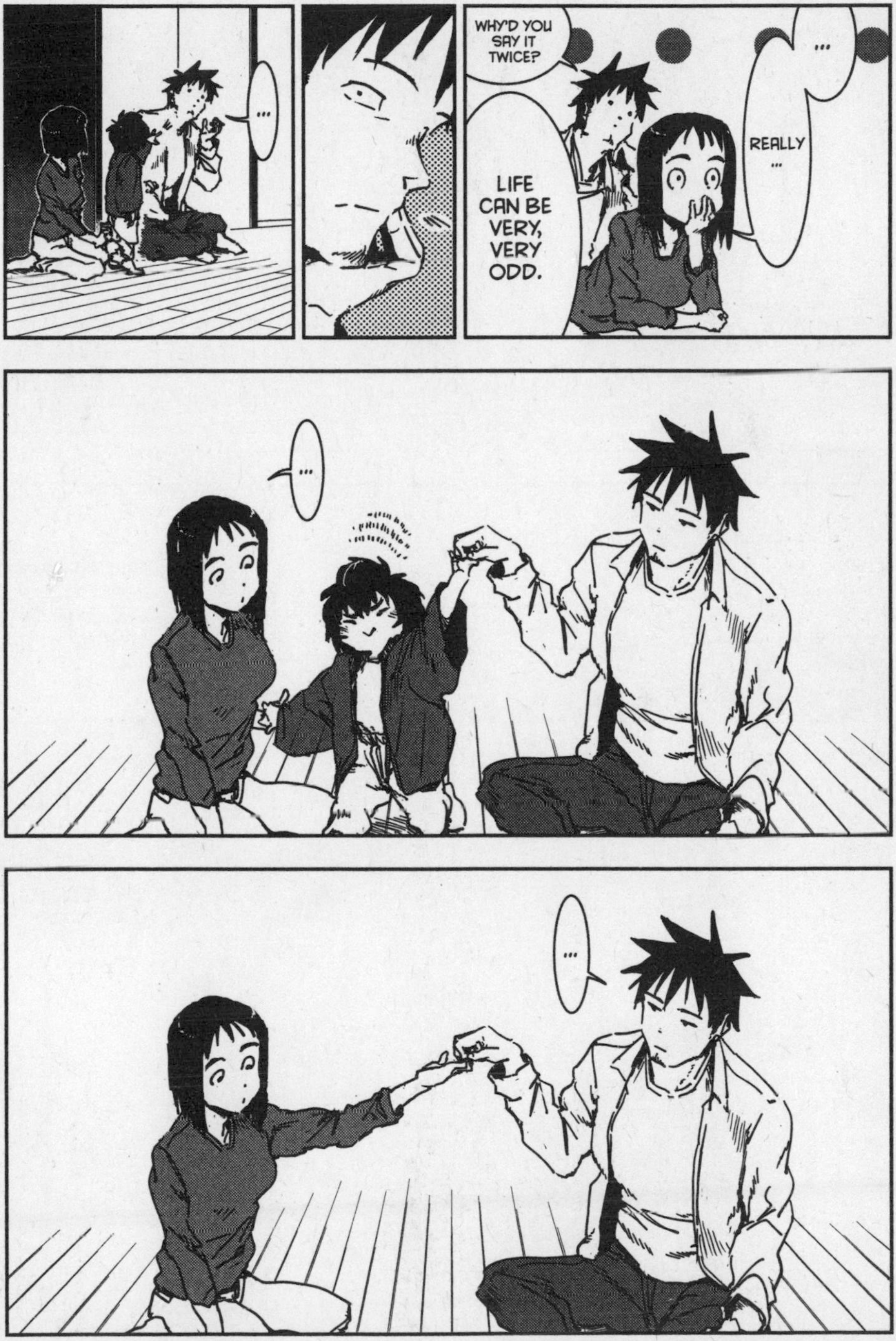
...
REALLY ...
WHY'D YOU SAY IT TWICE?
LIFE CAN BE VERY, VERY ODD.
...
...
...

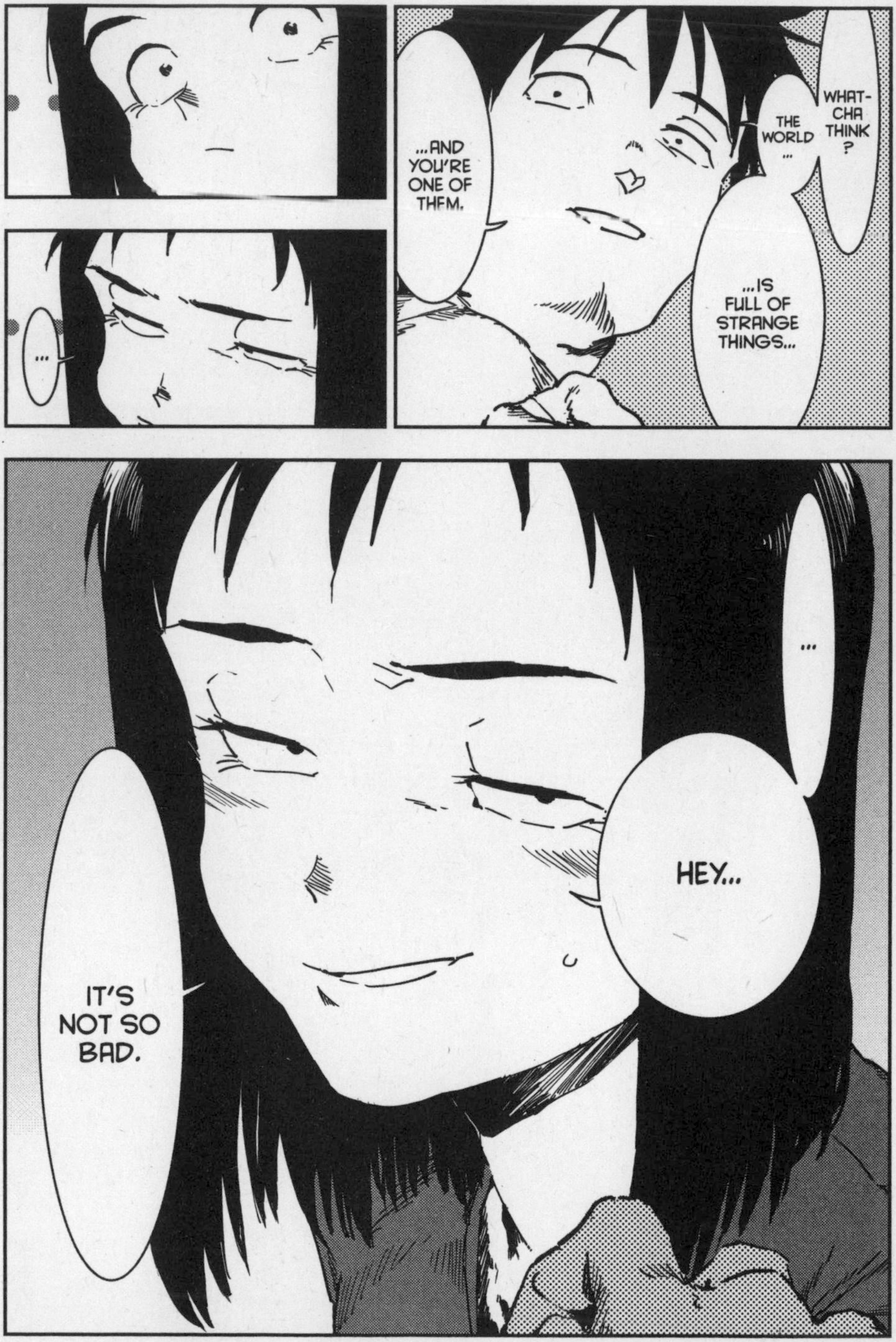
WHAT-CHA THINK?
THE WORLD ...
...IS FULL OF STRANGE THINGS...
...AND YOU'RE ONE OF THEM.
...
...
HEY...
IT'S NOT SO BAD.

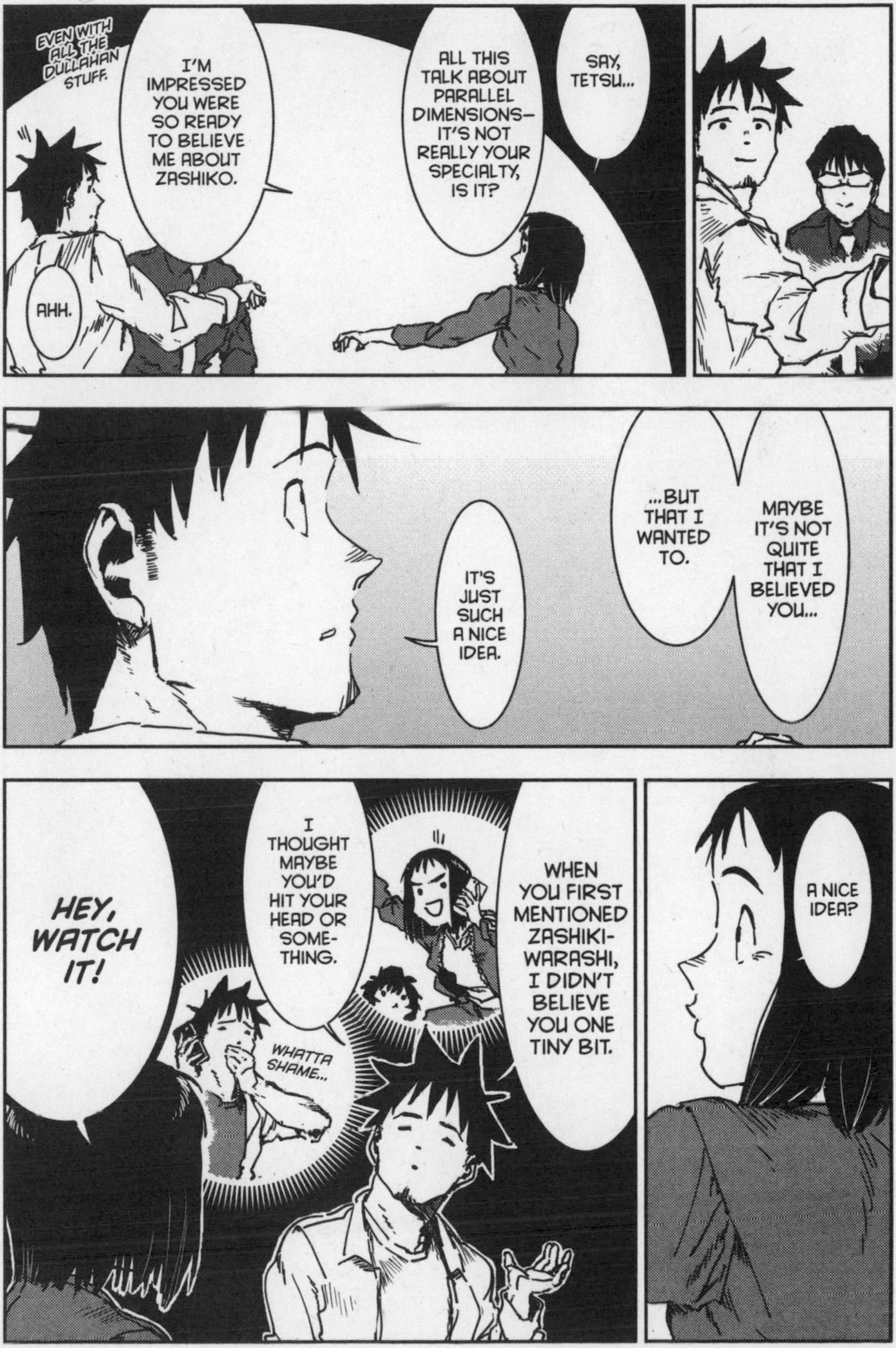
SAY, TETSU...
ALL THIS TALK ABOUT PARALLEL DIMENSIONS— IT'S NOT REALLY YOUR SPECIALTY, IS IT?
I'M IMPRESSED YOU WERE SO READY TO BELIEVE ME ABOUT ZASHIKO.
EVEN WITH ALL THE DULLAHAN STUFF.
AHH.
MAYBE IT'S NOT QUITE THAT I BELIEVED YOU...
...BUT THAT I WANTED TO.
IT'S JUST SUCH A NICE IDEA.
A NICE IDEA?
WHEN YOU FIRST MENTIONED ZASHIKI-WARASHI, I DIDN'T BELIEVE YOU ONE TINY BIT.
I THOUGHT MAYBE YOU'D HIT YOUR HEAD OR SOME-THING.
HEY, WATCH IT!
WHATTA SHAME...

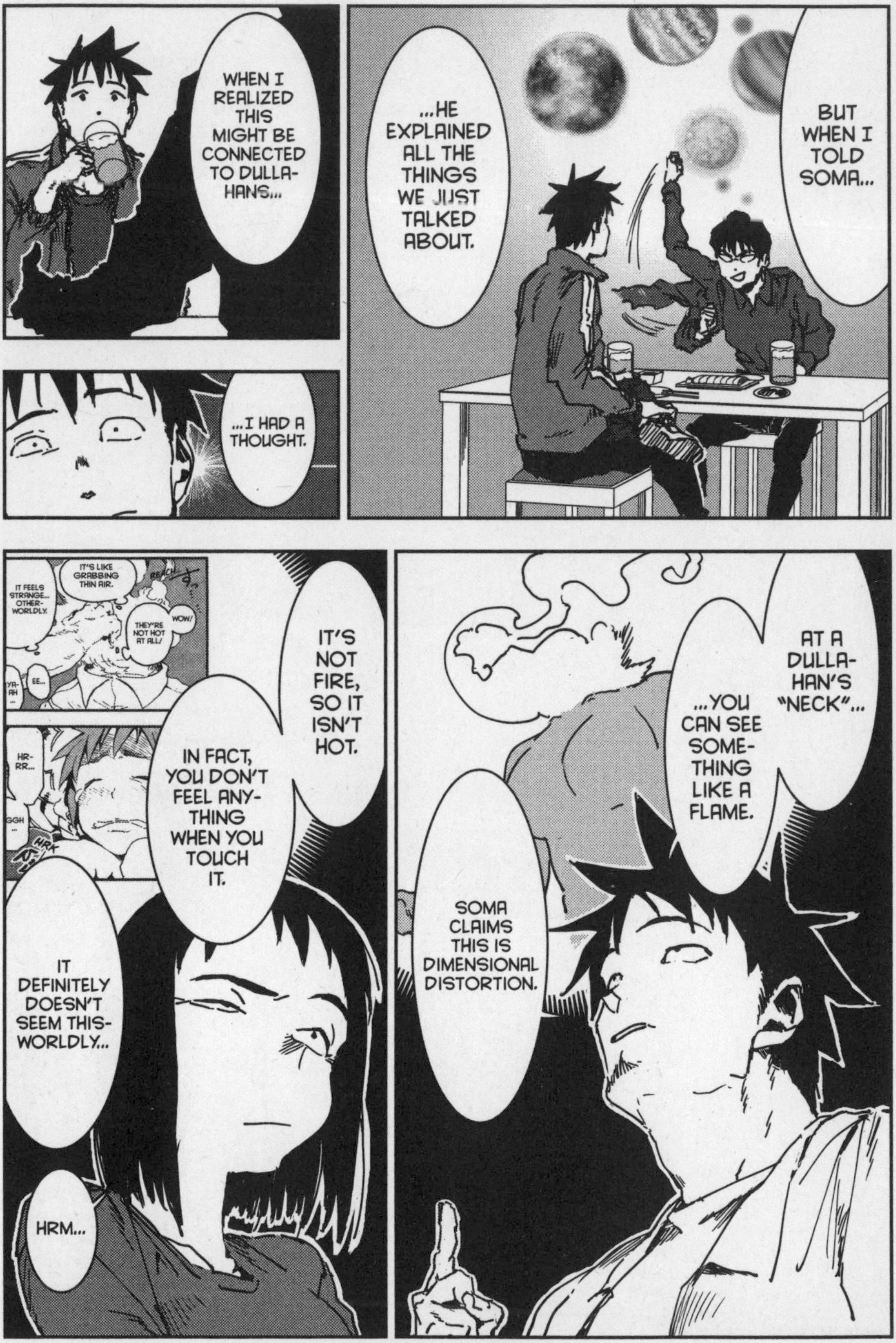
BUT WHEN I TOLD SOMA...
...HE EXPLAINED ALL THE THINGS WE JUST TALKED ABOUT.
WHEN I REALIZED THIS MIGHT BE CONNECTED TO DULLA-HANS...
...I HAD A THOUGHT.
AT A DULLA-HAN'S "NECK"...
...YOU CAN SEE SOME-THING LIKE A FLAME.
SOMA CLAIMS THIS IS DIMENSIONAL DISTORTION.
IT'S NOT FIRE, SO IT ISN'T HOT.
IN FACT, YOU DON'T FEEL ANY-THING WHEN YOU TOUCH IT.
REACH
WOW!
THEY'RE NOT HOT AT ALL!
IT'S LIKE GRABBING THIN AIR.
IT FEELS STRANGE... OTHER-WORLDLY.
EE...
YA-AH...
HR-RR...
GGH...
HRK
IT DEFINITELY DOESN'T SEEM THIS-WORLDLY...
HRM...

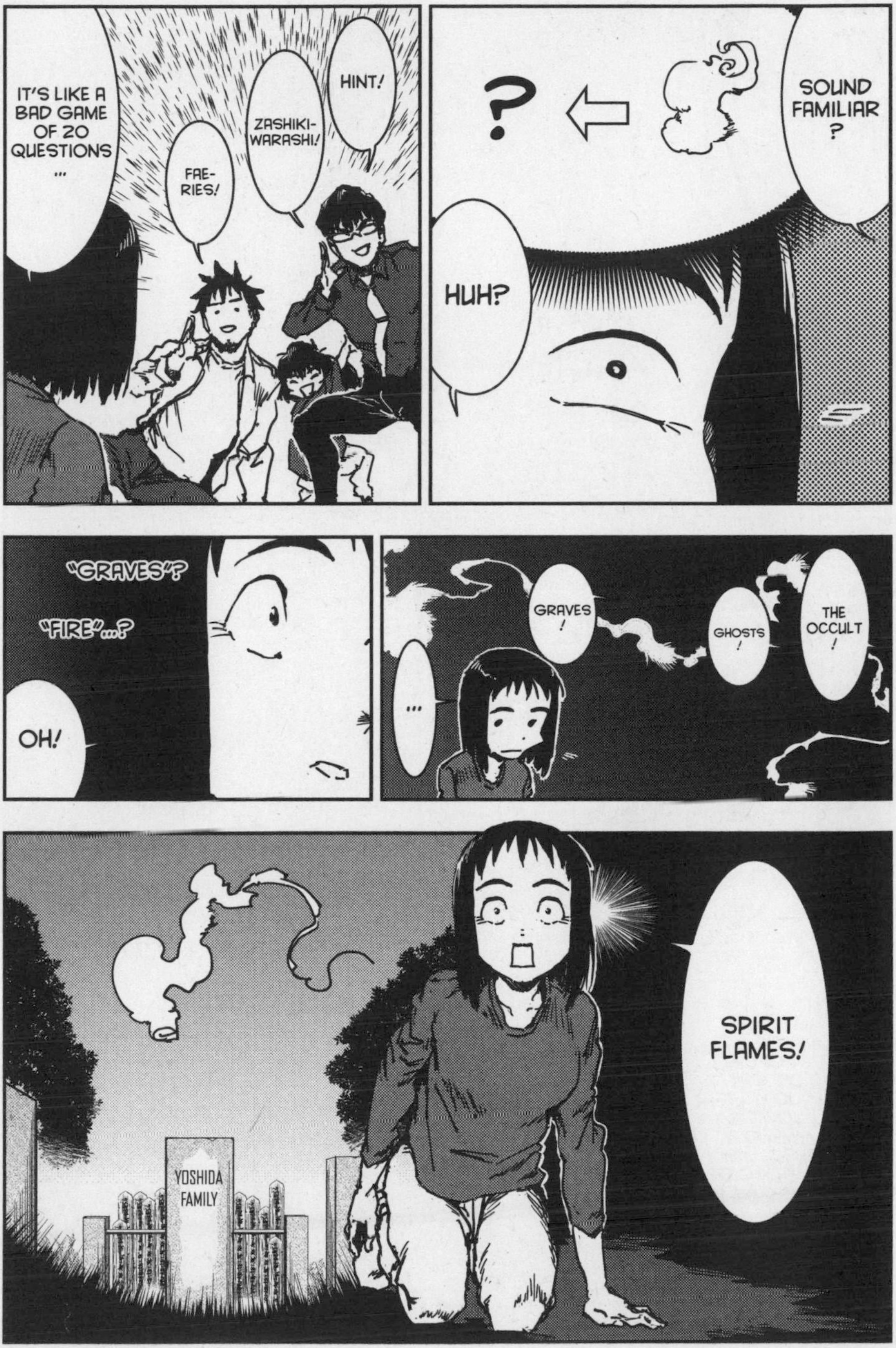
SOUND FAMILIAR ?
HUH?
HINT!
ZASHIKI-WARASHI!
FAE-RIES!
IT'S LIKE A BAD GAME OF 20 QUESTIONS ...
THE OCCULT !
GHOSTS !
GRAVES !
...
"GRAVES"?
"FIRE"...?
OH!
SPIRIT FLAMES!
YOSHIDA FAMILY

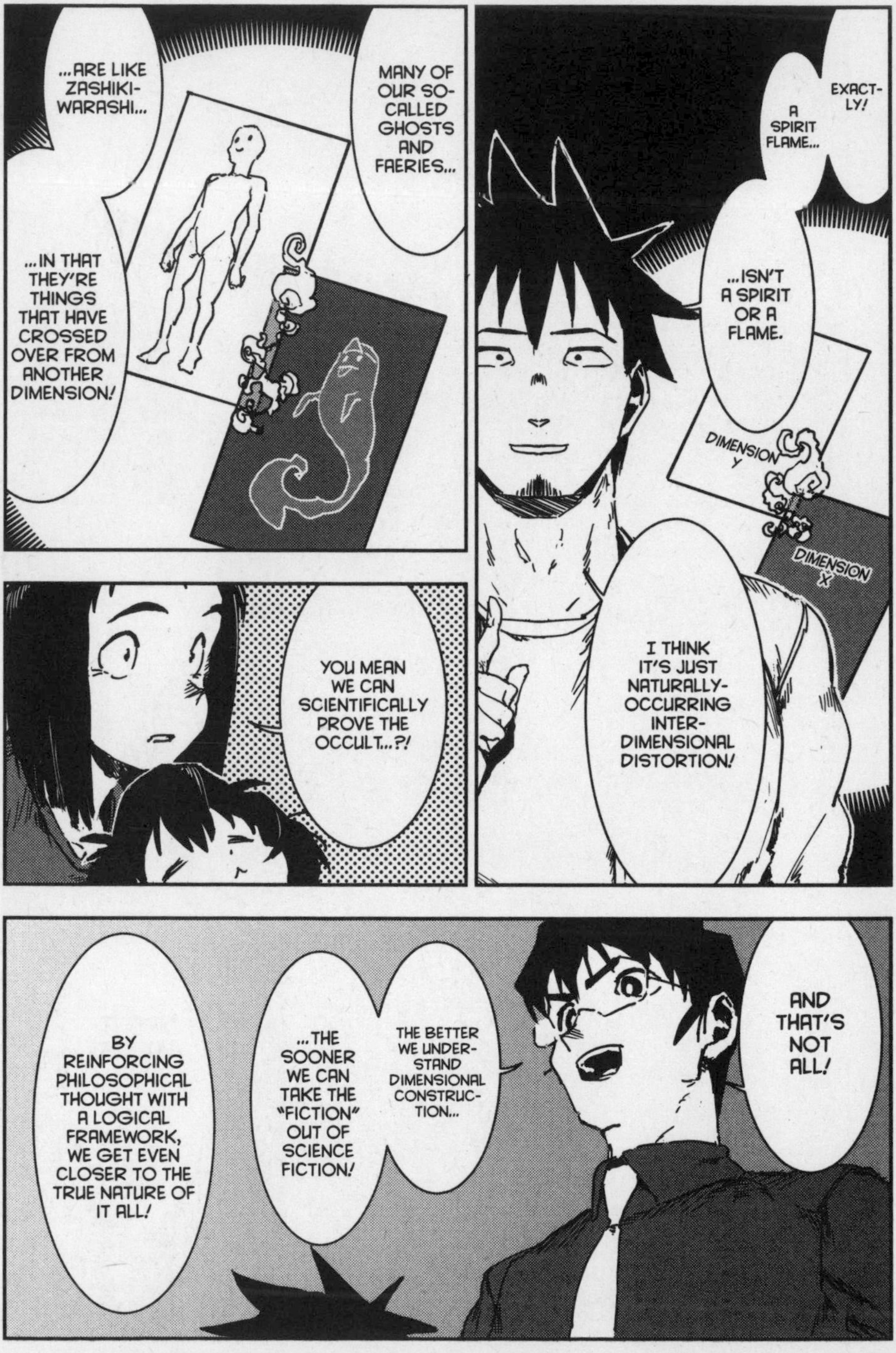
A SPIRIT FLAME...
EXACTLY!
...ISN'T A SPIRIT OR A FLAME.
DIMENSION Y
DIMENSION X
I THINK IT'S JUST NATURALLY-OCCURRING INTER-DIMENSIONAL DISTORTION!
MANY OF OUR SO-CALLED GHOSTS AND FAERIES...
...ARE LIKE ZASHIKI-WARASHI...
...IN THAT THEY'RE THINGS THAT HAVE CROSSED OVER FROM ANOTHER DIMENSION!
YOU MEAN WE CAN SCIENTIFICALLY PROVE THE OCCULT...?!
AND THAT'S NOT ALL!
THE BETTER WE UNDER-STAND DIMENSIONAL CONSTRUC-TION...
...THE SOONER WE CAN TAKE THE "FICTION" OUT OF SCIENCE FICTION!
BY REINFORCING PHILOSOPHICAL THOUGHT WITH A LOGICAL FRAMEWORK, WE GET EVEN CLOSER TO THE TRUE NATURE OF IT ALL!

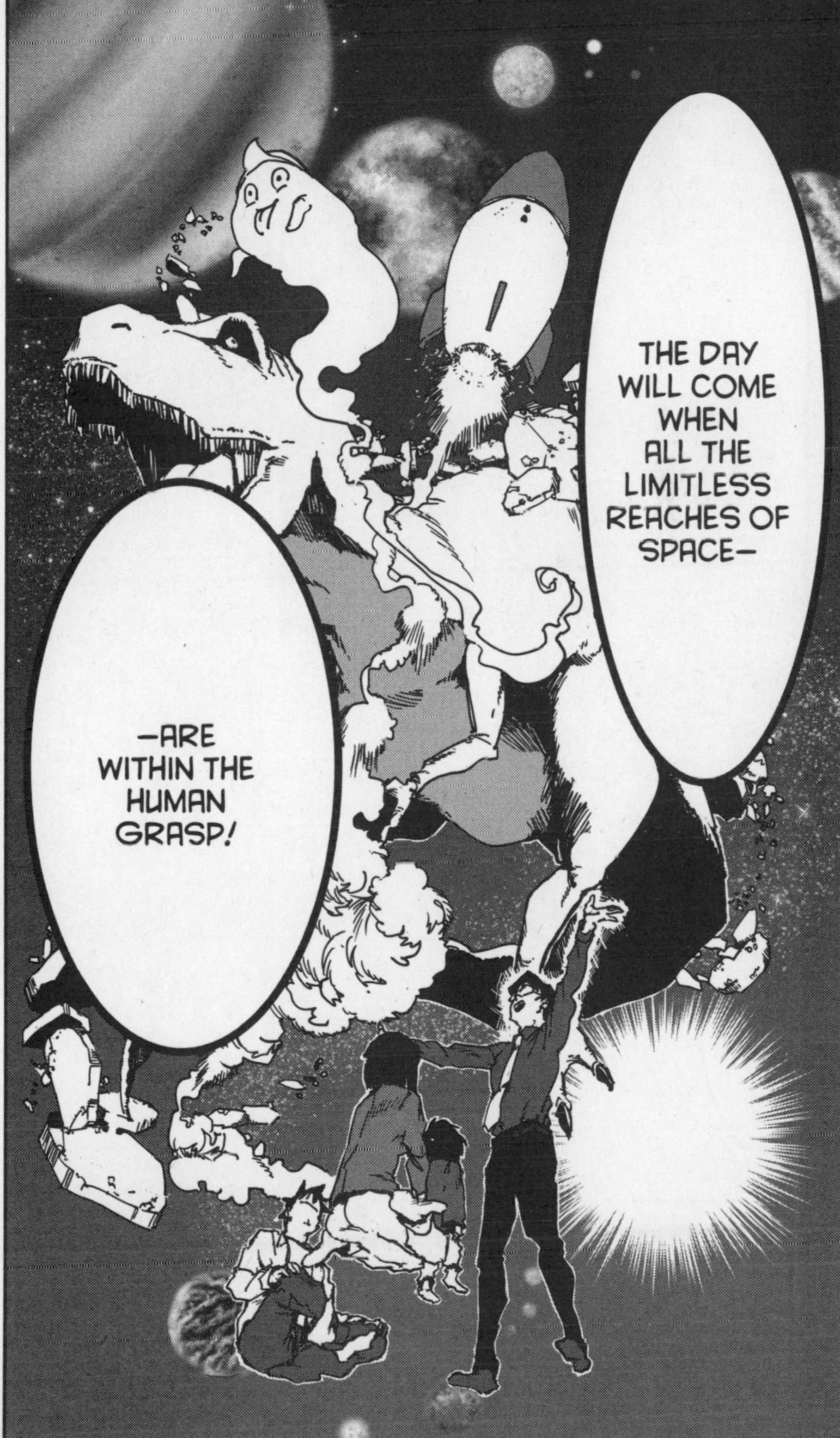
THE DAY WILL COME WHEN ALL THE LIMITLESS REACHES OF SPACE–
–ARE WITHIN THE HUMAN GRASP!

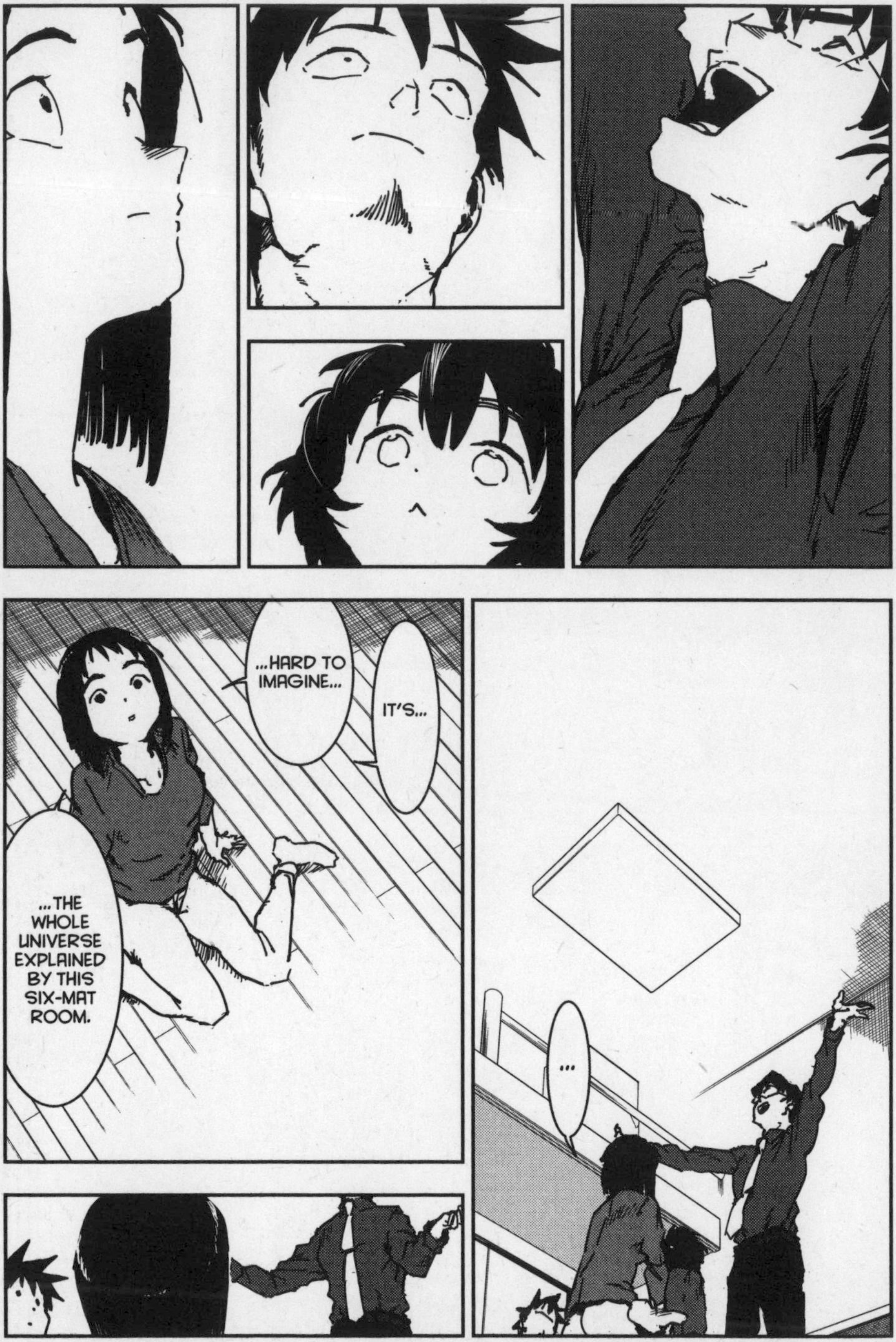
...
IT'S...
...HARD TO IMAGINE...
...THE WHOLE UNIVERSE EXPLAINED BY THIS SIX-MAT ROOM.

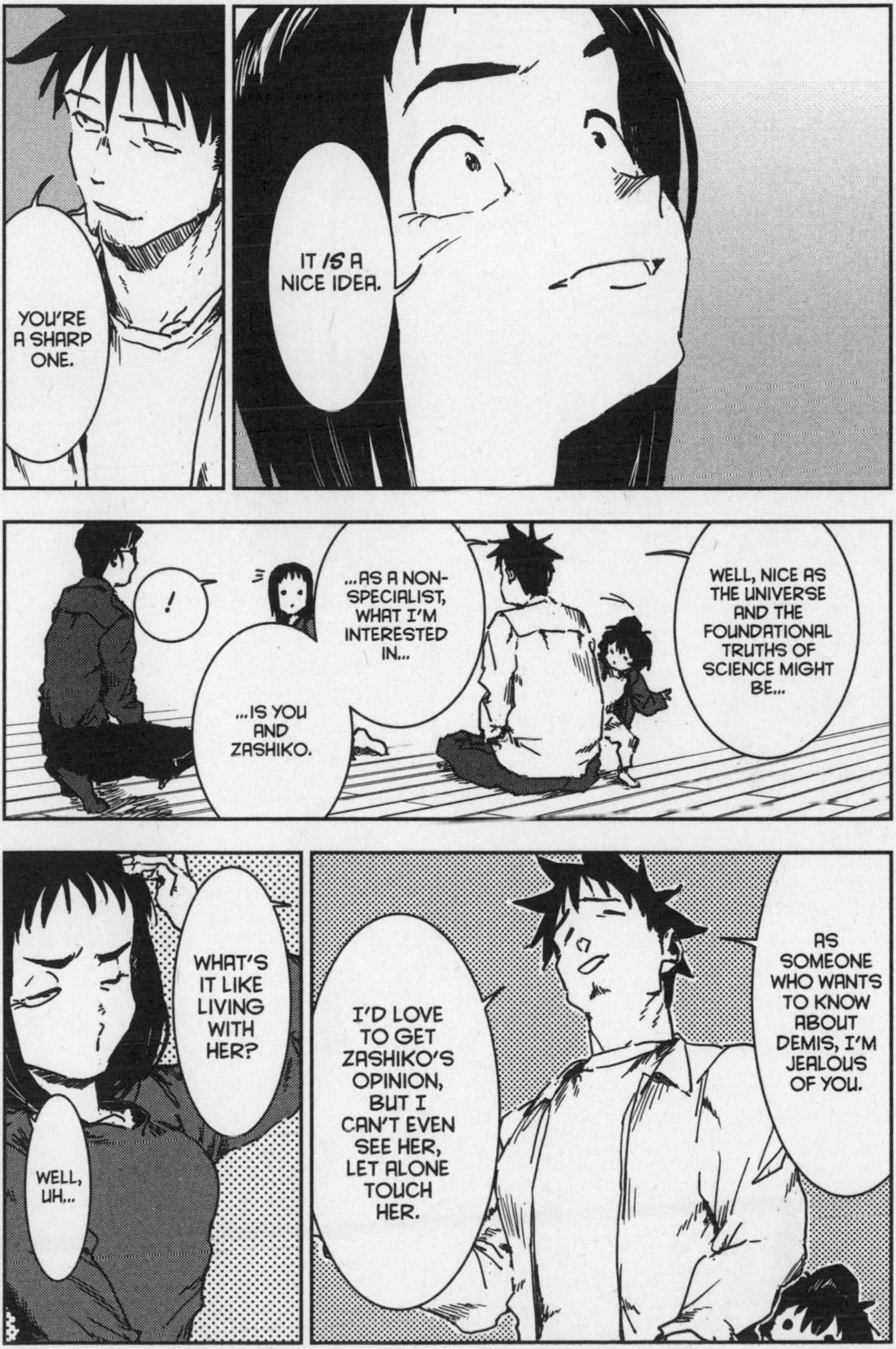
IT IS A NICE IDEA.
YOU'RE A SHARP ONE.
WELL, NICE AS THE UNIVERSE AND THE FOUNDATIONAL TRUTHS OF SCIENCE MIGHT BE...
...AS A NON-SPECIALIST, WHAT I'M INTERESTED IN...
...IS YOU AND ZASHIKO.
!
AS SOMEONE WHO WANTS TO KNOW ABOUT DEMIS, I'M JEALOUS OF YOU.
I'D LOVE TO GET ZASHIKO'S OPINION, BUT I CAN'T EVEN SEE HER, LET ALONE TOUCH HER.
WHAT'S IT LIKE LIVING WITH HER?
WELL, UH...

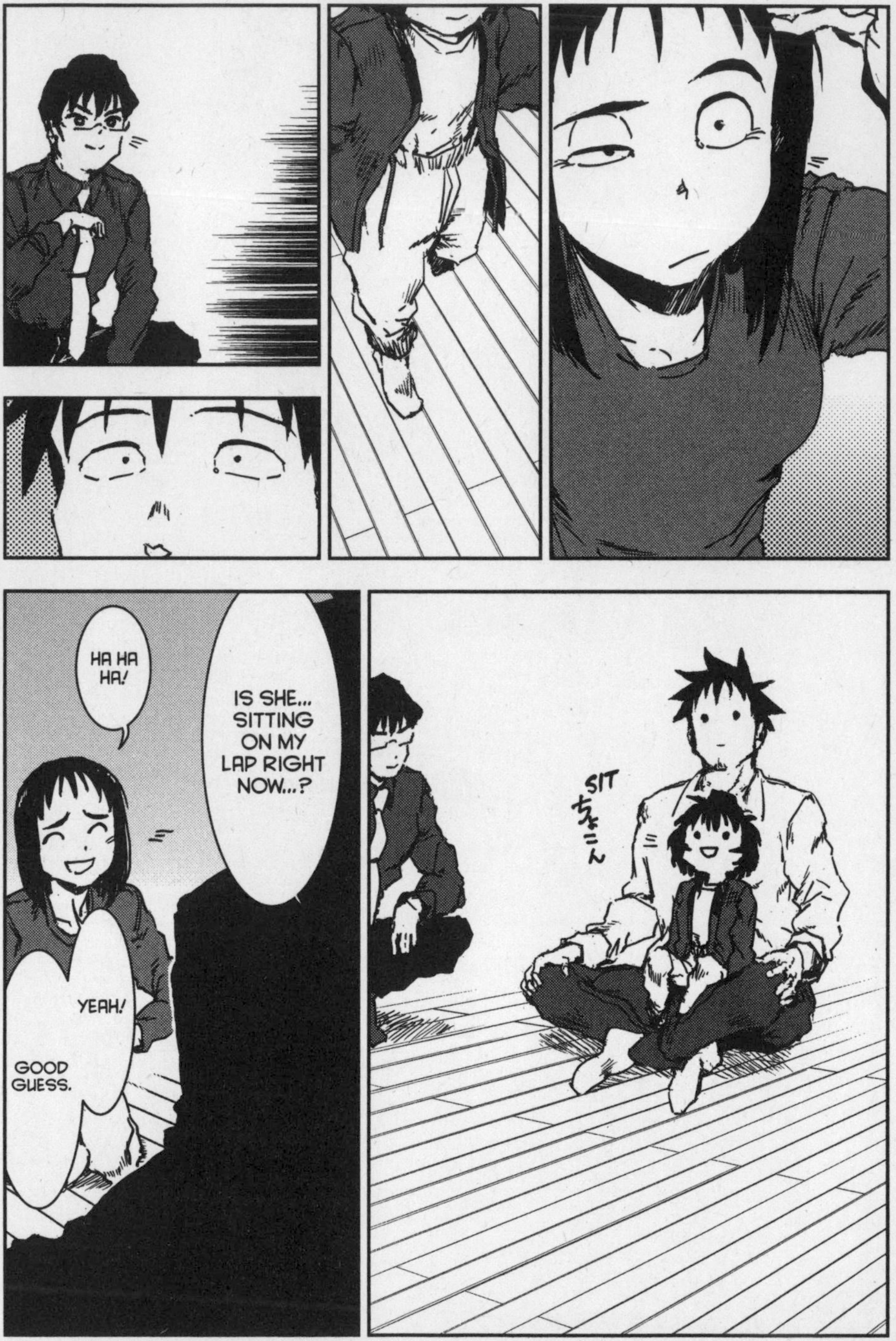
SIT
ちょこん
IS SHE... SITTING ON MY LAP RIGHT NOW...?
HA HA HA!
YEAH!
GOOD GUESS.

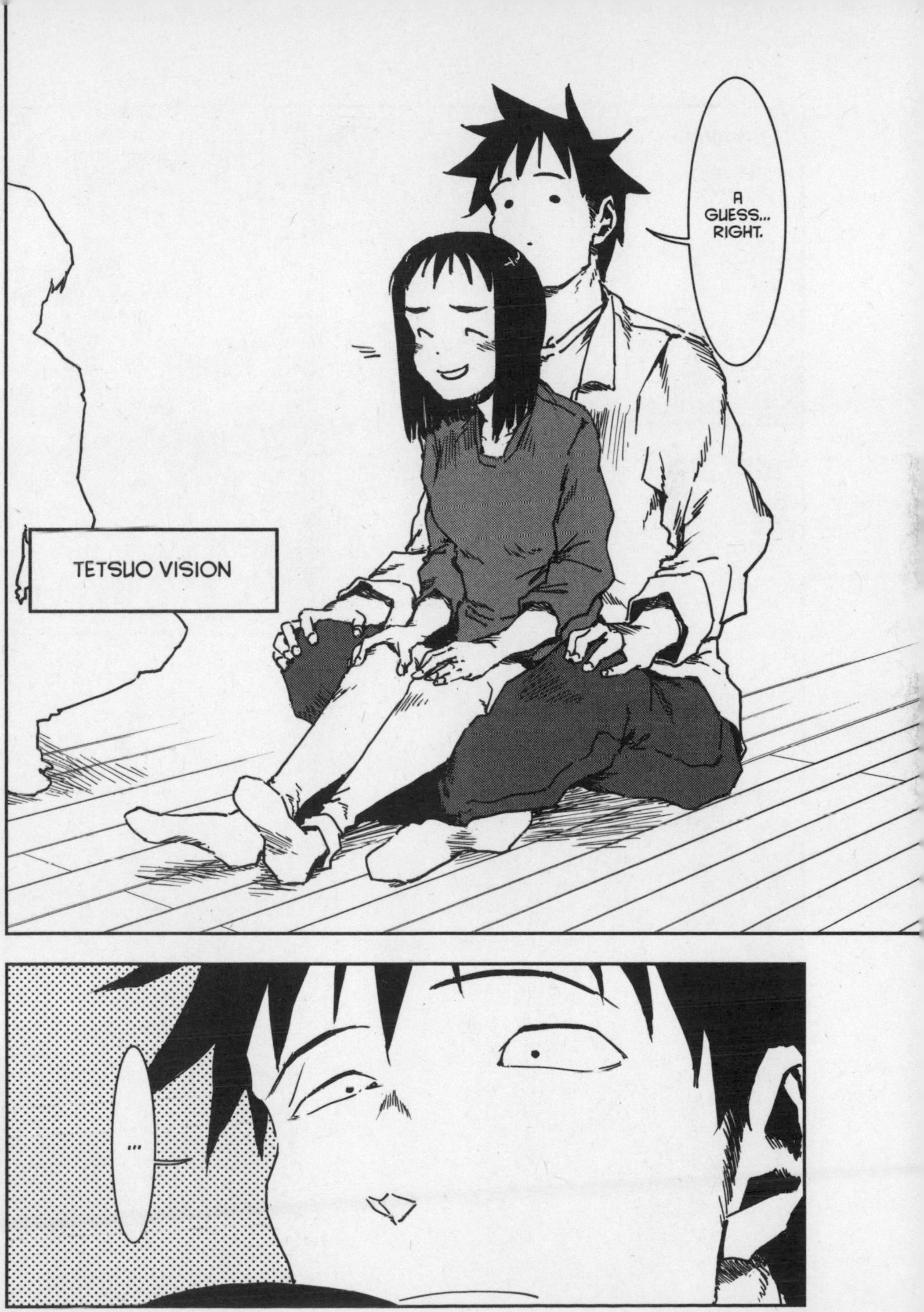
A GUESS... RIGHT.
TETSUO VISION
...

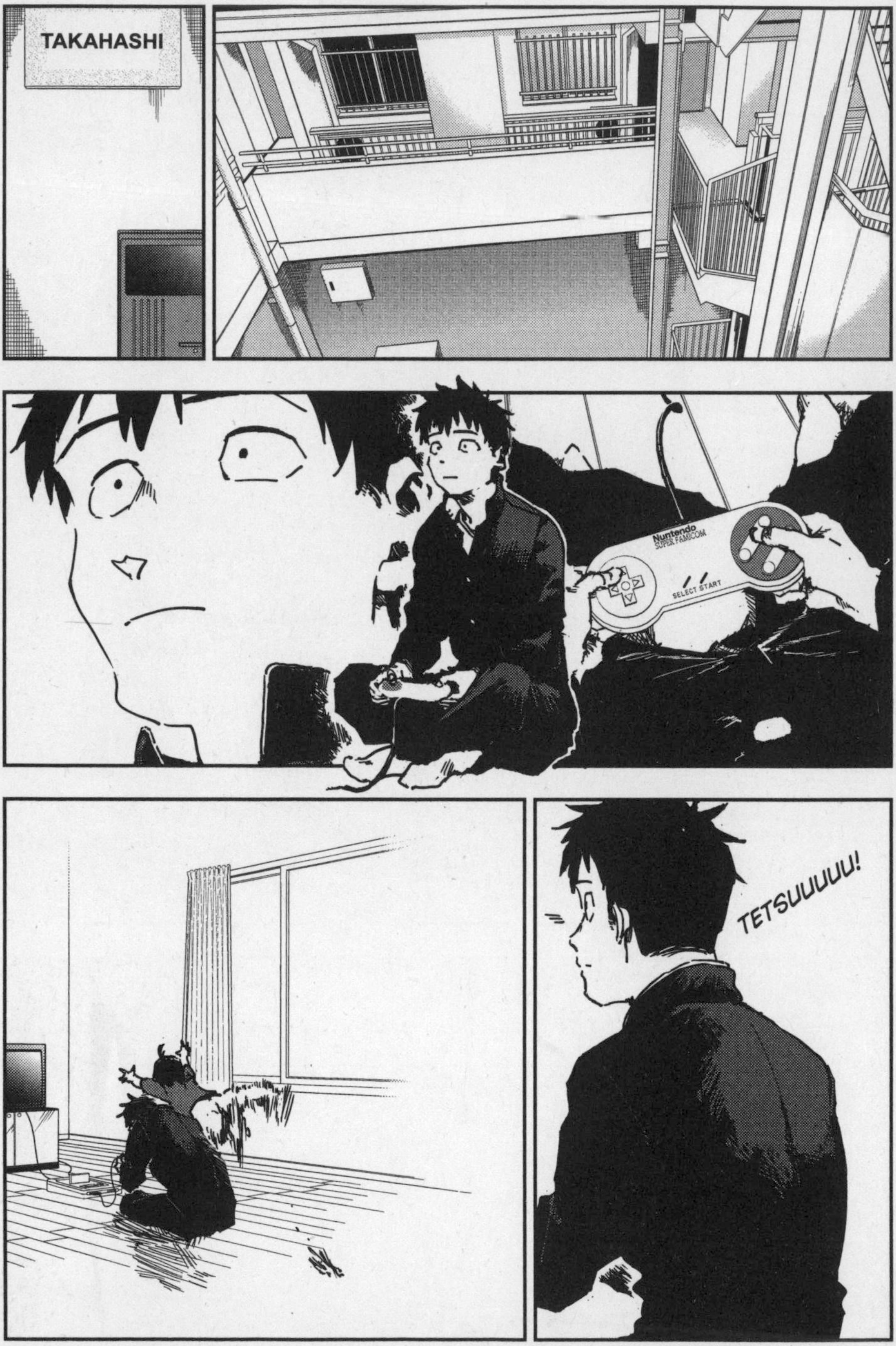
TAKAHASHI
Nuntendo
SUPER FAMICOM
SELECT START
TETSUUUUU!

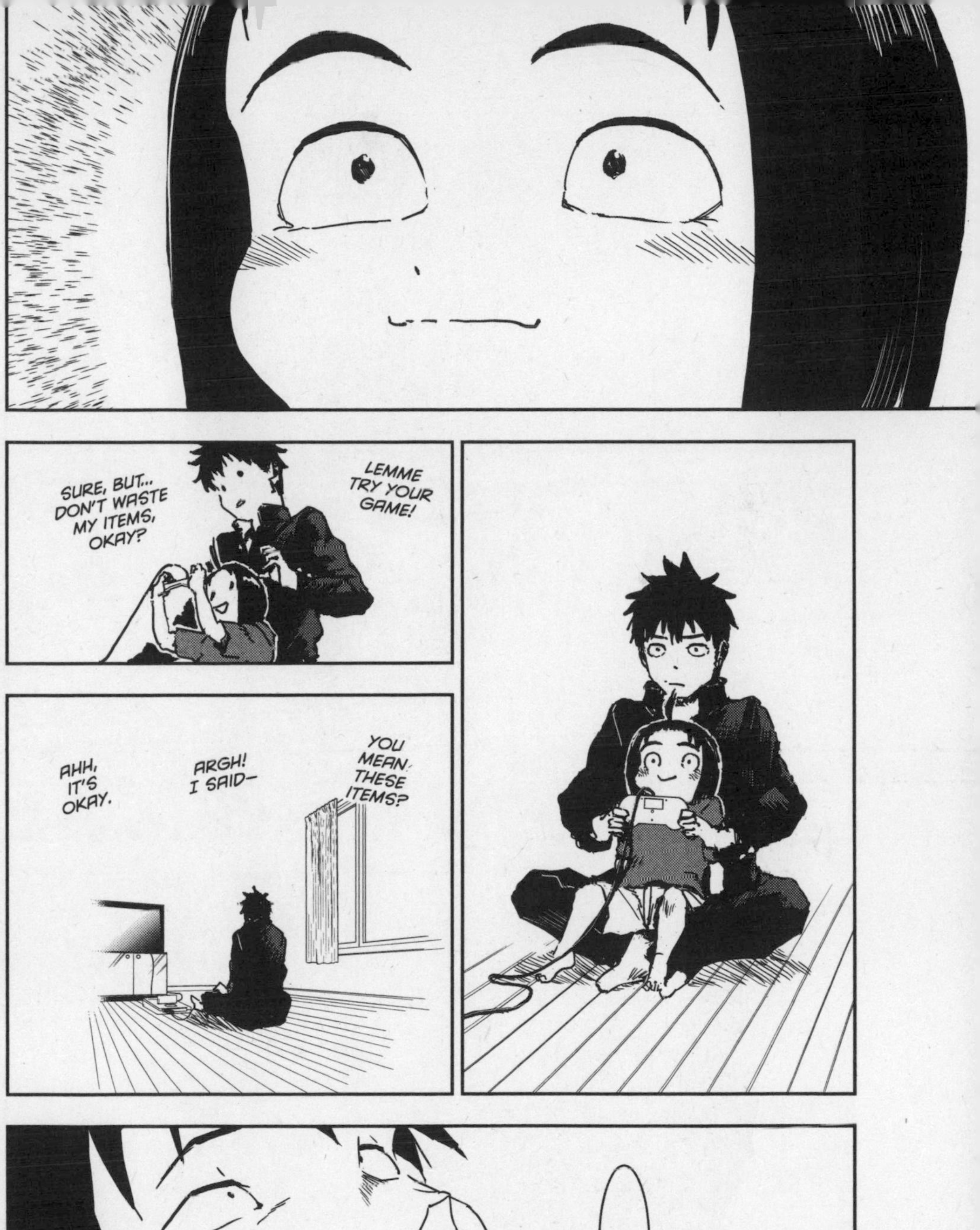
LEMME TRY YOUR GAME!
SURE, BUT... DON'T WASTE MY ITEMS, OKAY?
YOU MEAN THESE ITEMS?
ARGH! I SAID—
AHH, IT'S OKAY.
...

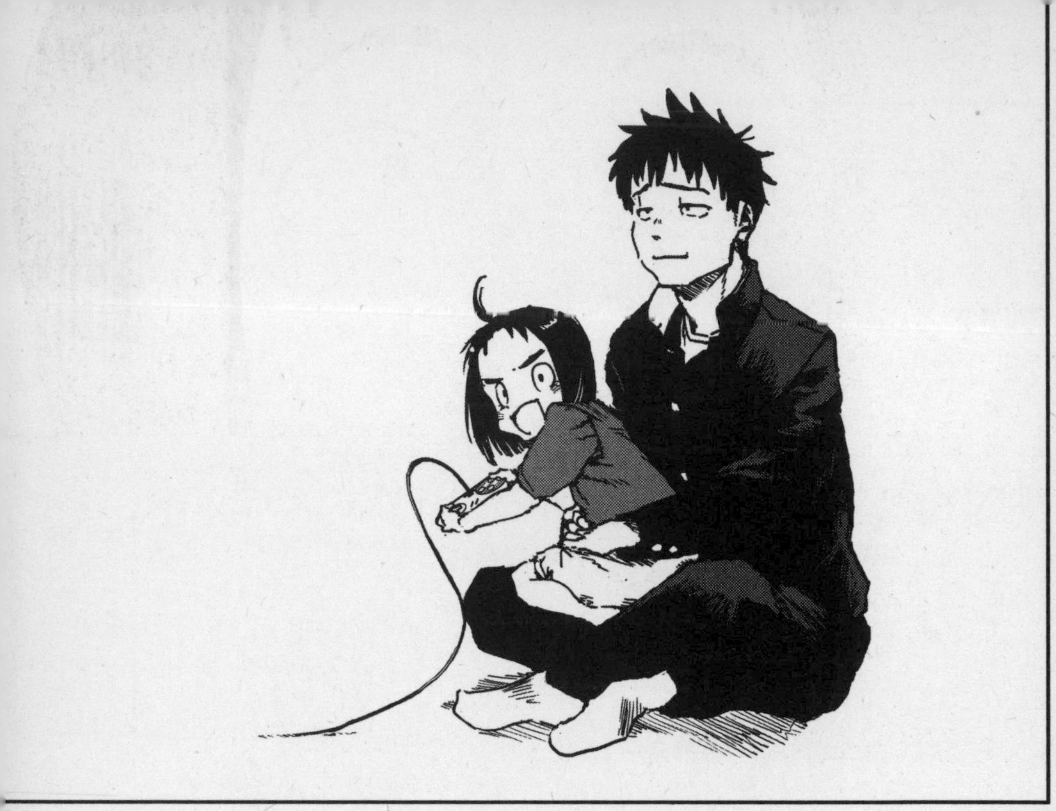
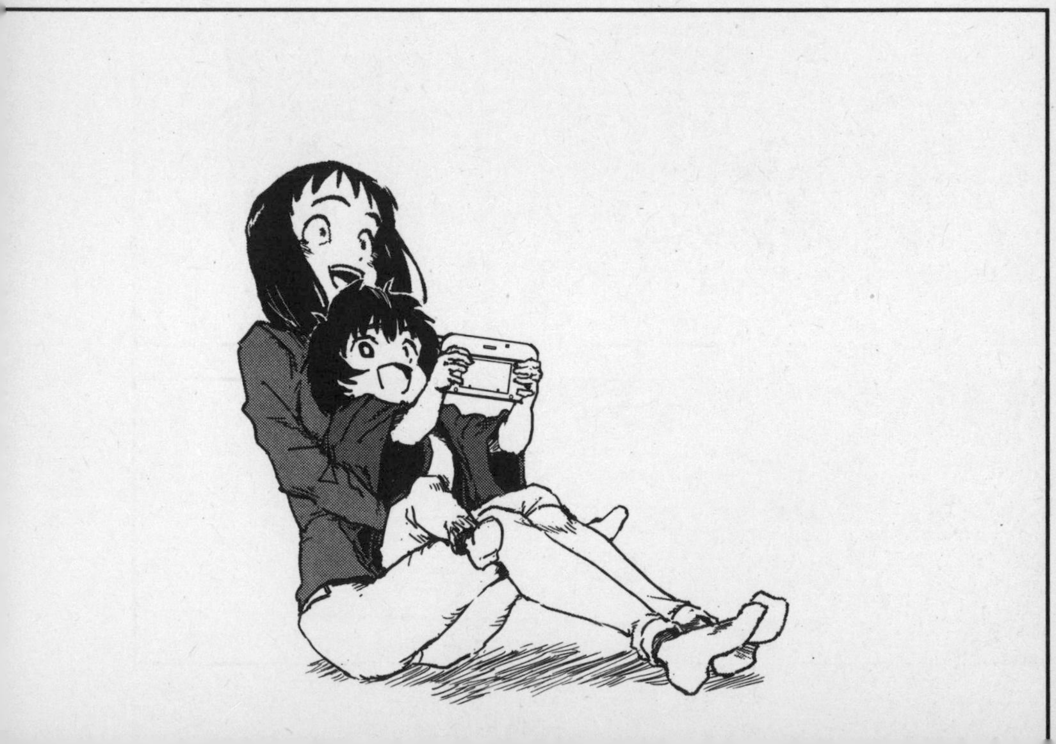

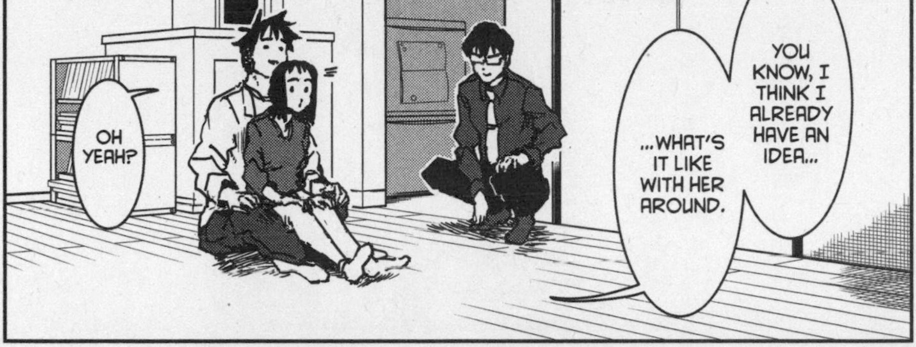
YOU KNOW, I THINK I ALREADY HAVE AN IDEA...
...WHAT'S IT LIKE WITH HER AROUND.
OH YEAH?

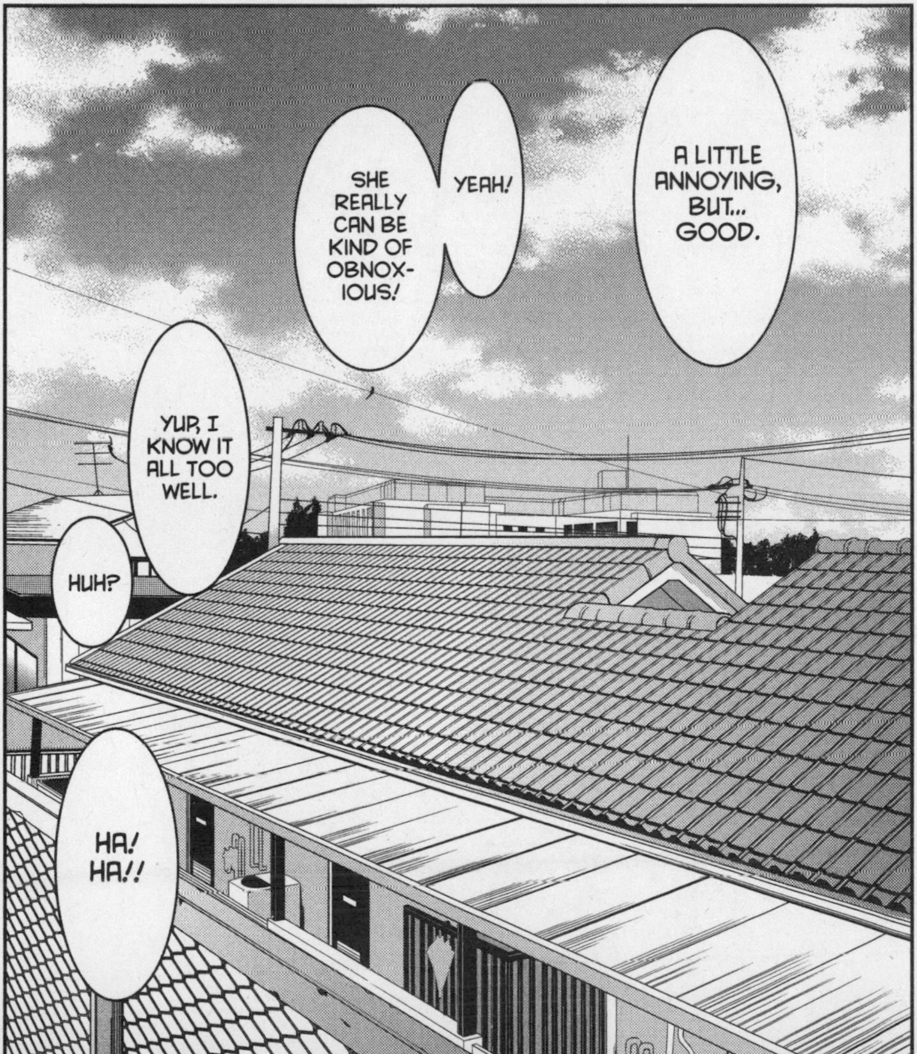
A LITTLE ANNOYING, BUT... GOOD.
YEAH!
SHE REALLY CAN BE KIND OF OBNOX-IOUS!
YUP, I KNOW IT ALL TOO WELL.
HUH?
HA! HA!!

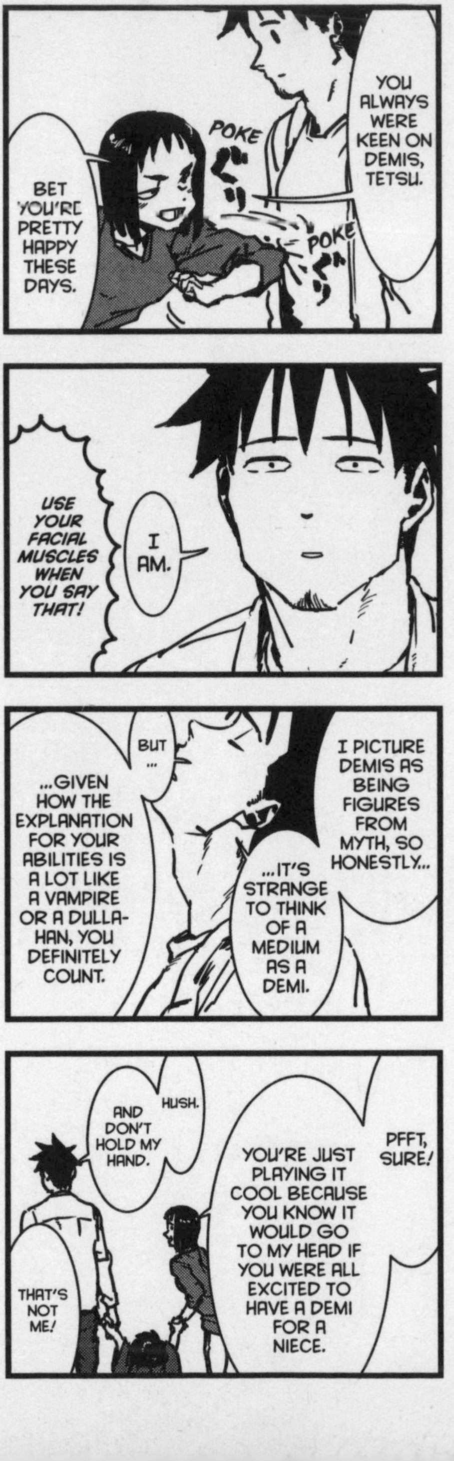
YOU ALWAYS WERE KEEN ON DEMIS, TETSU.
POKE
POKE
BET YOU'RE PRETTY HAPPY THESE DAYS.
I AM.
USE YOUR FACIAL MUSCLES WHEN YOU SAY THAT!
I PICTURE DEMIS AS BEING FIGURES FROM MYTH, SO HONESTLY...
...IT'S STRANGE TO THINK OF A MEDIUM AS A DEMI.
BUT...
...GIVEN HOW THE EXPLANATION FOR YOUR ABILITIES IS A LOT LIKE A VAMPIRE OR A DULLA-HAN, YOU DEFINITELY COUNT.
PFFT, SURE!
YOU'RE JUST PLAYING IT COOL BECAUSE YOU KNOW IT WOULD GO TO MY HEAD IF YOU WERE ALL EXCITED TO HAVE A DEMI FOR A NIECE.
HUSH.
AND DON'T HOLD MY HAND.
THAT'S NOT ME!

INTERVIEWS WITH MONSTER GIRLS

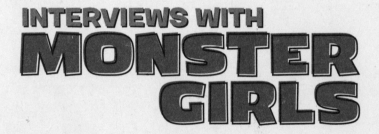

Chapter 40: Tetsuko Takahashi is a Biology Teacher

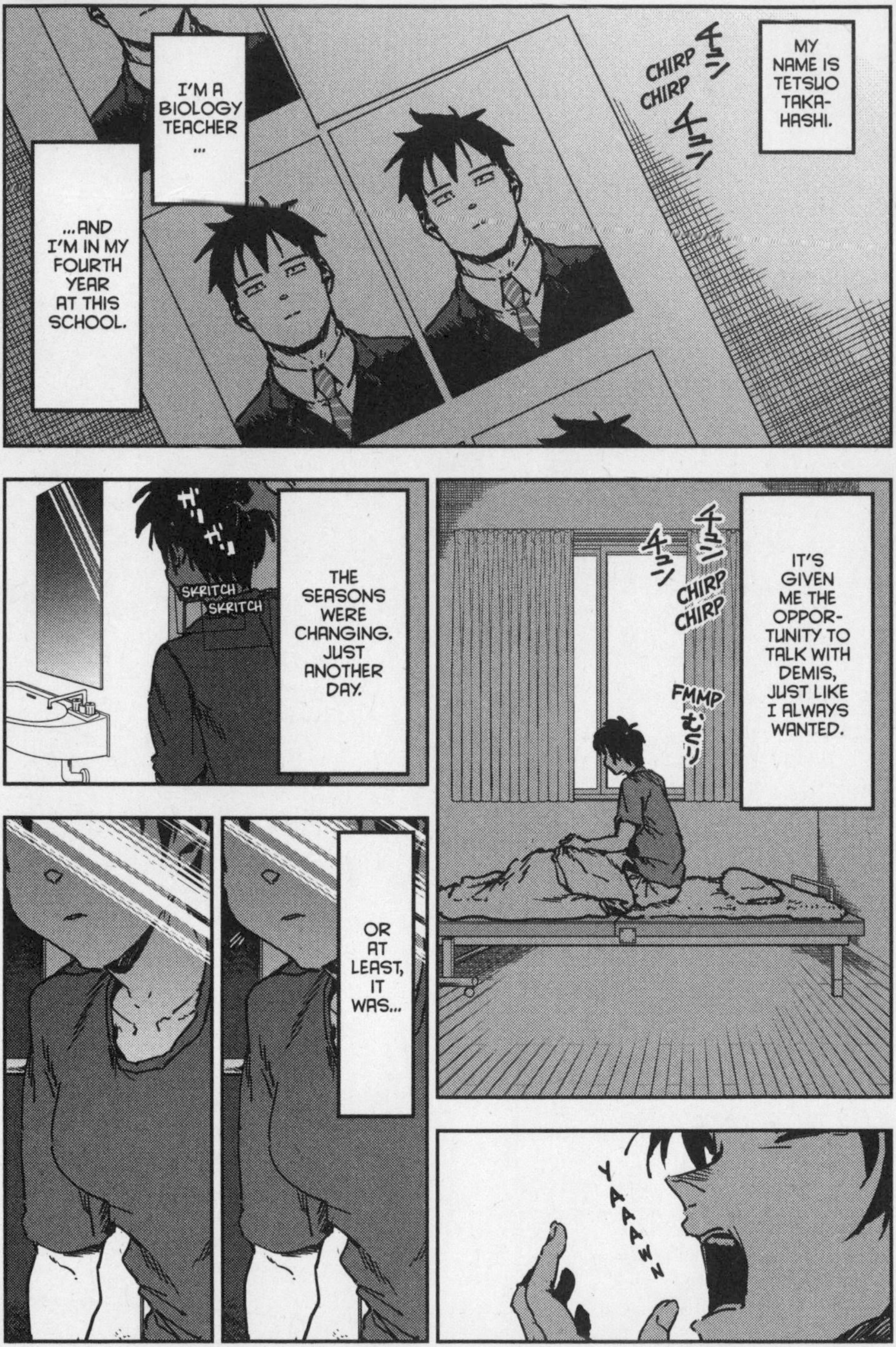
MY NAME IS TETSUO TAKA-HASHI.
チュン CHIRP
チュン CHIRP
I'M A BIOLOGY TEACHER ...
...AND I'M IN MY FOURTH YEAR AT THIS SCHOOL.
チュン チュン
CHIRP CHIRP
IT'S GIVEN ME THE OPPOR-TUNITY TO TALK WITH DEMIS, JUST LIKE I ALWAYS WANTED.
FMMP むくり
YAAAWN
ガリ ガリ
SKRITCH SKRITCH
THE SEASONS WERE CHANGING. JUST ANOTHER DAY.
OR AT LEAST, IT WAS...

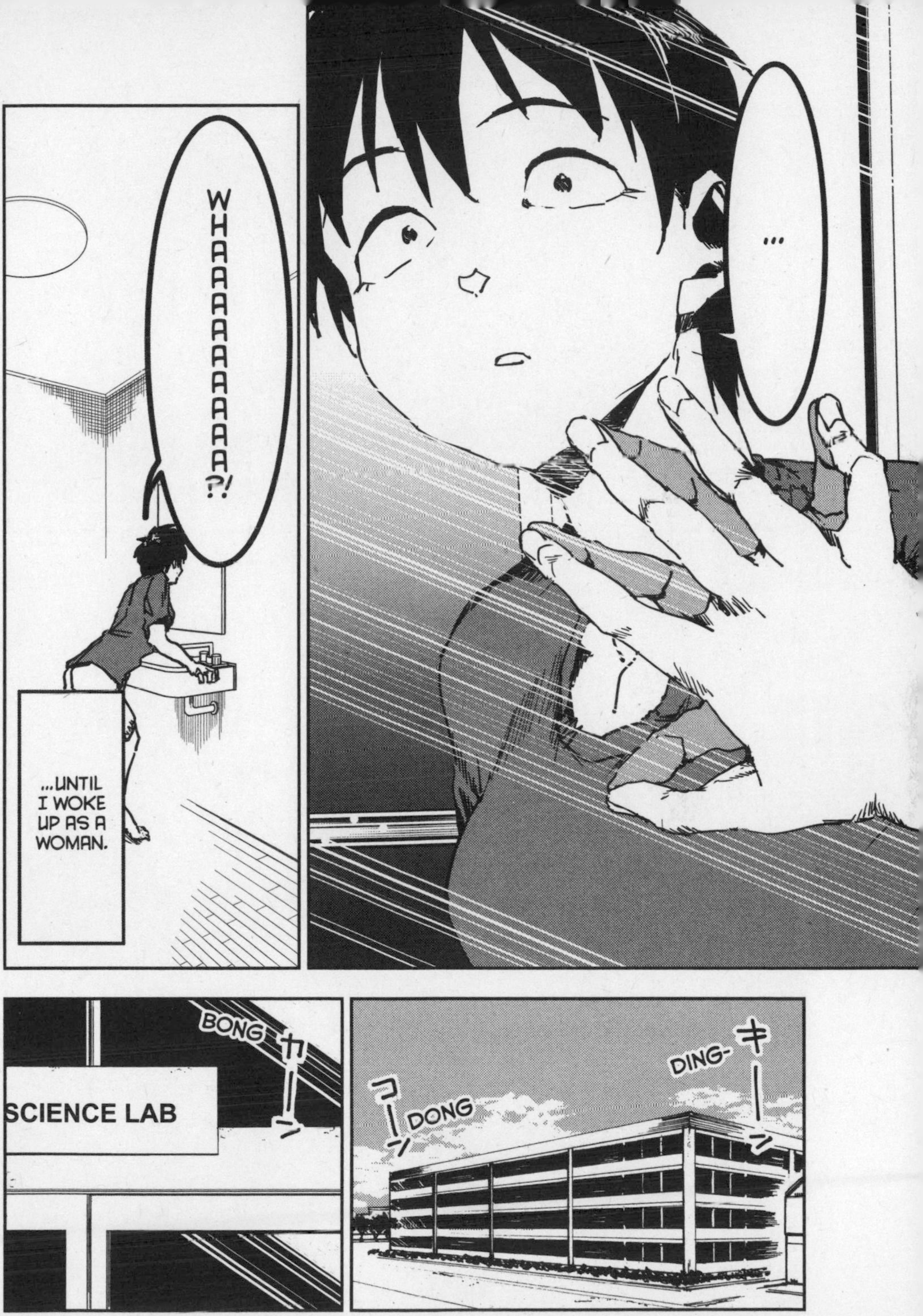
...
WHAAAAAAAAAAA?!
...UNTIL I WOKE UP AS A WOMAN.
DING-
キーン
DONG
コーン
BONG
カーン
SCIENCE LAB

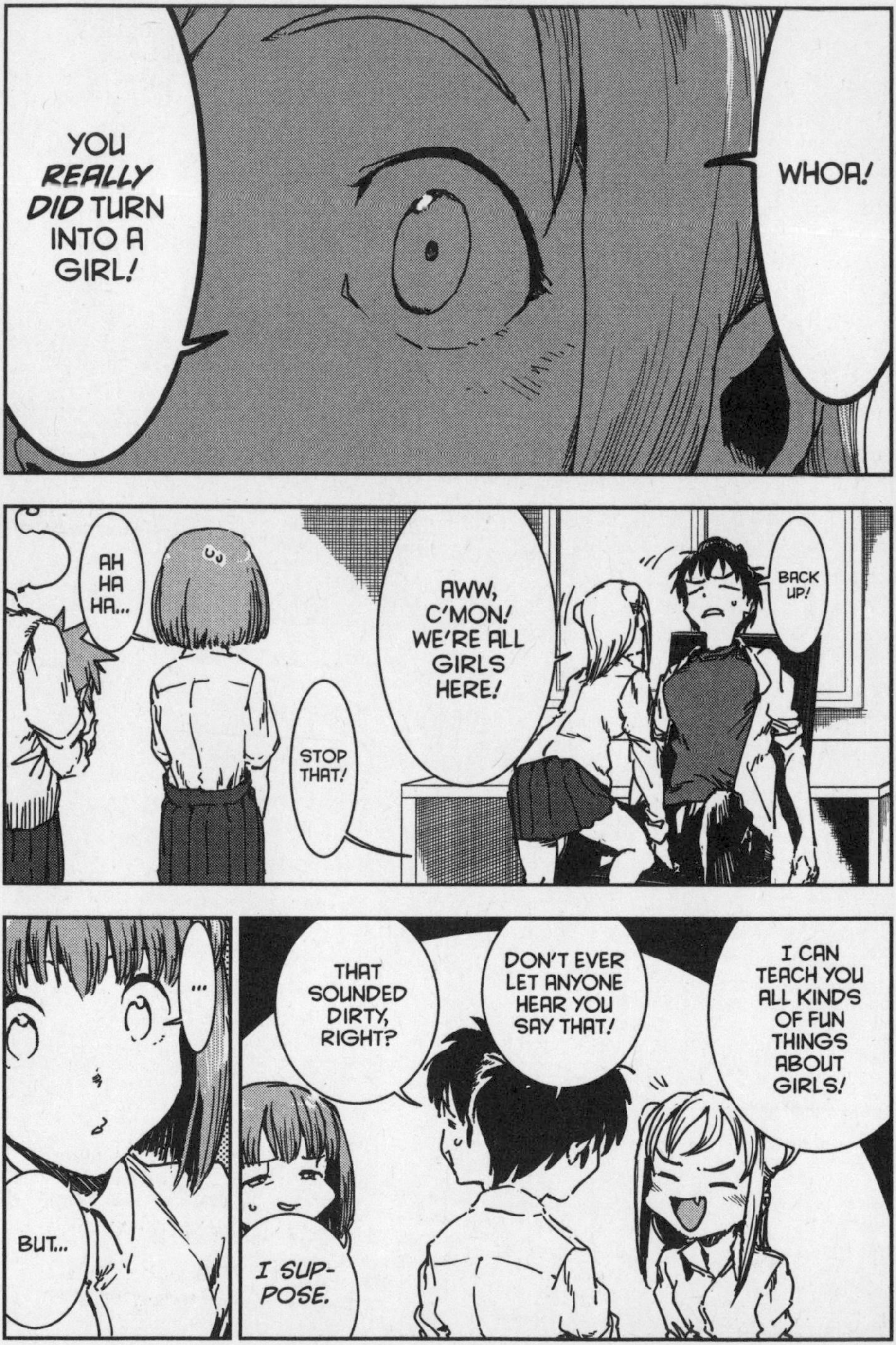
WHOA!
YOU *REALLY DID* TURN INTO A GIRL!
BACK UP!
AWW, C'MON! WE'RE ALL GIRLS HERE!
STOP THAT!
AH HA HA...
I CAN TEACH YOU ALL KINDS OF FUN THINGS ABOUT GIRLS!
DON'T EVER LET ANYONE HEAR YOU SAY THAT!
THAT SOUNDED DIRTY, RIGHT?
I SUP-POSE.
...
BUT...

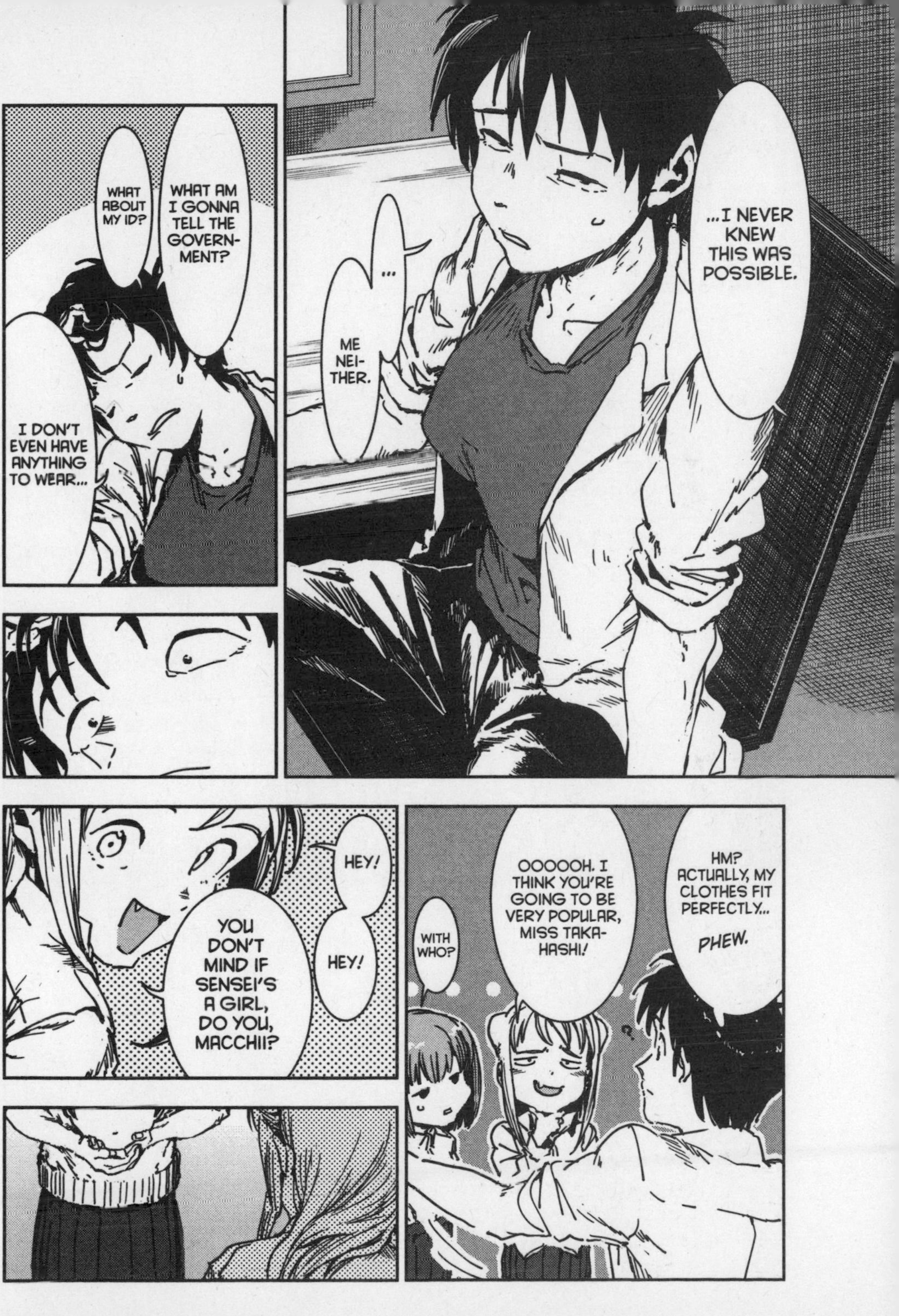
...I NEVER KNEW THIS WAS POSSIBLE.
...
ME NEITHER.
WHAT AM I GONNA TELL THE GOVERNMENT?
WHAT ABOUT MY ID?
I DON'T EVEN HAVE ANYTHING TO WEAR...
HM? ACTUALLY, MY CLOTHES FIT PERFECTLY...
PHEW.
OOOOOH. I THINK YOU'RE GOING TO BE VERY POPULAR, MISS TAKAHASHI!
WITH WHO?
HEY!
HEY!
YOU DON'T MIND IF SENSEI'S A GIRL, DO YOU, MACCHII?

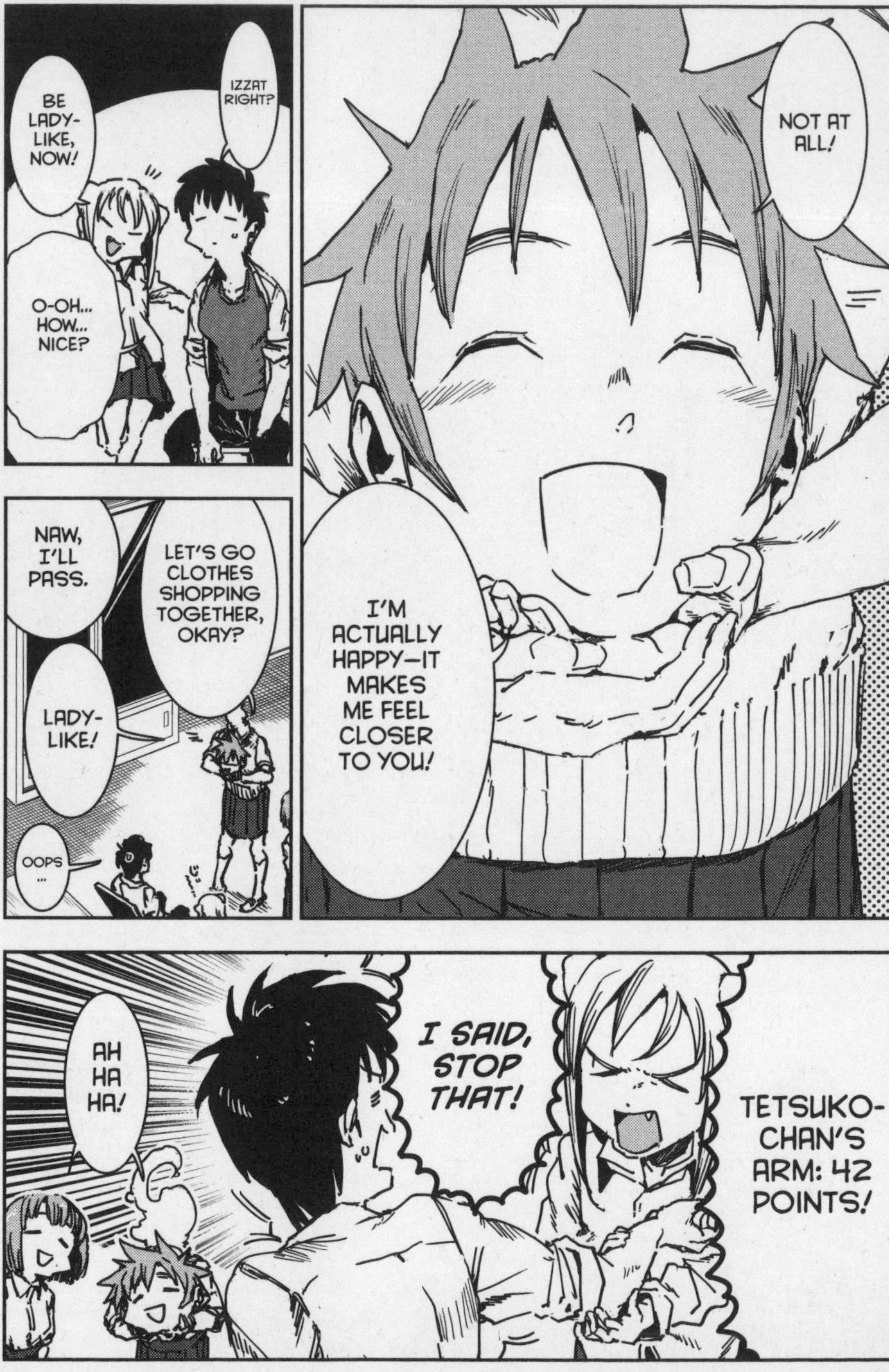
NOT AT ALL!
I'M ACTUALLY HAPPY—IT MAKES ME FEEL CLOSER TO YOU!
IZZAT RIGHT?
BE LADY-LIKE, NOW!
O-OH... HOW... NICE?
LET'S GO CLOTHES SHOPPING TOGETHER, OKAY?
NAW, I'LL PASS.
LADY-LIKE!
OOPS ...
TETSUKO-CHAN'S ARM: 42 POINTS!
I SAID, STOP THAT!
AH HA HA!

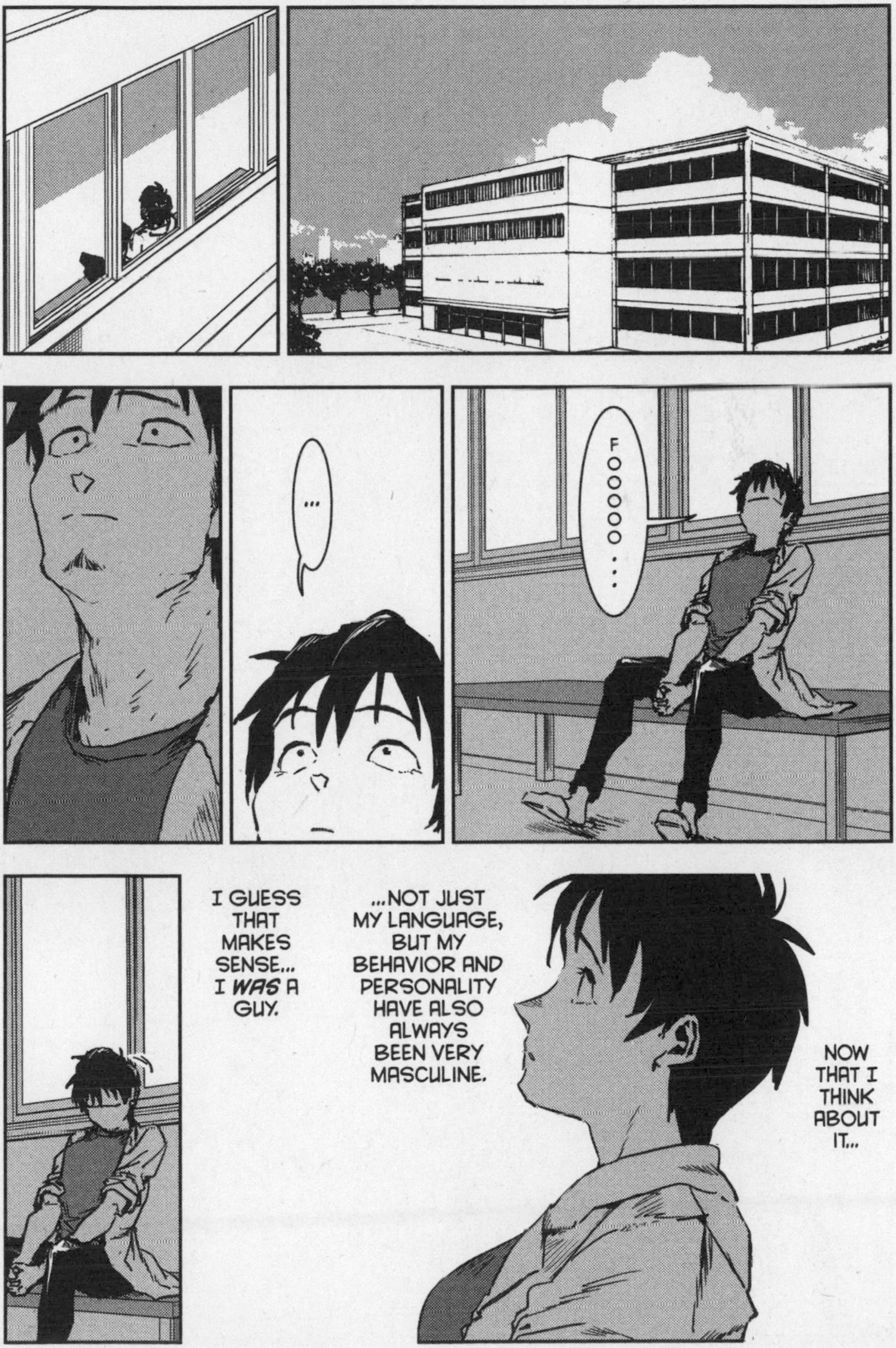
FOOOOO....
...
NOW THAT I THINK ABOUT IT...
...NOT JUST MY LANGUAGE, BUT MY BEHAVIOR AND PERSONALITY HAVE ALSO ALWAYS BEEN VERY MASCULINE.
I GUESS THAT MAKES SENSE... I *WAS* A GUY.

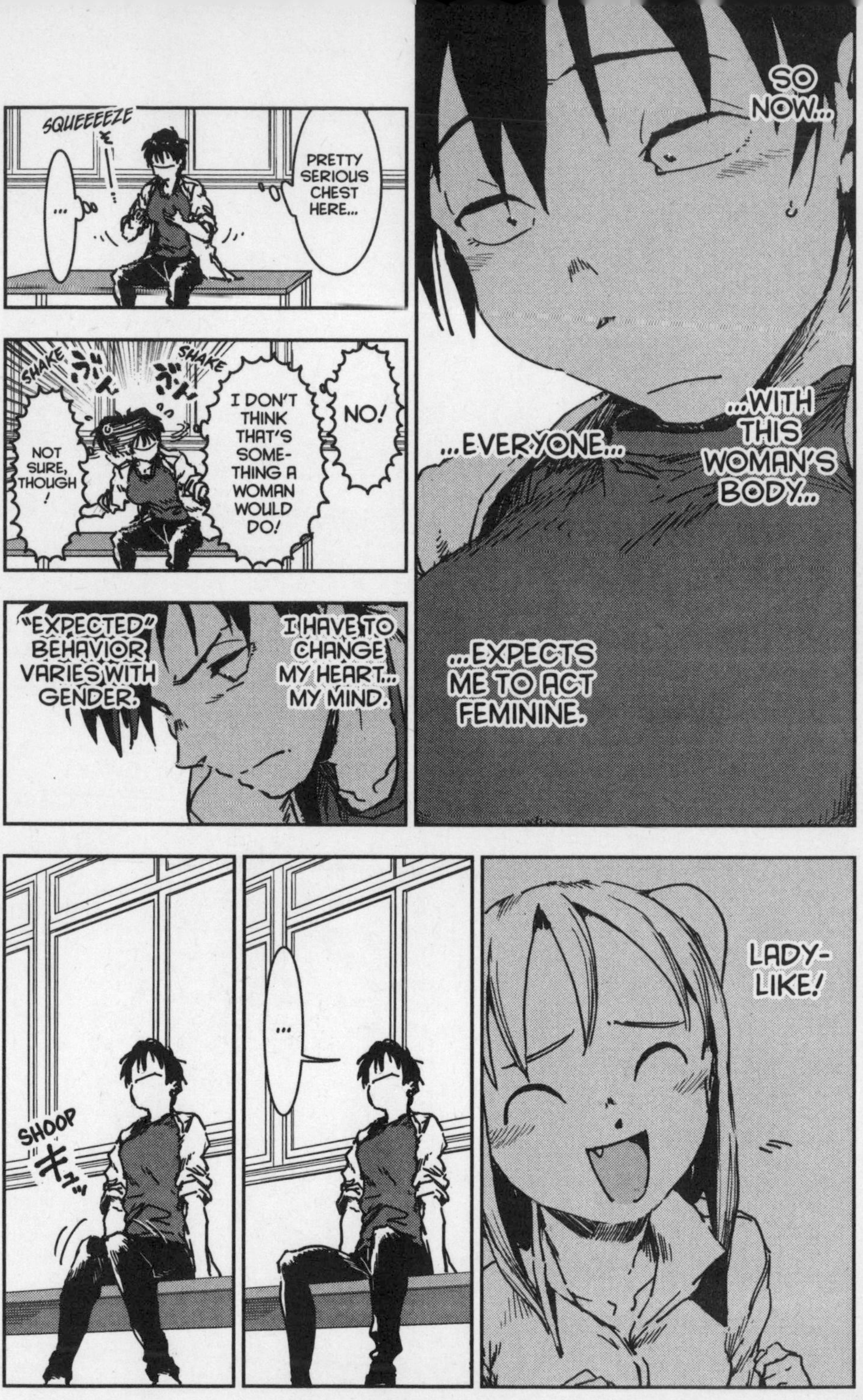
SO NOW...
...WITH THIS WOMAN'S BODY...
...EVERYONE...
...EXPECTS ME TO ACT FEMININE.
PRETTY SERIOUS CHEST HERE...
...
SQUEEEEZE
NO!
I DON'T THINK THAT'S SOME-THING A WOMAN WOULD DO!
SHAKE
SHAKE
NOT SURE, THOUGH!
I HAVE TO CHANGE MY HEART... MY MIND.
"EXPECTED" BEHAVIOR VARIES WITH GENDER.
LADY-LIKE!
...
SHOOP

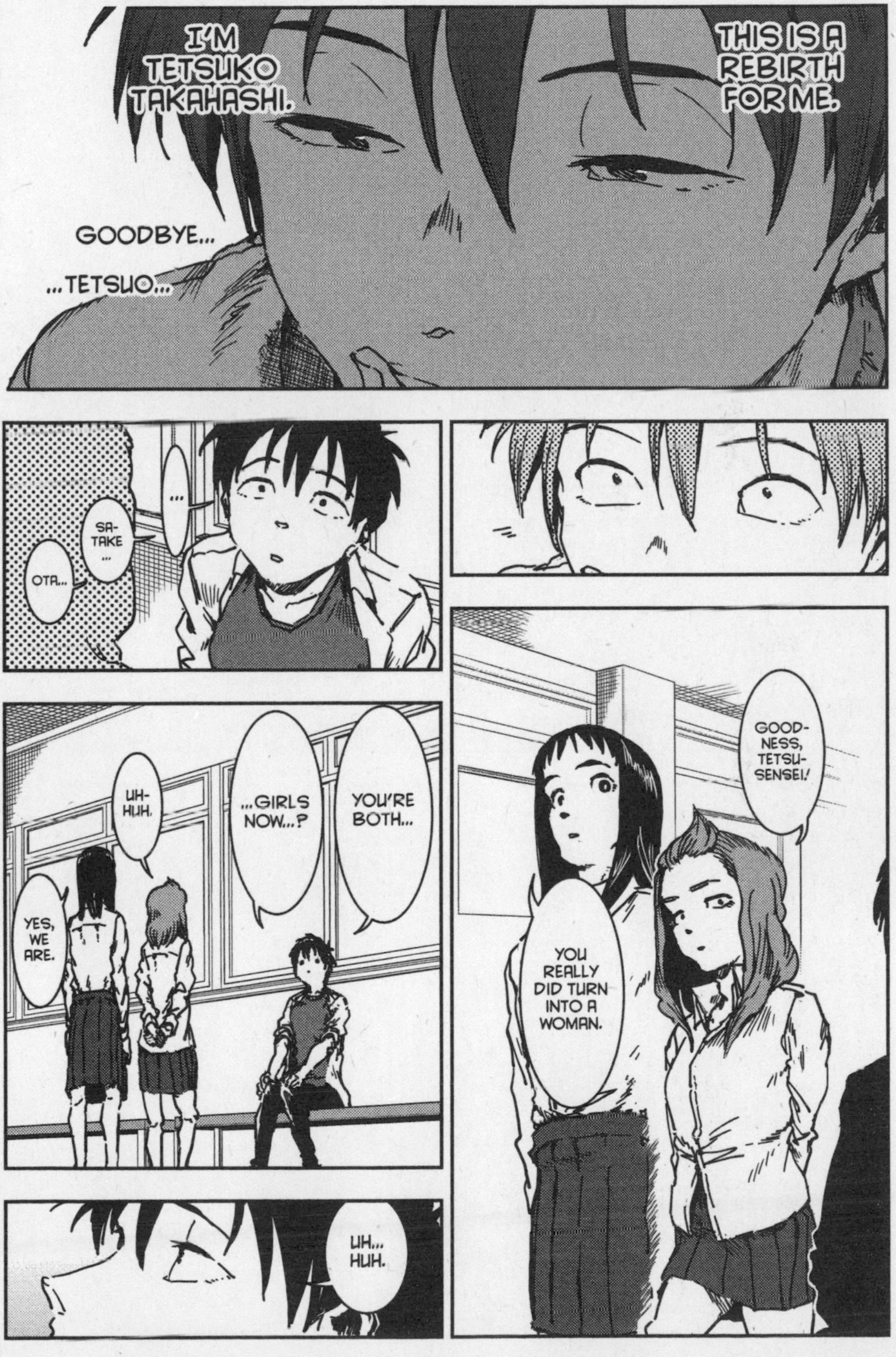
THIS IS A REBIRTH FOR ME.
I'M TETSUKO TAKAHASHI.
GOODBYE...
...TETSUO...
...
SA-TAKE...
OTA...
GOOD-NESS, TETSU-SENSEI!
YOU REALLY DID TURN INTO A WOMAN.
YOU'RE BOTH...
...GIRLS NOW...?
UH-HUH.
YES, WE ARE.
UH... HUH.

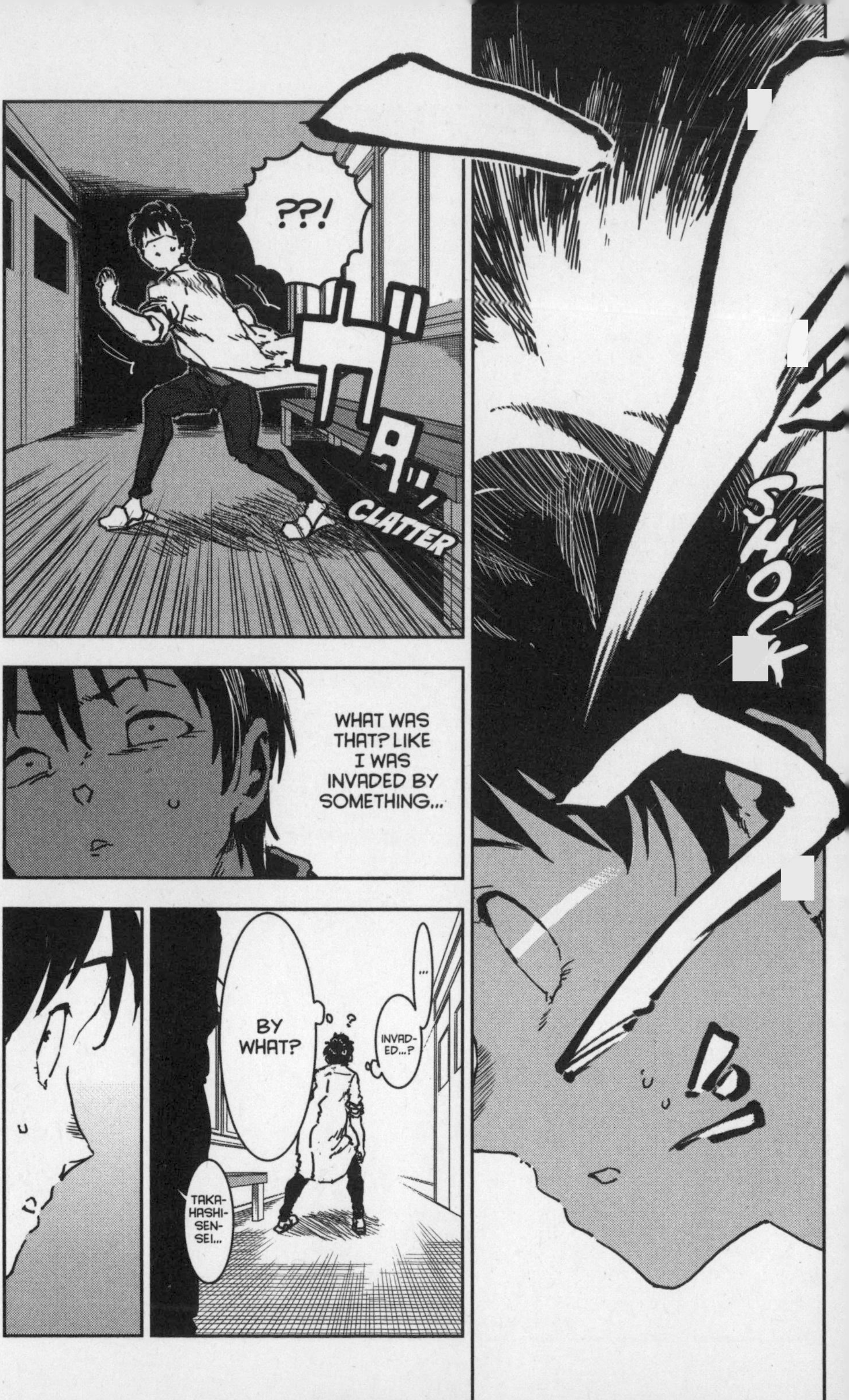
SHOCK
??!
ガタッ
CLATTER
WHAT WAS THAT? LIKE I WAS INVADED BY SOMETHING...
...
INVADED...?
BY WHAT?
TAKAHASHI-SENSEI...

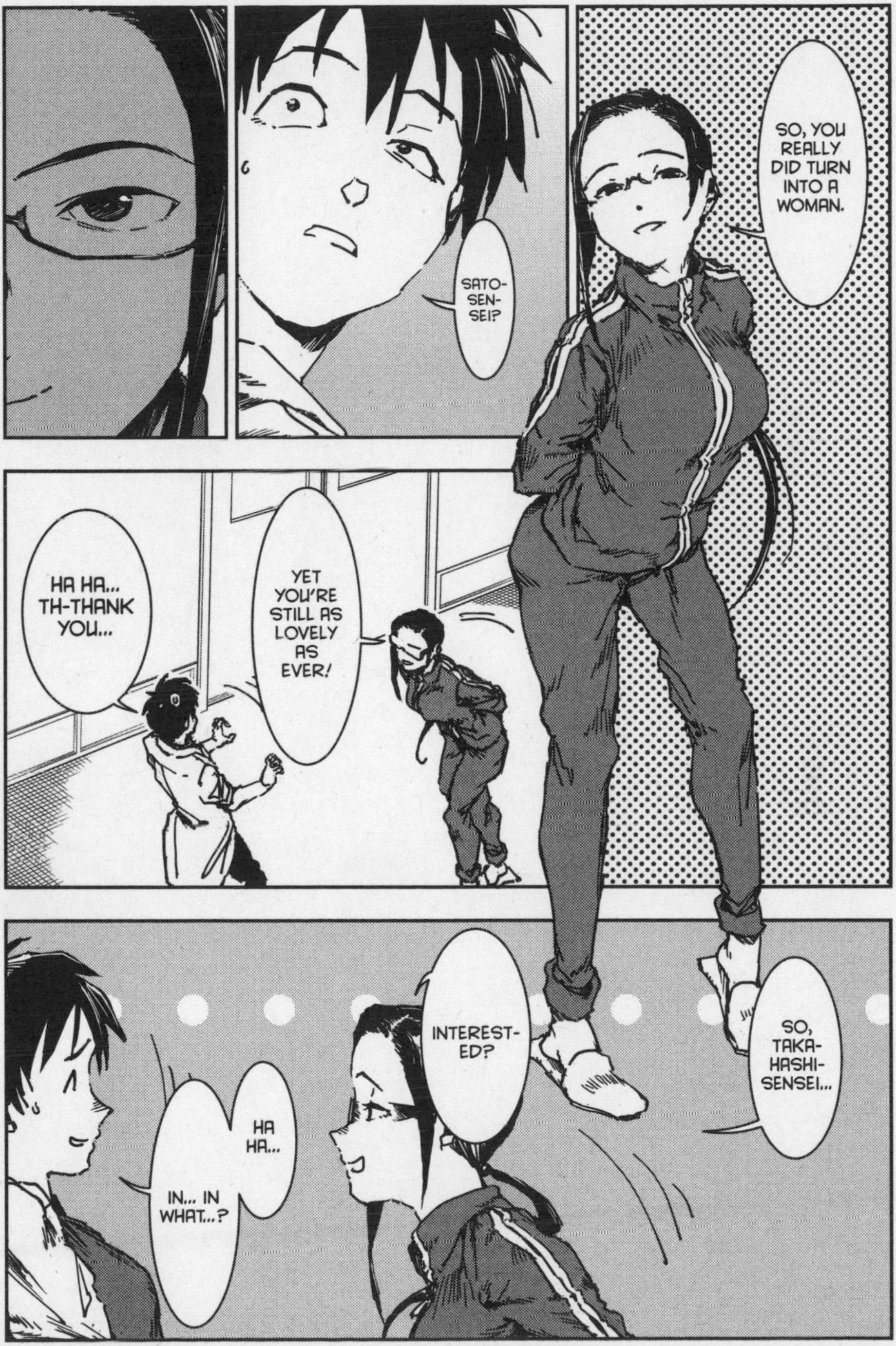
SO, YOU REALLY DID TURN INTO A WOMAN.
SATO-SEN-SEI?
YET YOU'RE STILL AS LOVELY AS EVER!
HA HA... TH-THANK YOU...
SO, TAKA-HASHI-SENSEI...
INTEREST-ED?
HA HA...
IN... IN WHAT...?

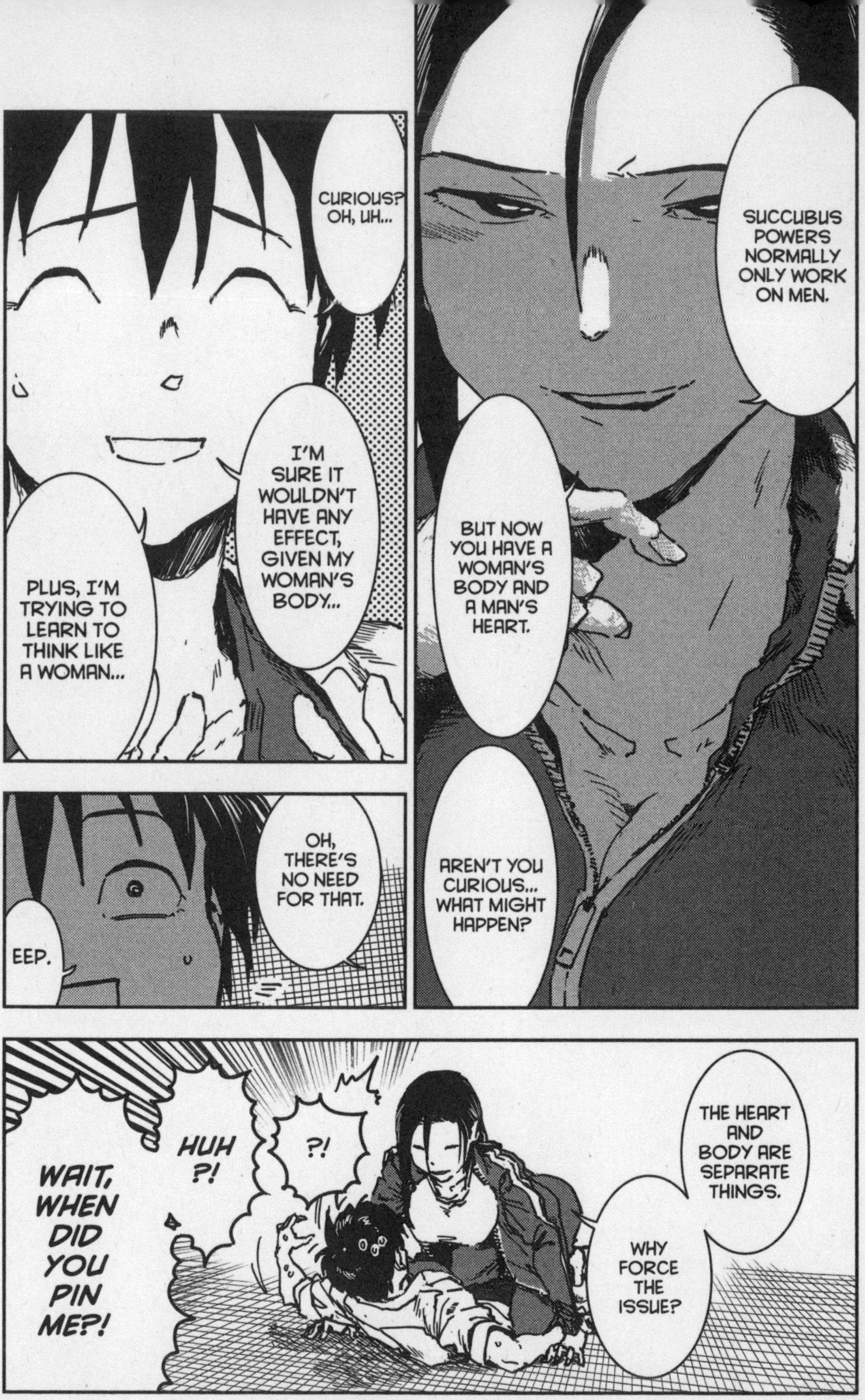
SUCCUBUS POWERS NORMALLY ONLY WORK ON MEN.
BUT NOW YOU HAVE A WOMAN'S BODY AND A MAN'S HEART.
AREN'T YOU CURIOUS... WHAT MIGHT HAPPEN?
CURIOUS? OH, UH...
I'M SURE IT WOULDN'T HAVE ANY EFFECT, GIVEN MY WOMAN'S BODY...
PLUS, I'M TRYING TO LEARN TO THINK LIKE A WOMAN...
OH, THERE'S NO NEED FOR THAT.
EEP.
THE HEART AND BODY ARE SEPARATE THINGS.
WHY FORCE THE ISSUE?
?!
HUH ?!
WAIT, WHEN DID YOU PIN ME?!

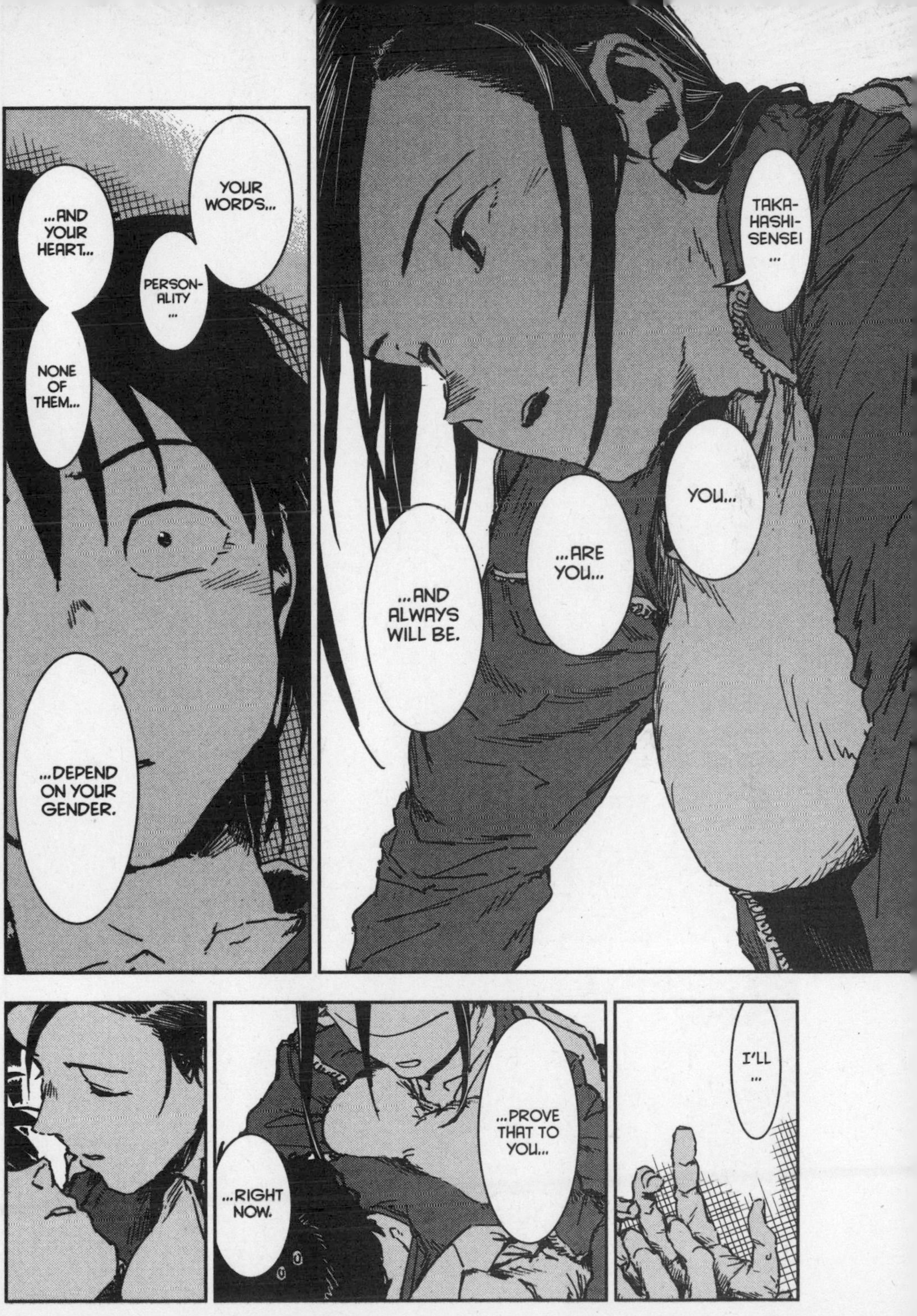
TAKA-HASHI-SENSEI...
YOU...
...ARE YOU...
...AND ALWAYS WILL BE.
YOUR WORDS...
PERSON-ALITY...
...AND YOUR HEART...
NONE OF THEM...
...DEPEND ON YOUR GENDER.
I'LL...
...PROVE THAT TO YOU...
...RIGHT NOW.

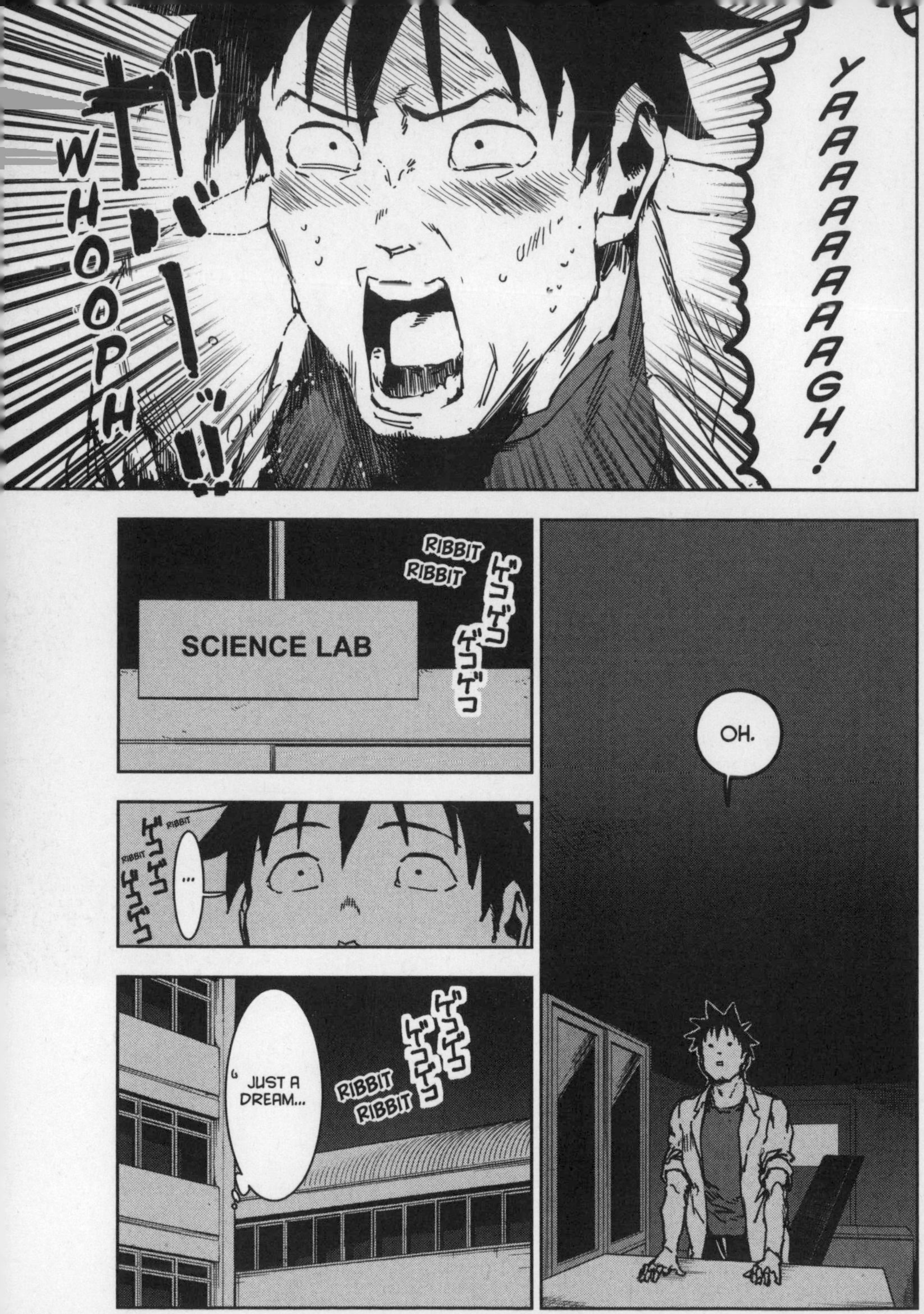
YAAAAAAAAGH!
WHOOMPH!!
OH.
SCIENCE LAB
RIBBIT RIBBIT
ゲコゲコ ゲコゲコ
...
RIBBIT RIBBIT
JUST A DREAM...
RIBBIT RIBBIT

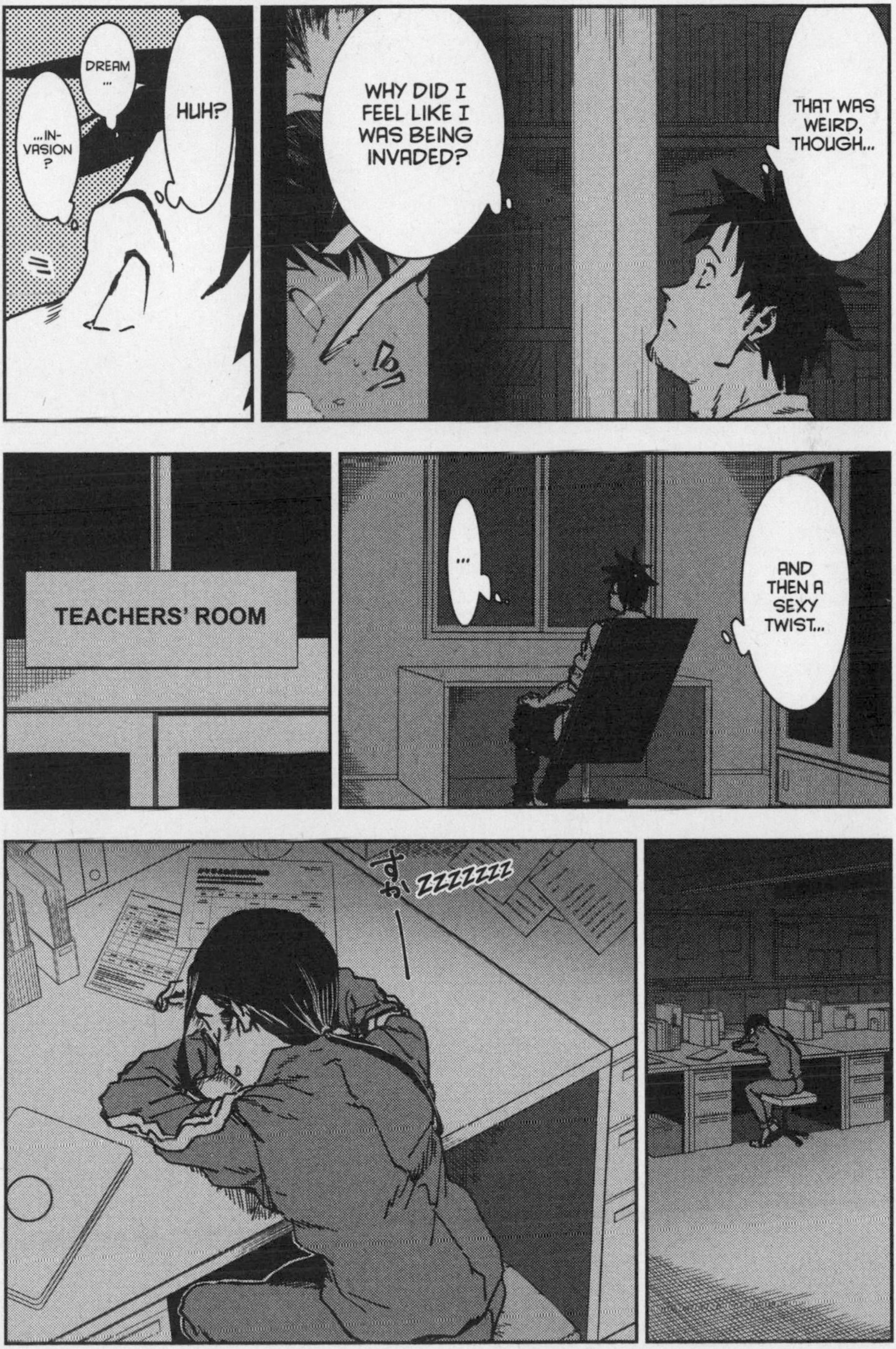
THAT WAS WEIRD, THOUGH...
WHY DID I FEEL LIKE I WAS BEING INVADED?
HUH?
DREAM ...
...IN-VASION ?
AND THEN A SEXY TWIST...
...
TEACHERS' ROOM
ZZZZZZZ

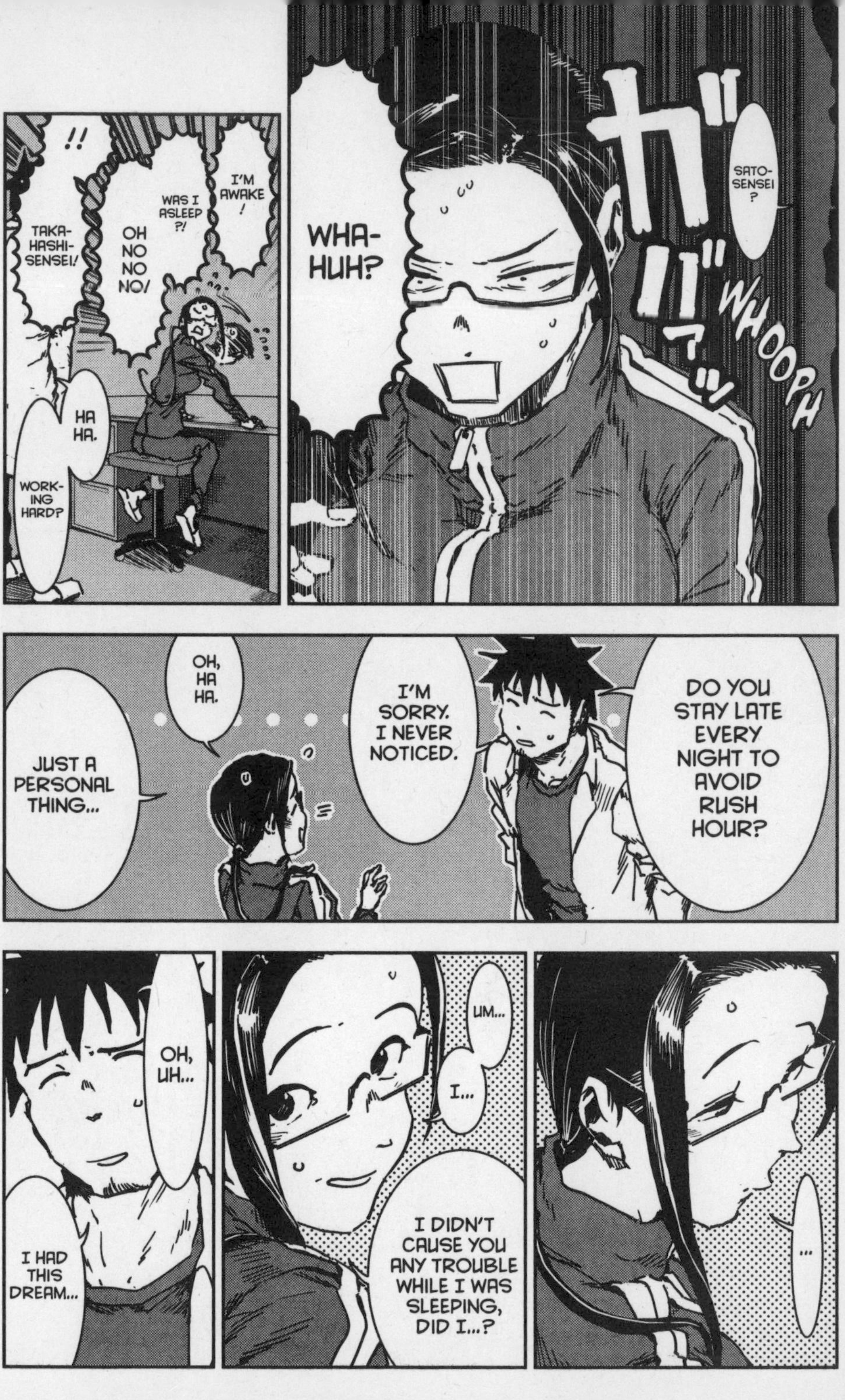
SATO-SENSEI?
ガバッ
WHOOPH
WHA-HUH?
I'M AWAKE!
WAS I ASLEEP?!
OH NO NO NO!
!!
TAKAHASHI-SENSEI!
HA HA.
WORKING HARD?
DO YOU STAY LATE EVERY NIGHT TO AVOID RUSH HOUR?
I'M SORRY. I NEVER NOTICED.
OH, HA HA.
JUST A PERSONAL THING...
...
UM...
I...
I DIDN'T CAUSE YOU ANY TROUBLE WHILE I WAS SLEEPING, DID I...?
OH, UH...
I HAD THIS DREAM...

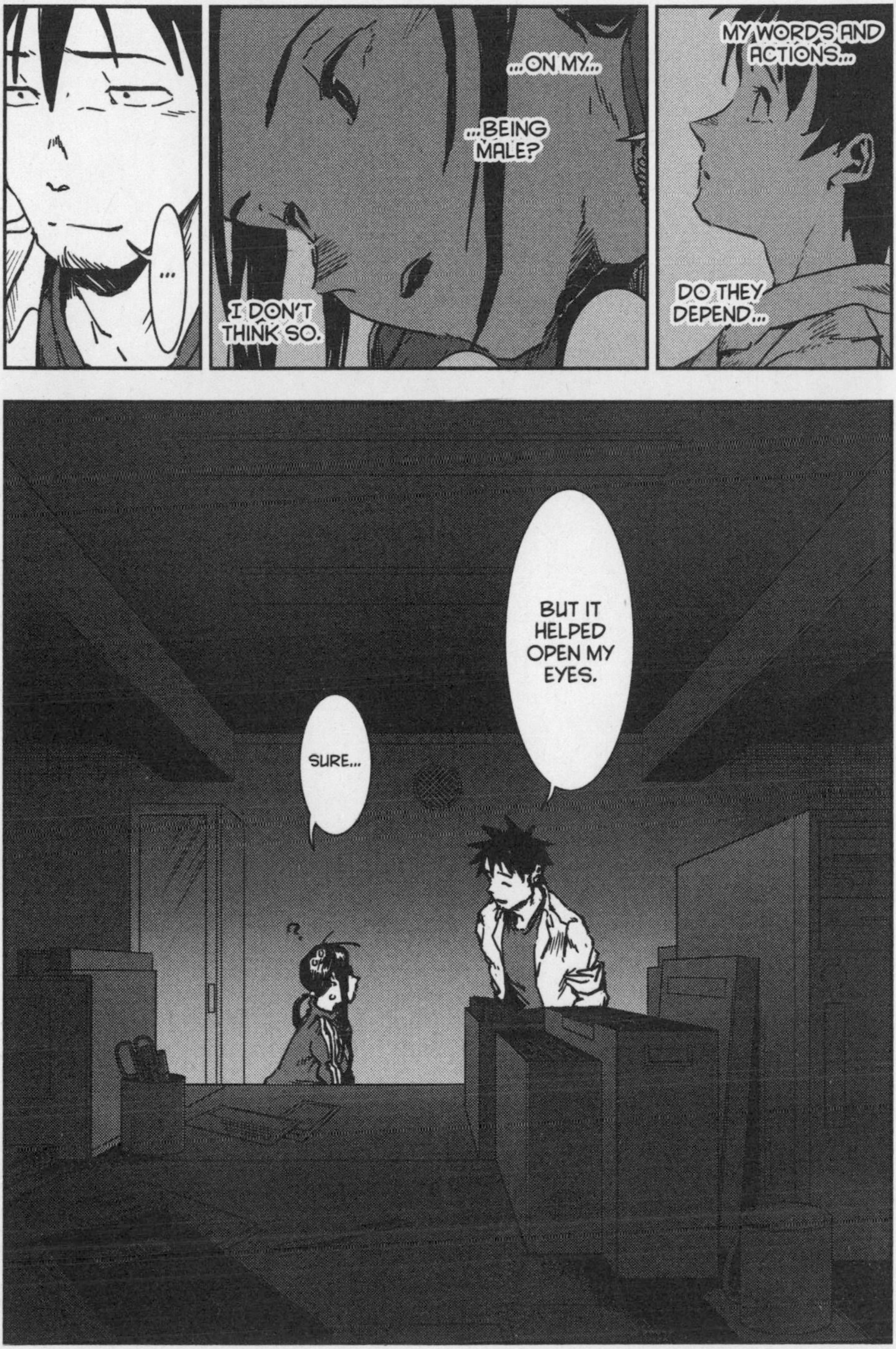
MY WORDS AND ACTIONS...
DO THEY DEPEND...
...ON MY...
...BEING MALE?
I DON'T THINK SO.
...
BUT IT HELPED OPEN MY EYES.
SURE...

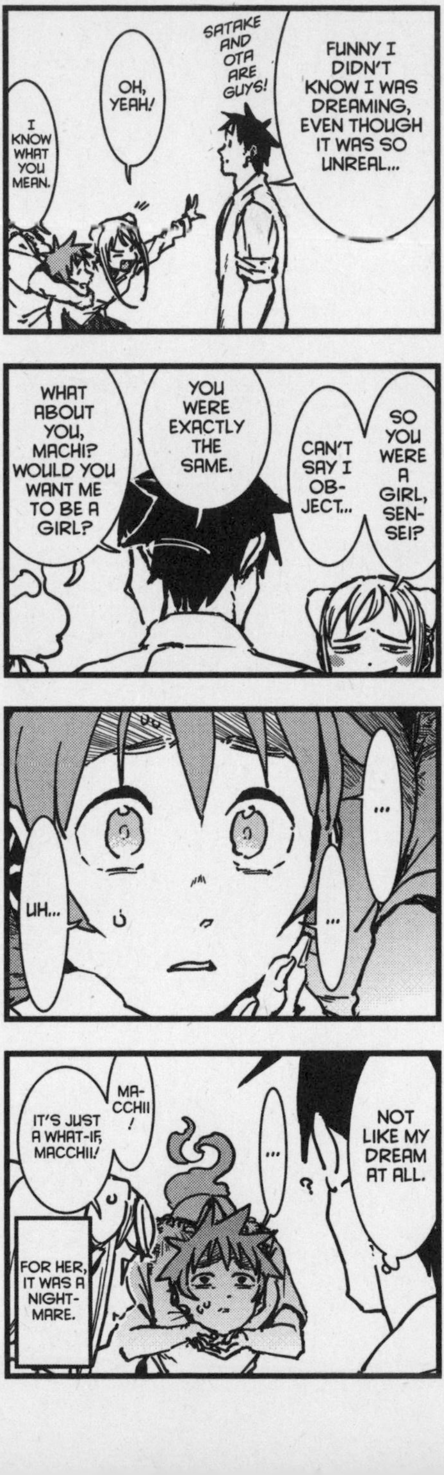
FUNNY I DIDN'T KNOW I WAS DREAMING, EVEN THOUGH IT WAS SO UNREAL...
SATAKE AND OTA ARE GUYS!
OH, YEAH!
I KNOW WHAT YOU MEAN.
SO YOU WERE A GIRL, SEN-SEI?
CAN'T SAY I OB-JECT...
YOU WERE EXACTLY THE SAME.
WHAT ABOUT YOU, MACHI? WOULD YOU WANT ME TO BE A GIRL?
...
...
UH...
NOT LIKE MY DREAM AT ALL.
...
MA-CCHII!
IT'S JUST A WHAT-IF, MACCHII!
FOR HER, IT WAS A NIGHT-MARE.

INTERVIEWS WITH MONSTER GIRLS

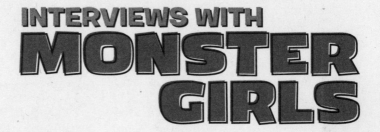

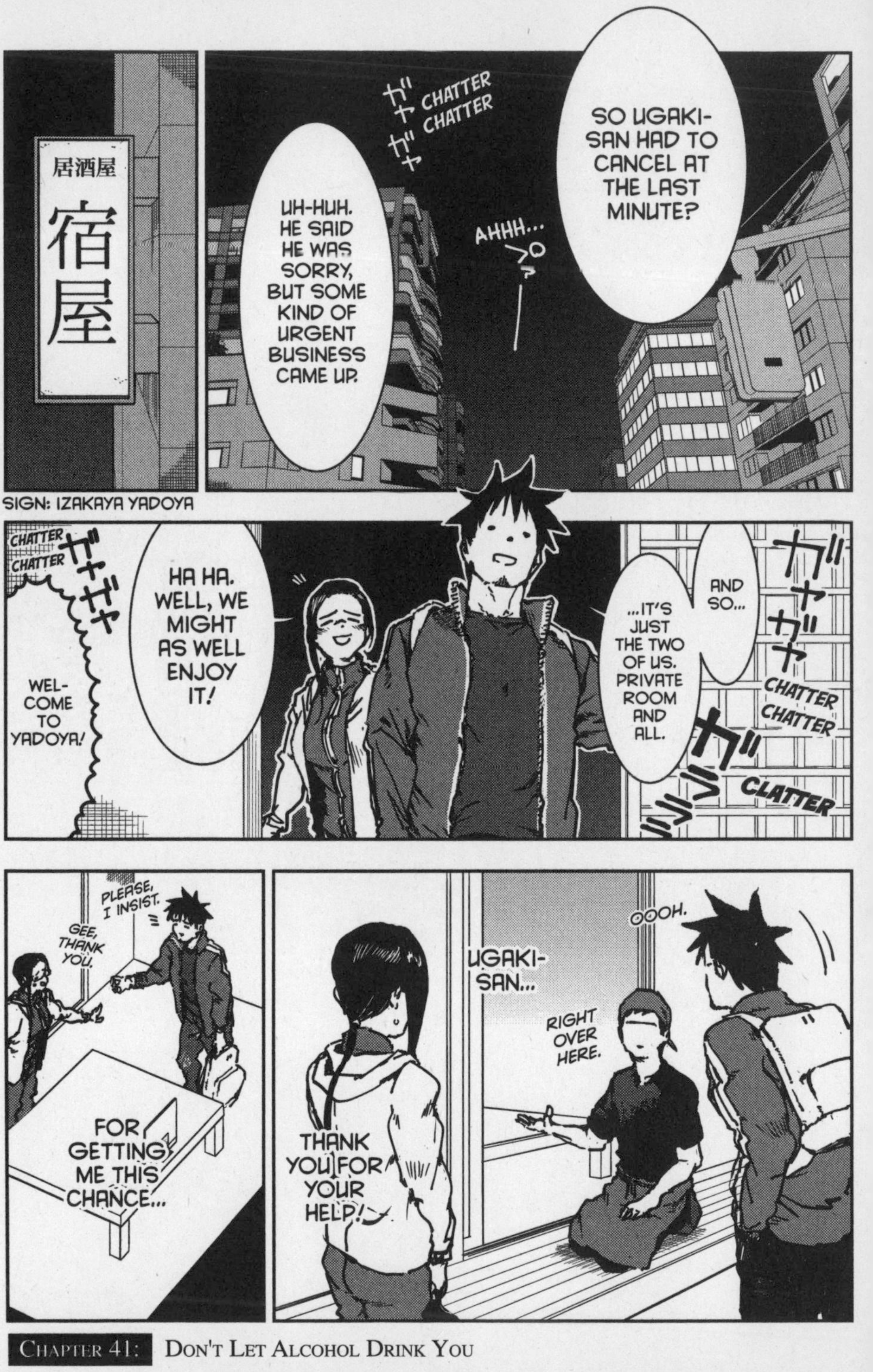
SO UGAKI-SAN HAD TO CANCEL AT THE LAST MINUTE?
CHATTER CHATTER
AHHH...
UH-HUH. HE SAID HE WAS SORRY, BUT SOME KIND OF URGENT BUSINESS CAME UP.
居酒屋
宿屋
SIGN: IZAKAYA YADOYA
CHATTER CHATTER
CLATTER
AND SO...
...IT'S JUST THE TWO OF US. PRIVATE ROOM AND ALL.
HA HA. WELL, WE MIGHT AS WELL ENJOY IT!
WEL-COME TO YADOYA!
CHATTER CHATTER
OOOH.
UGAKI-SAN...
RIGHT OVER HERE.
THANK YOU FOR YOUR HELP!
PLEASE, I INSIST.
GEE, THANK YOU.
FOR GETTING ME THIS CHANCE...

Chapter 41: Don't Let Alcohol Drink You

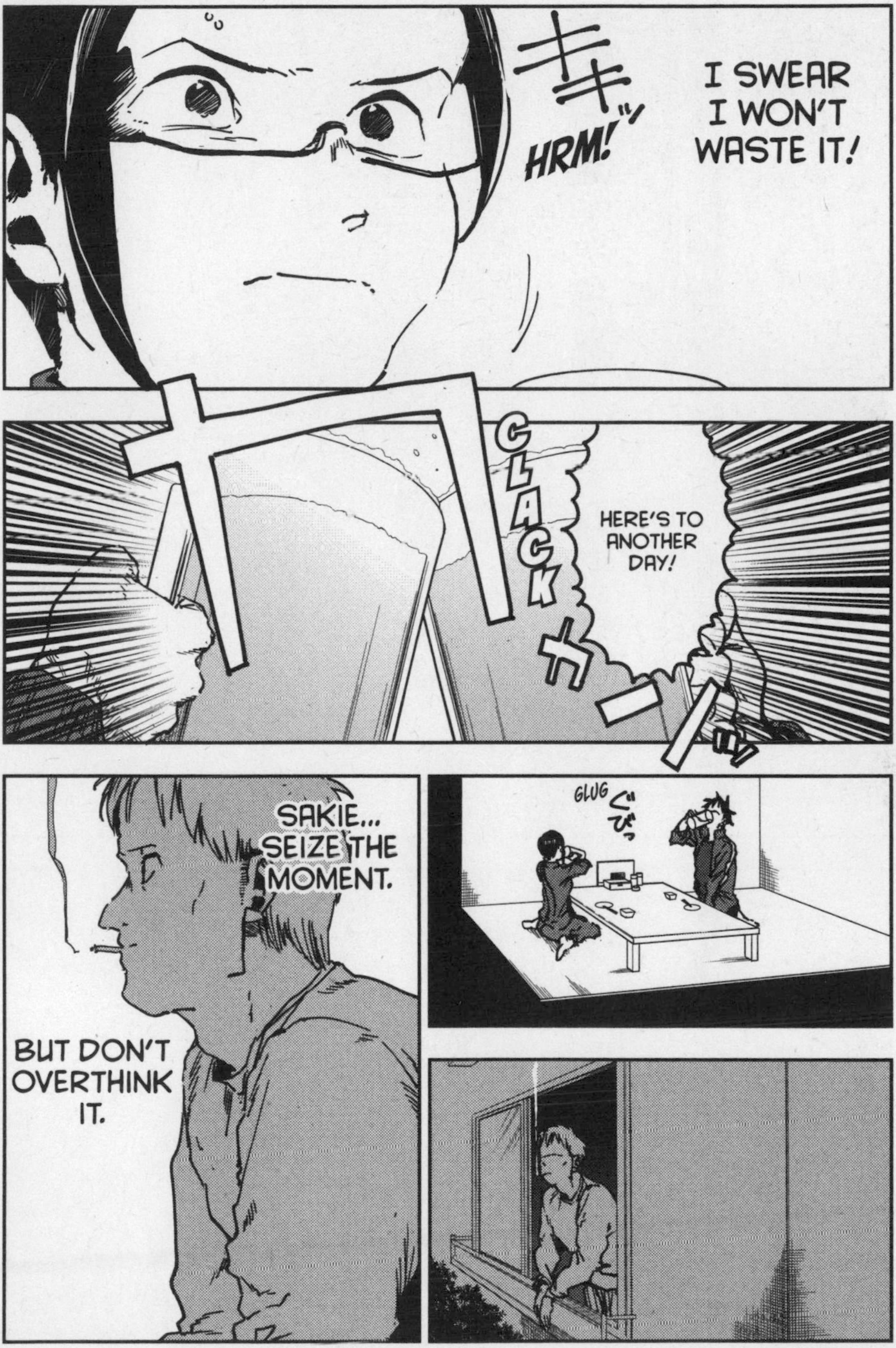
I SWEAR I WON'T WASTE IT!
HRM!
CLACK
HERE'S TO ANOTHER DAY!
GLUG
ぐびっ
SAKIE... SEIZE THE MOMENT.
BUT DON'T OVERTHINK IT.

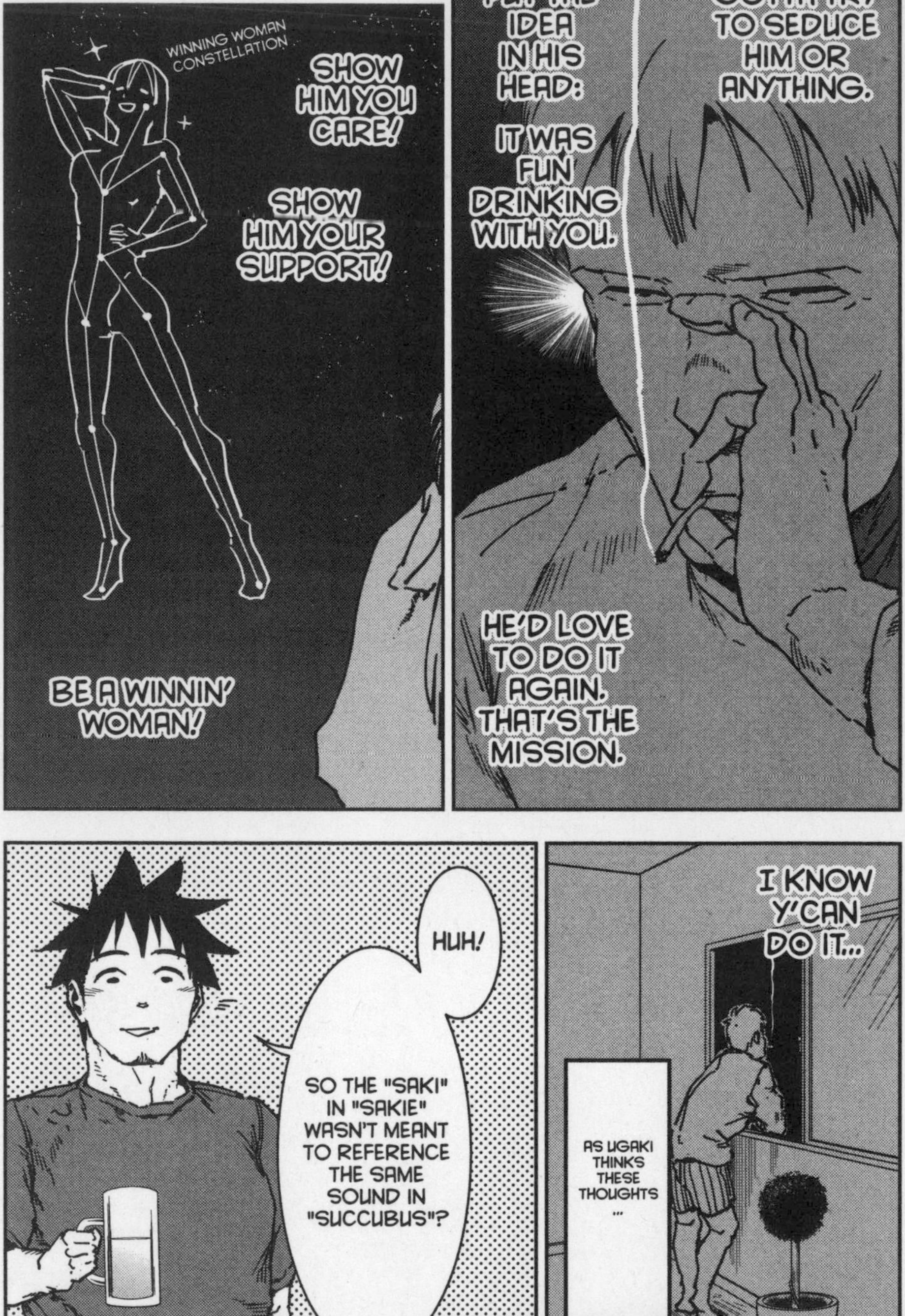
DON'T GOTTA TRY TO SEDUCE HIM OR ANYTHING.
JUST PUT THE IDEA IN HIS HEAD:
IT WAS FUN DRINKING WITH YOU.
HE'D LOVE TO DO IT AGAIN. THAT'S THE MISSION.
WINNING WOMAN CONSTELLATION
SHOW HIM YOU CARE!
SHOW HIM YOUR SUPPORT!
BE A WINNIN' WOMAN!
I KNOW Y'CAN DO IT...
AS UGAKI THINKS THESE THOUGHTS ...
HUH!
SO THE "SAKI" IN "SAKIE" WASN'T MEANT TO REFERENCE THE SAME SOUND IN "SUCCUBUS"?

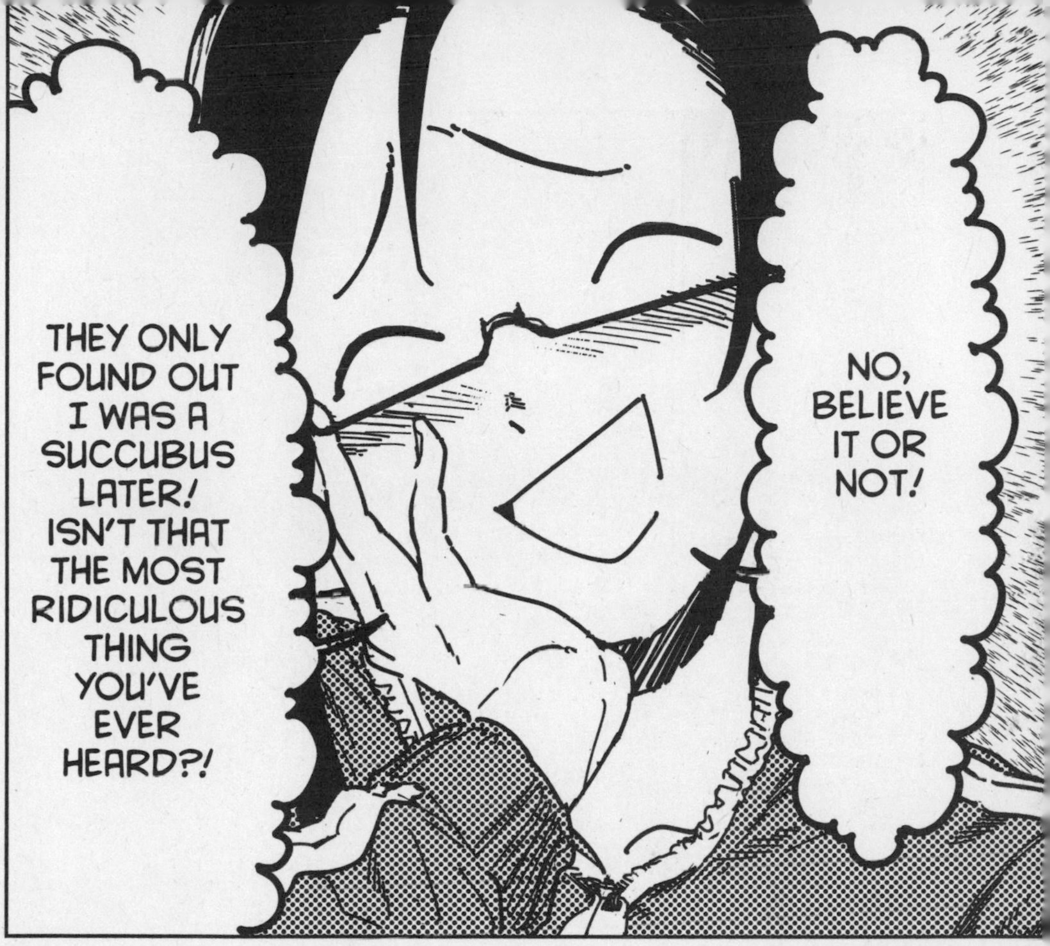
NO, BELIEVE IT OR NOT!
THEY ONLY FOUND OUT I WAS A SUCCUBUS LATER! ISN'T THAT THE MOST RIDICULOUS THING YOU'VE EVER HEARD?!

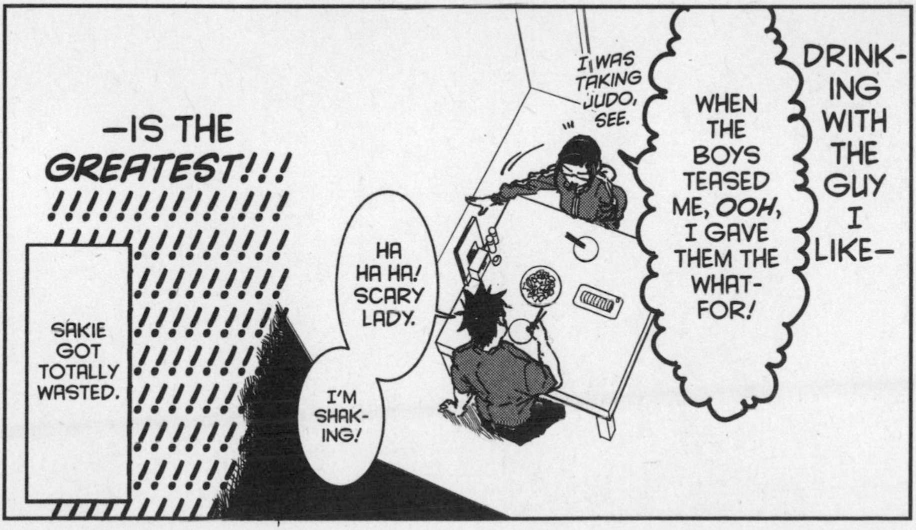
DRINKING WITH THE GUY I LIKE—
I WAS TAKING JUDO, SEE.
WHEN THE BOYS TEASED ME, *OOH*, I GAVE THEM THE WHATFOR!
HA HA HA! SCARY LADY.
I'M SHAKING!
—IS THE *GREATEST!!!* !!!!!!!!!!!!!!!!
SAKIE GOT TOTALLY WASTED.

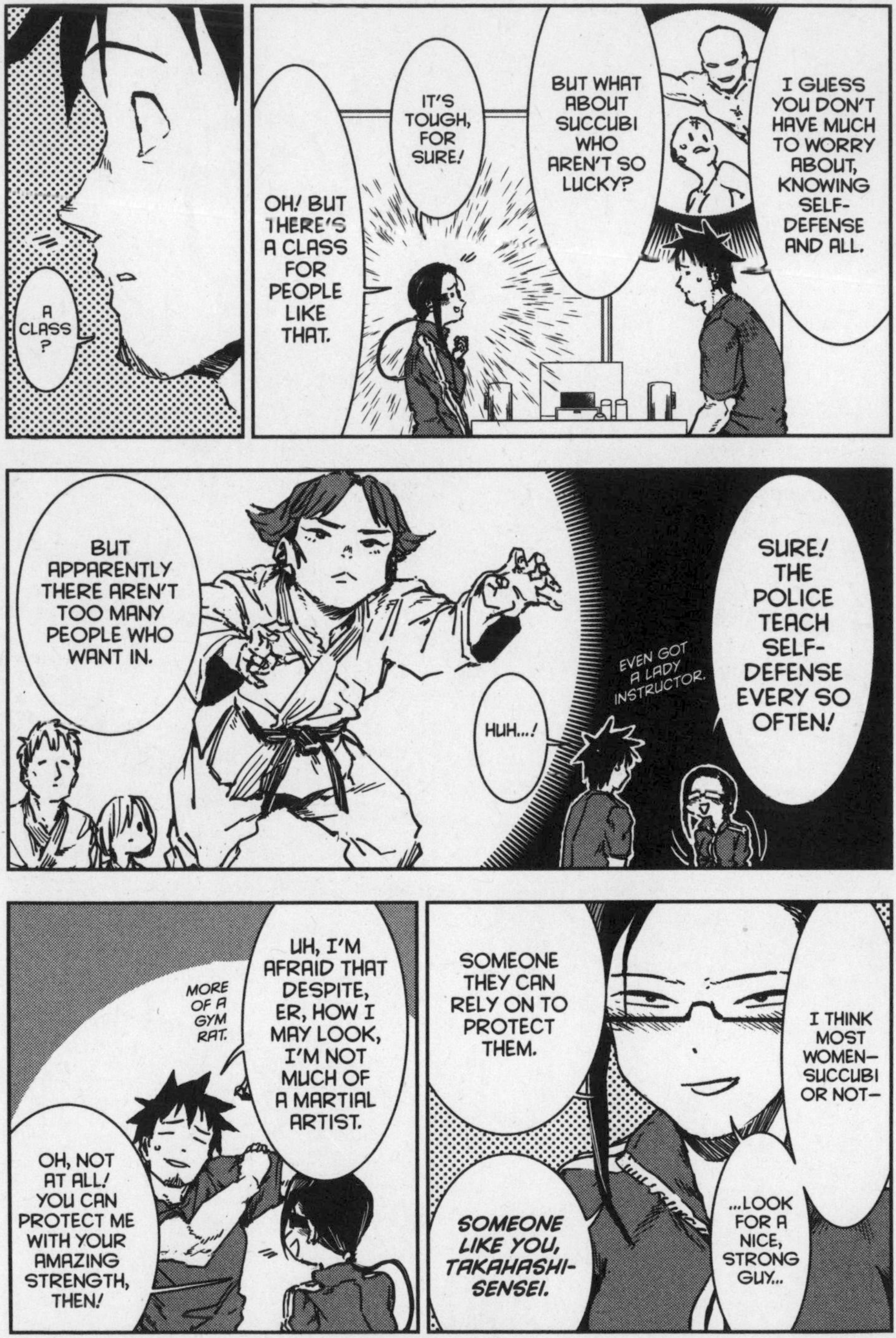
I GUESS YOU DON'T HAVE MUCH TO WORRY ABOUT, KNOWING SELF-DEFENSE AND ALL.
BUT WHAT ABOUT SUCCUBI WHO AREN'T SO LUCKY?
IT'S TOUGH, FOR SURE!
OH! BUT THERE'S A CLASS FOR PEOPLE LIKE THAT.
A CLASS?
SURE! THE POLICE TEACH SELF-DEFENSE EVERY SO OFTEN!
EVEN GOT A LADY INSTRUCTOR.
HUH...!
BUT APPARENTLY THERE AREN'T TOO MANY PEOPLE WHO WANT IN.
I THINK MOST WOMEN—SUCCUBI OR NOT—
...LOOK FOR A NICE, STRONG GUY...
SOMEONE THEY CAN RELY ON TO PROTECT THEM.
SOMEONE LIKE YOU, TAKAHASHI-SENSEI.
UH, I'M AFRAID THAT DESPITE, ER, HOW I MAY LOOK, I'M NOT MUCH OF A MARTIAL ARTIST.
MORE OF A GYM RAT.
OH, NOT AT ALL! YOU CAN PROTECT ME WITH YOUR AMAZING STRENGTH, THEN!

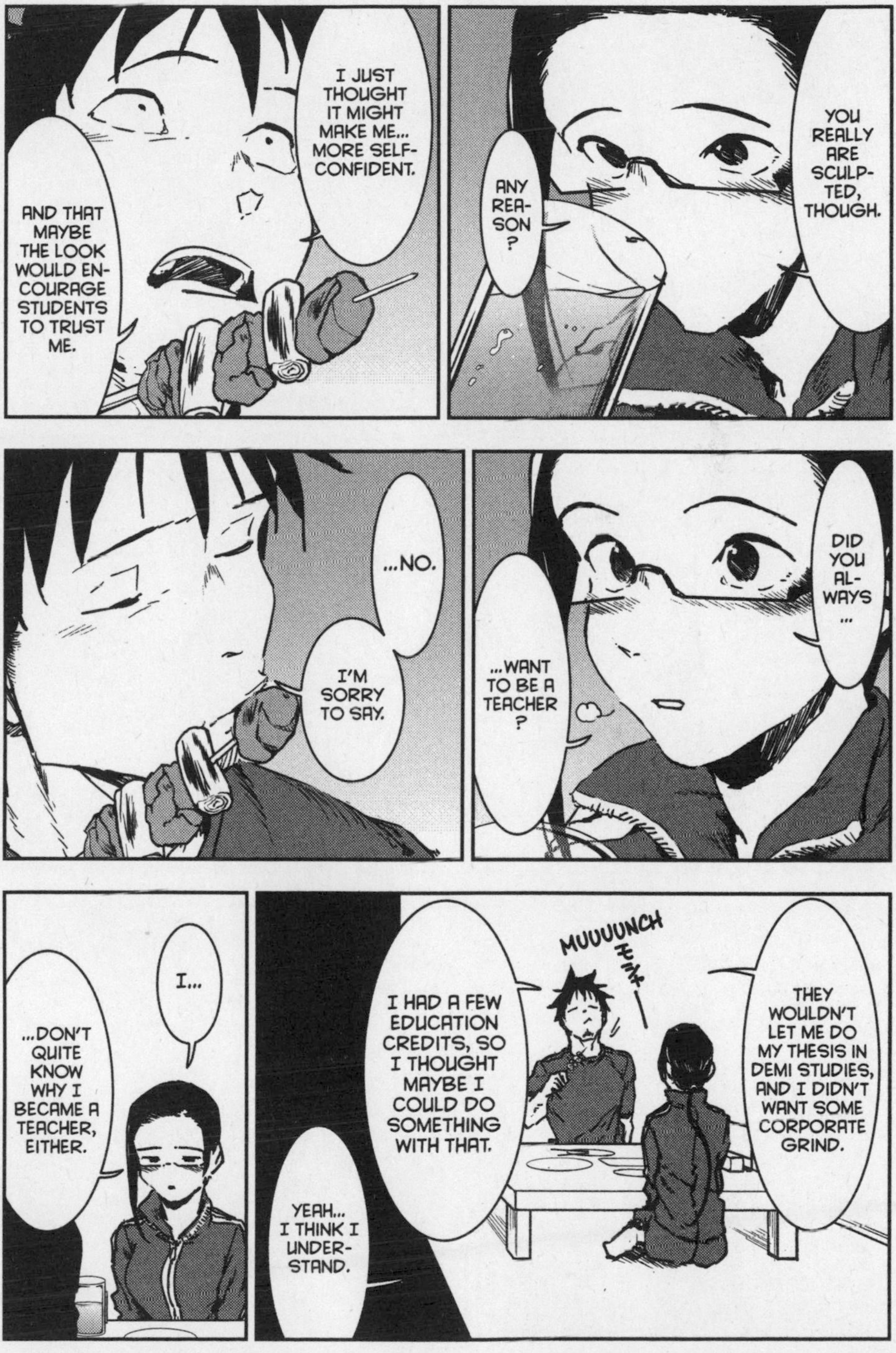
YOU REALLY ARE SCULPTED, THOUGH.
ANY REASON?
I JUST THOUGHT IT MIGHT MAKE ME... MORE SELF-CONFIDENT.
AND THAT MAYBE THE LOOK WOULD ENCOURAGE STUDENTS TO TRUST ME.
DID YOU ALWAYS...
...WANT TO BE A TEACHER?
...NO.
I'M SORRY TO SAY.
THEY WOULDN'T LET ME DO MY THESIS IN DEMI STUDIES, AND I DIDN'T WANT SOME CORPORATE GRIND.
MUUUUNCH
I HAD A FEW EDUCATION CREDITS, SO I THOUGHT MAYBE I COULD DO SOMETHING WITH THAT.
YEAH... I THINK I UNDERSTAND.
I...
...DON'T QUITE KNOW WHY I BECAME A TEACHER, EITHER.

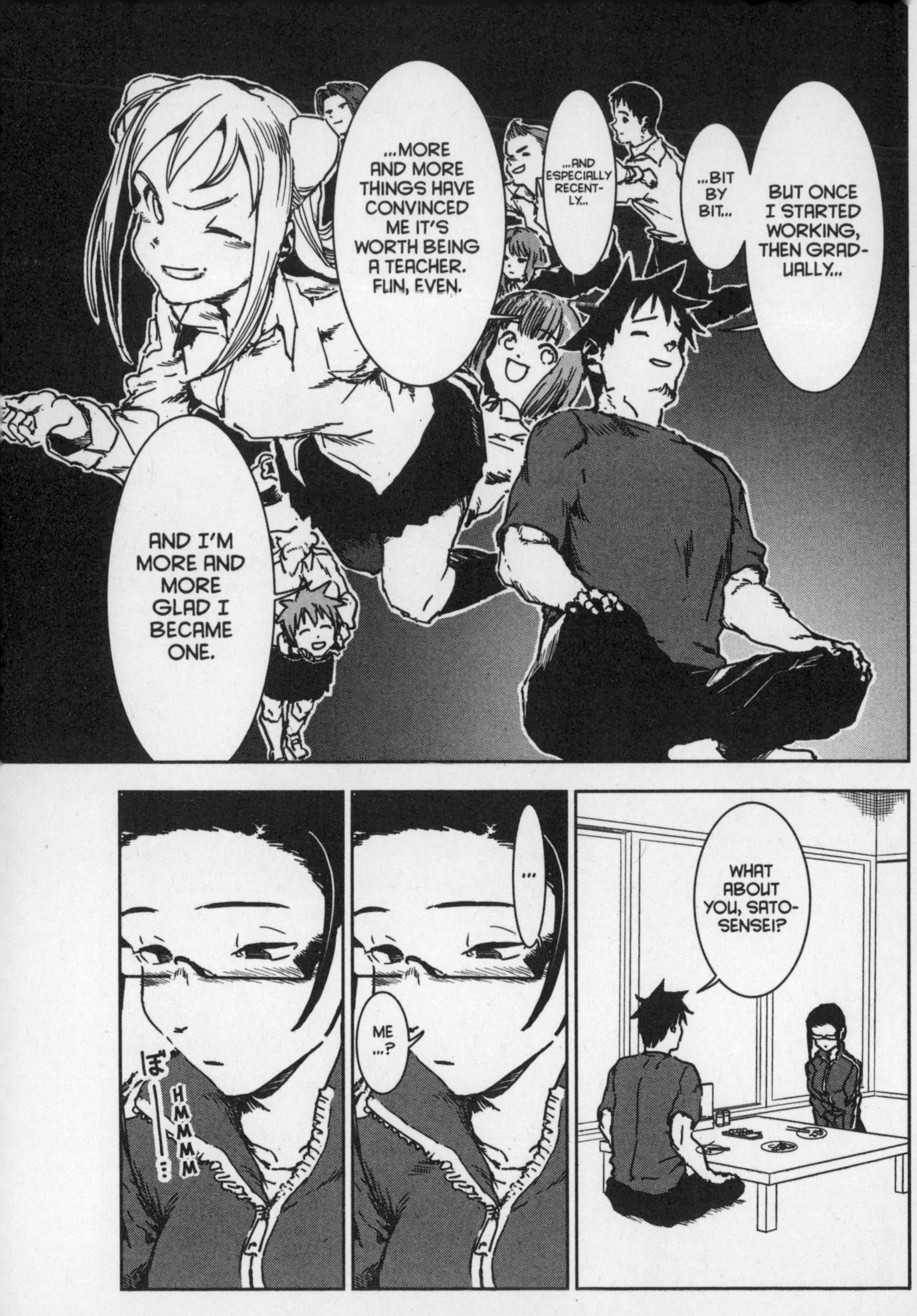
BUT ONCE I STARTED WORKING, THEN GRAD-UALLY...
...BIT BY BIT...
...AND ESPECIALLY RECENT-LY...
...MORE AND MORE THINGS HAVE CONVINCED ME IT'S WORTH BEING A TEACHER. FUN, EVEN.
AND I'M MORE AND MORE GLAD I BECAME ONE.
WHAT ABOUT YOU, SATO-SENSEI?
...
ME ...?
ぼー
HMMMM...

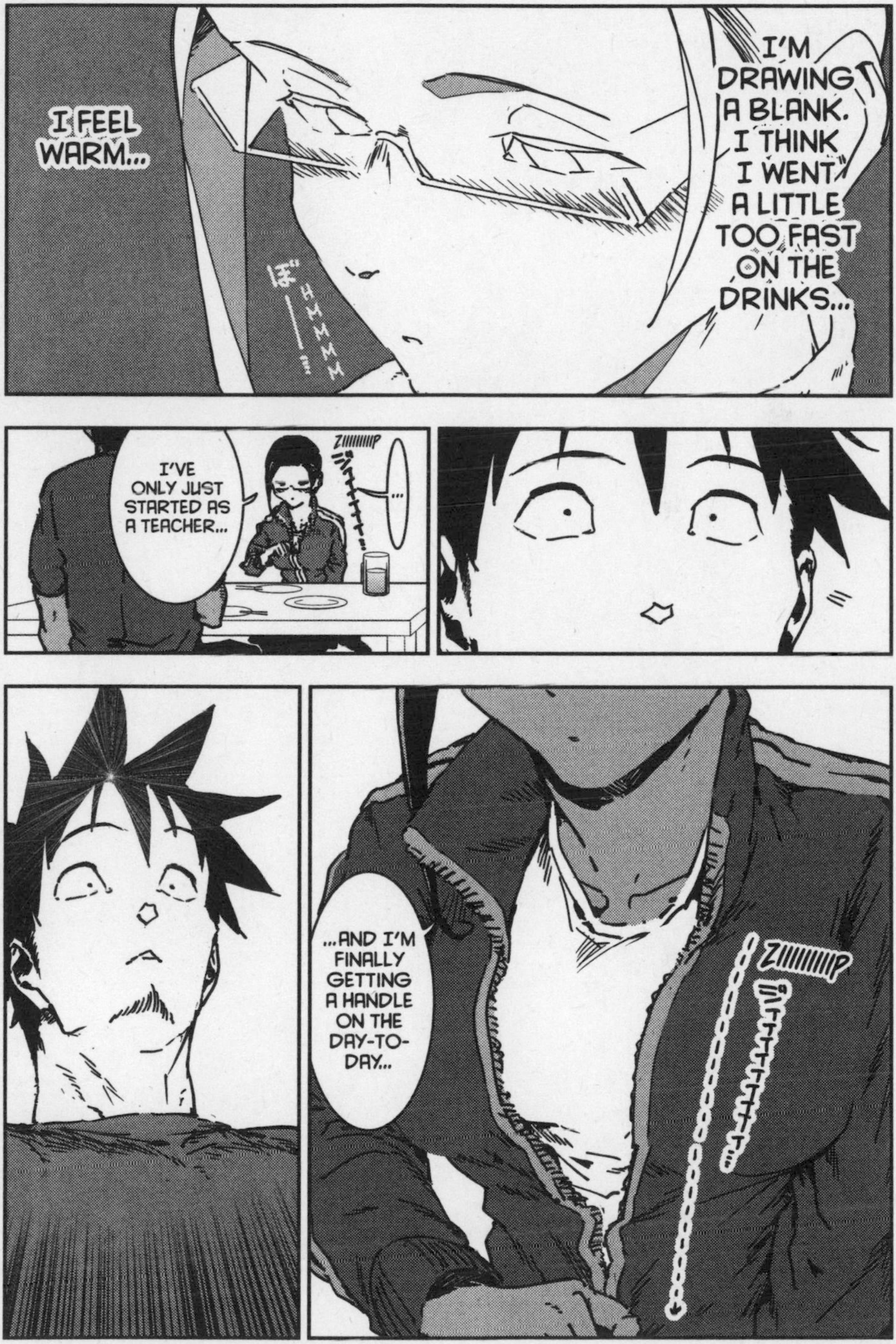
I'M DRAWING A BLANK. I THINK I WENT A LITTLE TOO FAST ON THE DRINKS...
I FEEL WARM...
ぼ—!! HMMMM
ZIIIIIIP
...
I'VE ONLY JUST STARTED AS A TEACHER...
ZIIIIIIP
...AND I'M FINALLY GETTING A HANDLE ON THE DAY-TO-DAY...

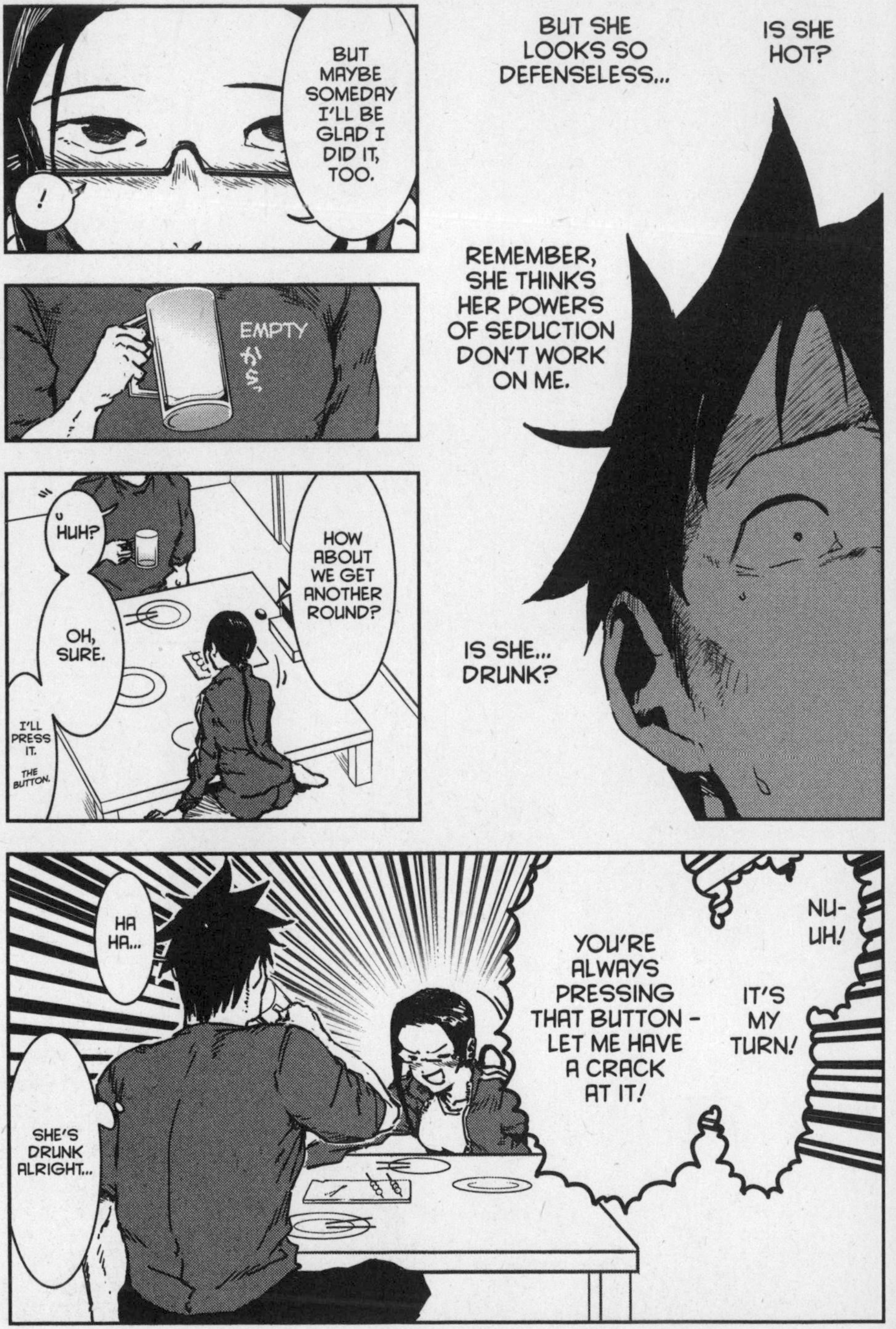
IS SHE HOT?
BUT SHE LOOKS SO DEFENSELESS...
REMEMBER, SHE THINKS HER POWERS OF SEDUCTION DON'T WORK ON ME.
IS SHE... DRUNK?
BUT MAYBE SOMEDAY I'LL BE GLAD I DID IT, TOO.
!
EMPTY
HOW ABOUT WE GET ANOTHER ROUND?
HUH?
OH, SURE.
I'LL PRESS IT.
THE BUTTON.
NU-UH!
IT'S MY TURN!
YOU'RE ALWAYS PRESSING THAT BUTTON - LET ME HAVE A CRACK AT IT!
HA HA...
SHE'S DRUNK ALRIGHT...

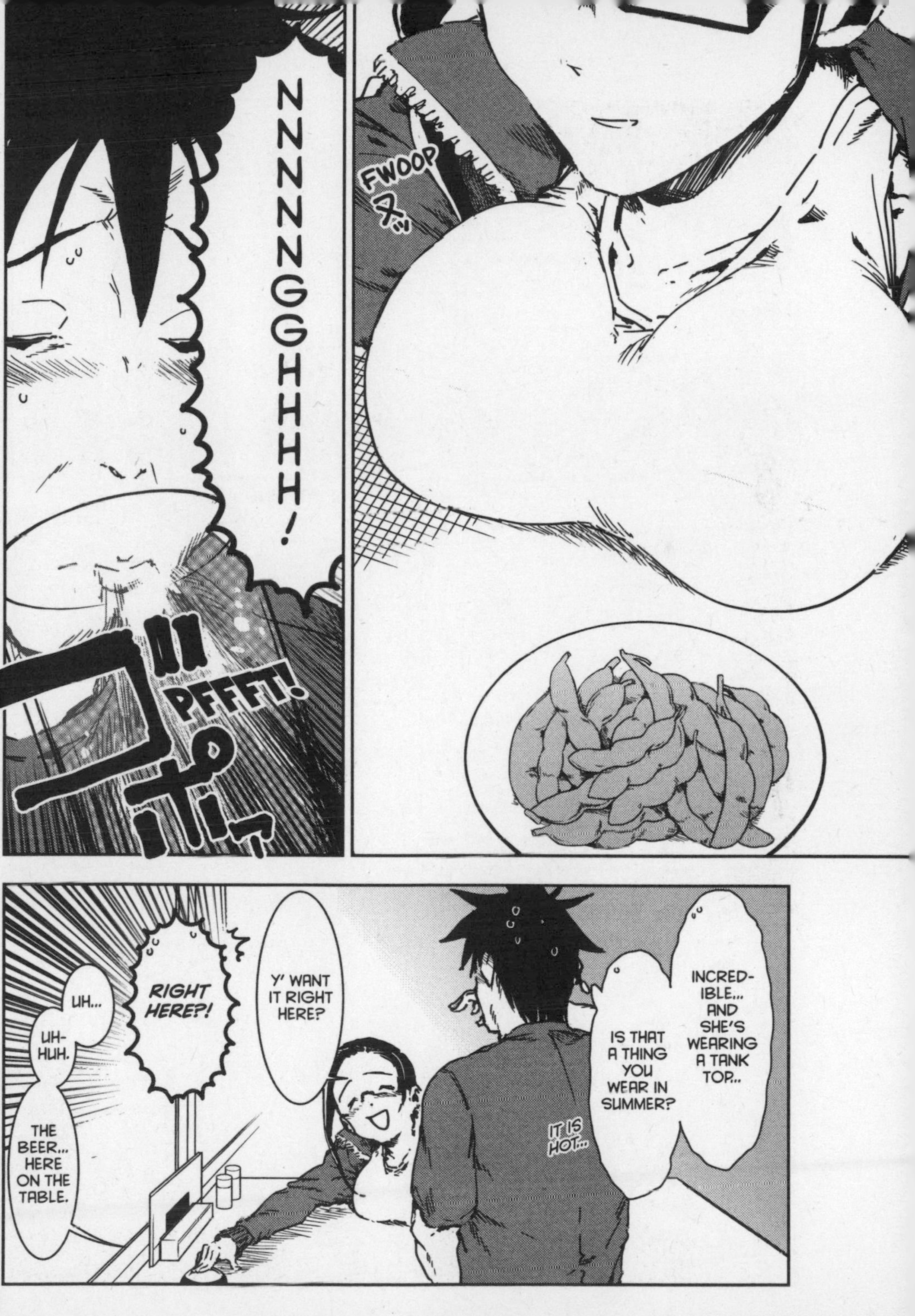
FWOOP
ズッ
NNNNNNGHHHH!
PFFFT!
プーッ
INCRED-IBLE... AND SHE'S WEARING A TANK TOP...
IS THAT A THING YOU WEAR IN SUMMER?
IT IS HOT...
Y' WANT IT RIGHT HERE?
RIGHT HERE?!
UH...
UH-HUH.
THE BEER... HERE ON THE TABLE.

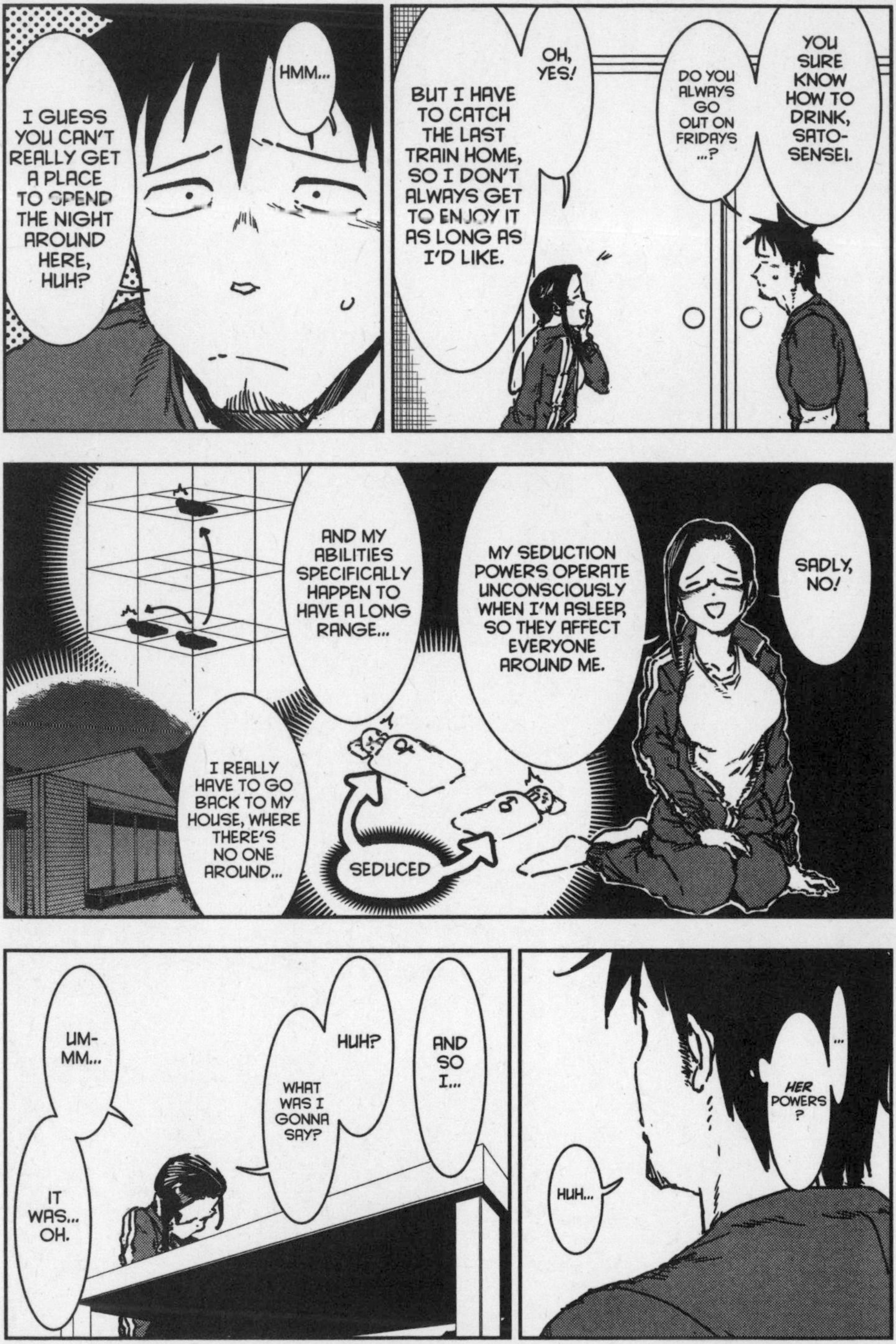
YOU SURE KNOW HOW TO DRINK, SATO-SENSEI.
DO YOU ALWAYS GO OUT ON FRIDAYS ...?
OH, YES!
BUT I HAVE TO CATCH THE LAST TRAIN HOME, SO I DON'T ALWAYS GET TO ENJOY IT AS LONG AS I'D LIKE.
HMM...
I GUESS YOU CAN'T REALLY GET A PLACE TO SPEND THE NIGHT AROUND HERE, HUH?
SADLY, NO!
MY SEDUCTION POWERS OPERATE UNCONSCIOUSLY WHEN I'M ASLEEP, SO THEY AFFECT EVERYONE AROUND ME.
AND MY ABILITIES SPECIFICALLY HAPPEN TO HAVE A LONG RANGE...
I REALLY HAVE TO GO BACK TO MY HOUSE, WHERE THERE'S NO ONE AROUND...
SEDUCED
...
HER POWERS?
HUH...
AND SO I...
HUH?
WHAT WAS I GONNA SAY?
UMM-MM...
IT WAS... OH.

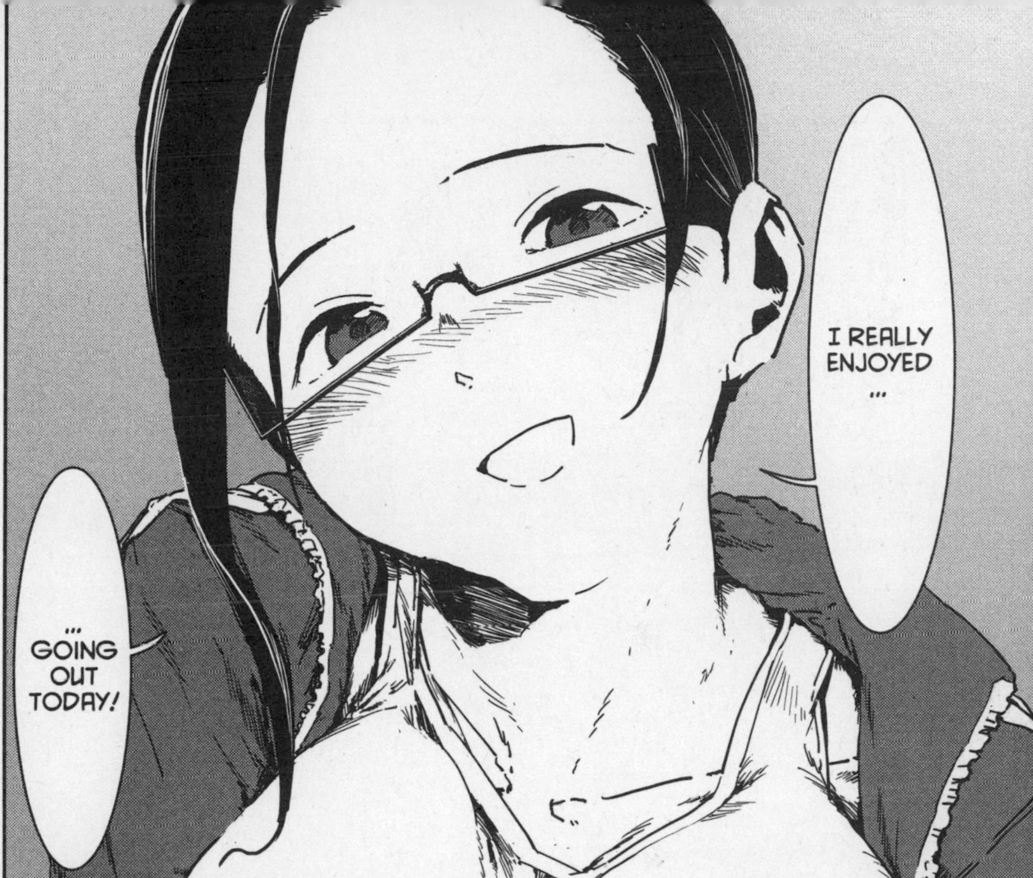
I REALLY ENJOYED ...
... GOING OUT TODAY!

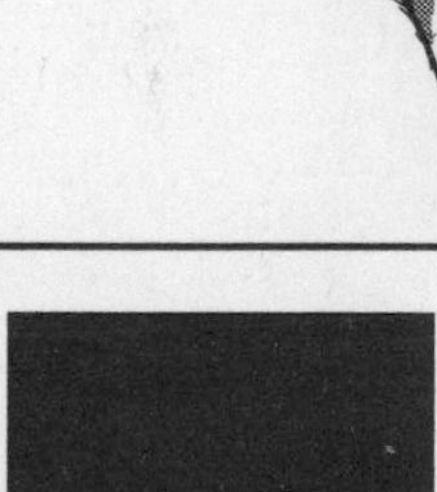

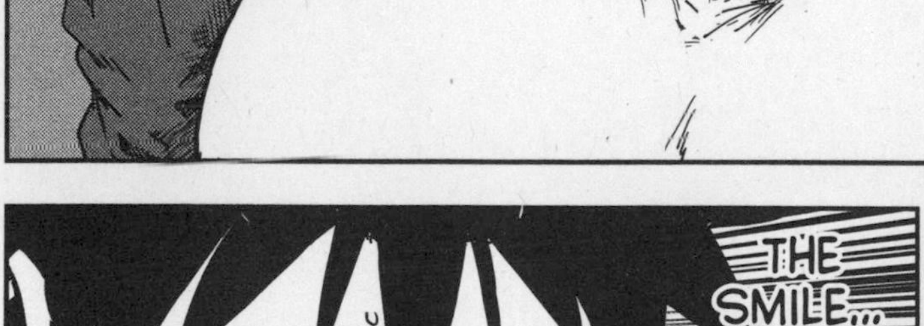
THE SMILE... THE TANK TOP...
HRRRGH...
HAS PECULIAR TURN-ONS

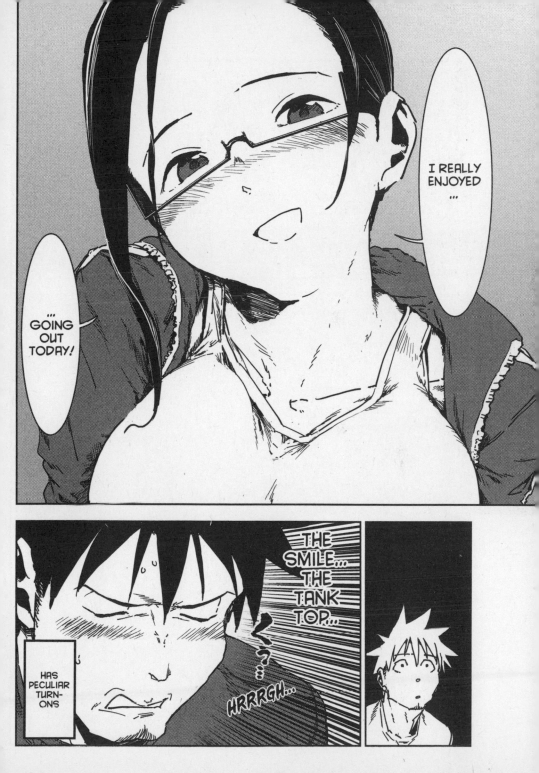

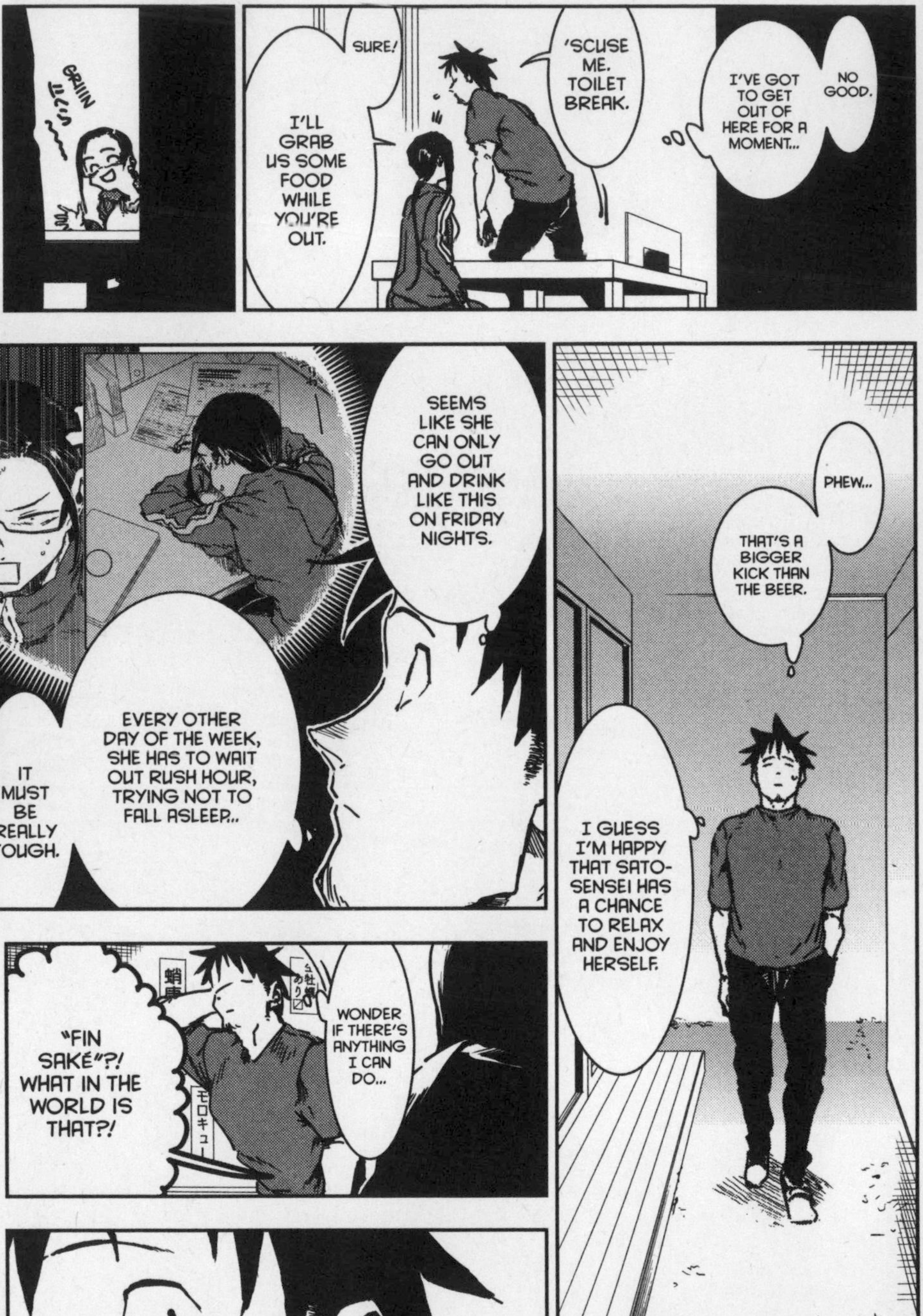
NO GOOD.
I'VE GOT TO GET OUT OF HERE FOR A MOMENT...
'SCUSE ME. TOILET BREAK.
SURE!
I'LL GRAB US SOME FOOD WHILE YOU'RE OUT.
GRIIN
PHEW...
THAT'S A BIGGER KICK THAN THE BEER.
I GUESS I'M HAPPY THAT SATO-SENSEI HAS A CHANCE TO RELAX AND ENJOY HERSELF.
SEEMS LIKE SHE CAN ONLY GO OUT AND DRINK LIKE THIS ON FRIDAY NIGHTS.
EVERY OTHER DAY OF THE WEEK, SHE HAS TO WAIT OUT RUSH HOUR, TRYING NOT TO FALL ASLEEP...
IT MUST BE REALLY TOUGH.
WONDER IF THERE'S ANYTHING I CAN DO...
モロキュー
"FIN SAKÉ"?! WHAT IN THE WORLD IS THAT?!

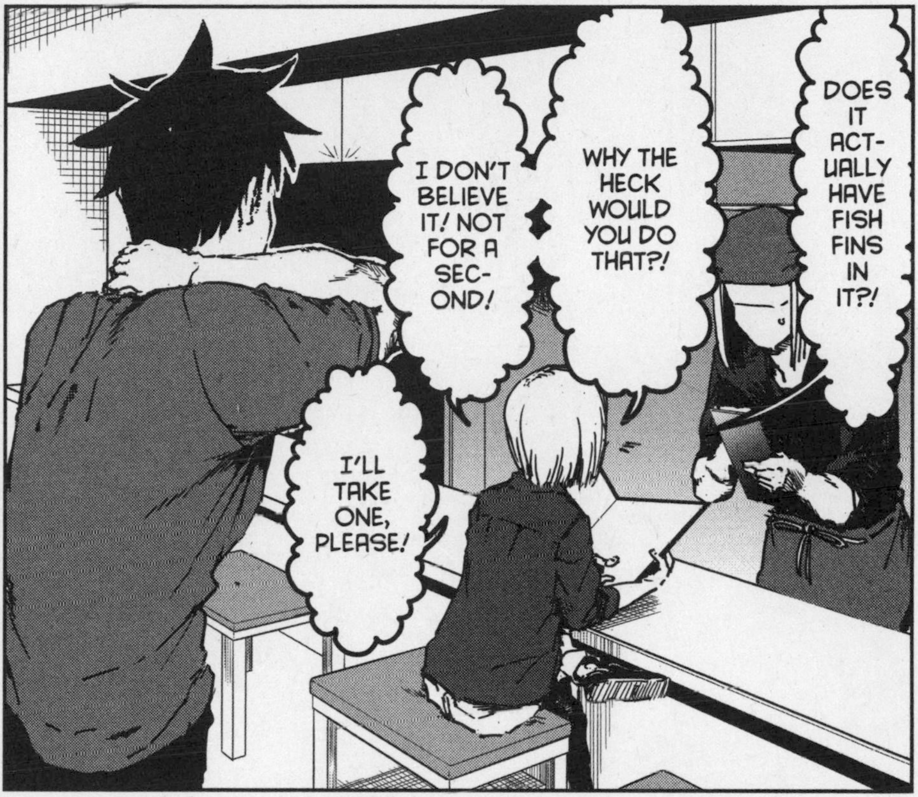
DOES IT ACTUALLY HAVE FISH FINS IN IT?!
WHY THE HECK WOULD YOU DO THAT?!
I DON'T BELIEVE IT! NOT FOR A SECOND!
I'LL TAKE ONE, PLEASE!

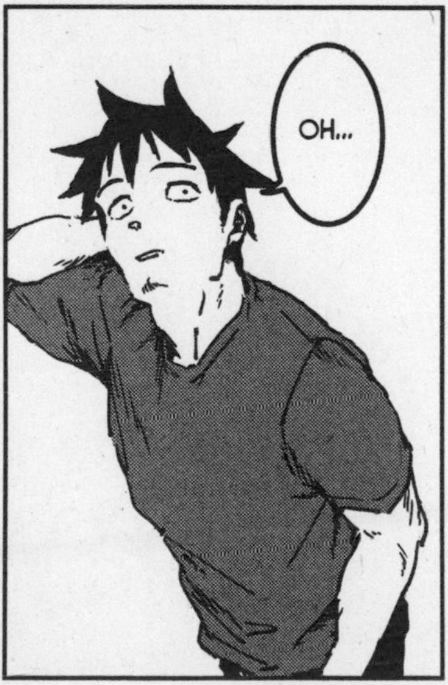
OH...

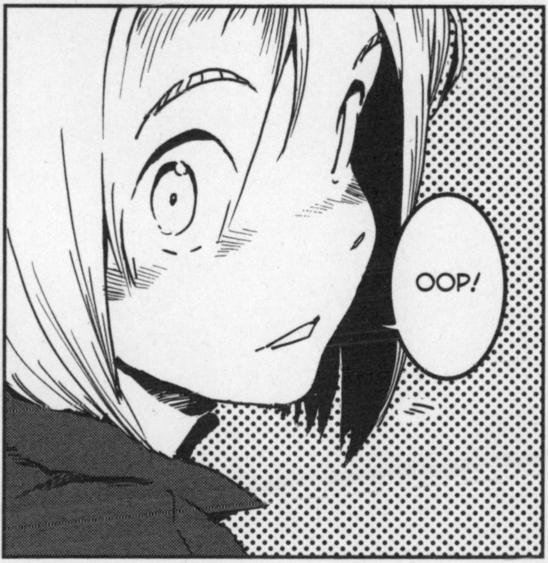
OOP!

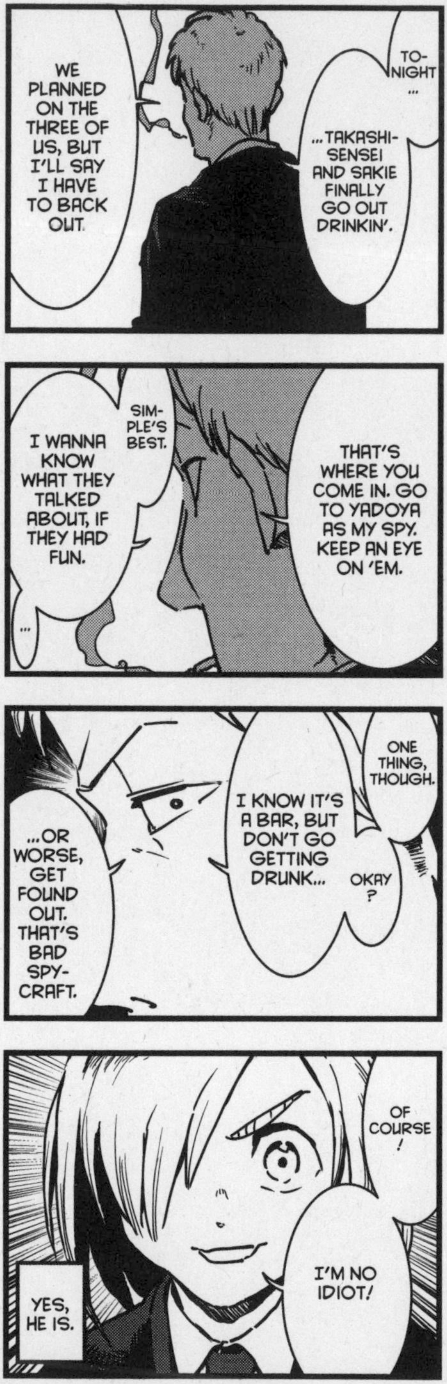
TONIGHT...
...TAKASHI-SENSEI AND SAKIE FINALLY GO OUT DRINKIN'.
WE PLANNED ON THE THREE OF US, BUT I'LL SAY I HAVE TO BACK OUT.
THAT'S WHERE YOU COME IN. GO TO YADOYA AS MY SPY. KEEP AN EYE ON 'EM.
SIMPLE'S BEST.
I WANNA KNOW WHAT THEY TALKED ABOUT, IF THEY HAD FUN.
...
ONE THING, THOUGH.
I KNOW IT'S A BAR, BUT DON'T GO GETTING DRUNK...
OKAY?
...OR WORSE, GET FOUND OUT. THAT'S BAD SPY-CRAFT.
OF COURSE!
I'M NO IDIOT!
YES, HE IS.

INTERVIEWS WITH MONSTER GIRLS

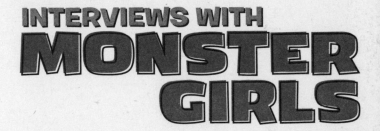

Chapter 42: Good Things Come to Those Who Sleep

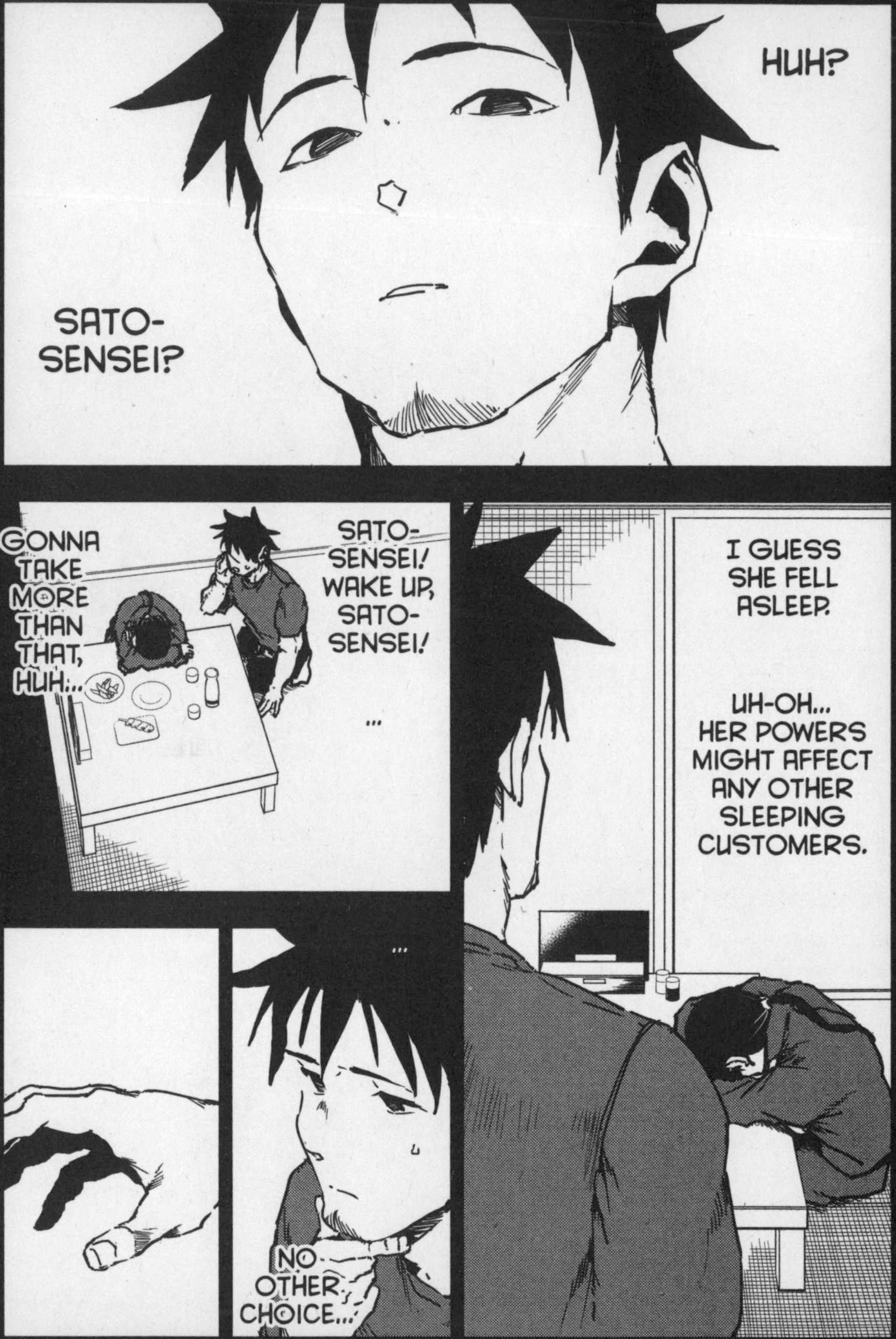
HUH?
SATO-SENSEI?
I GUESS SHE FELL ASLEEP.
UH-OH... HER POWERS MIGHT AFFECT ANY OTHER SLEEPING CUSTOMERS.
SATO-SENSEI! WAKE UP, SATO-SENSEI!
...
GONNA TAKE MORE THAN THAT, HUH...
...
NO OTHER CHOICE...

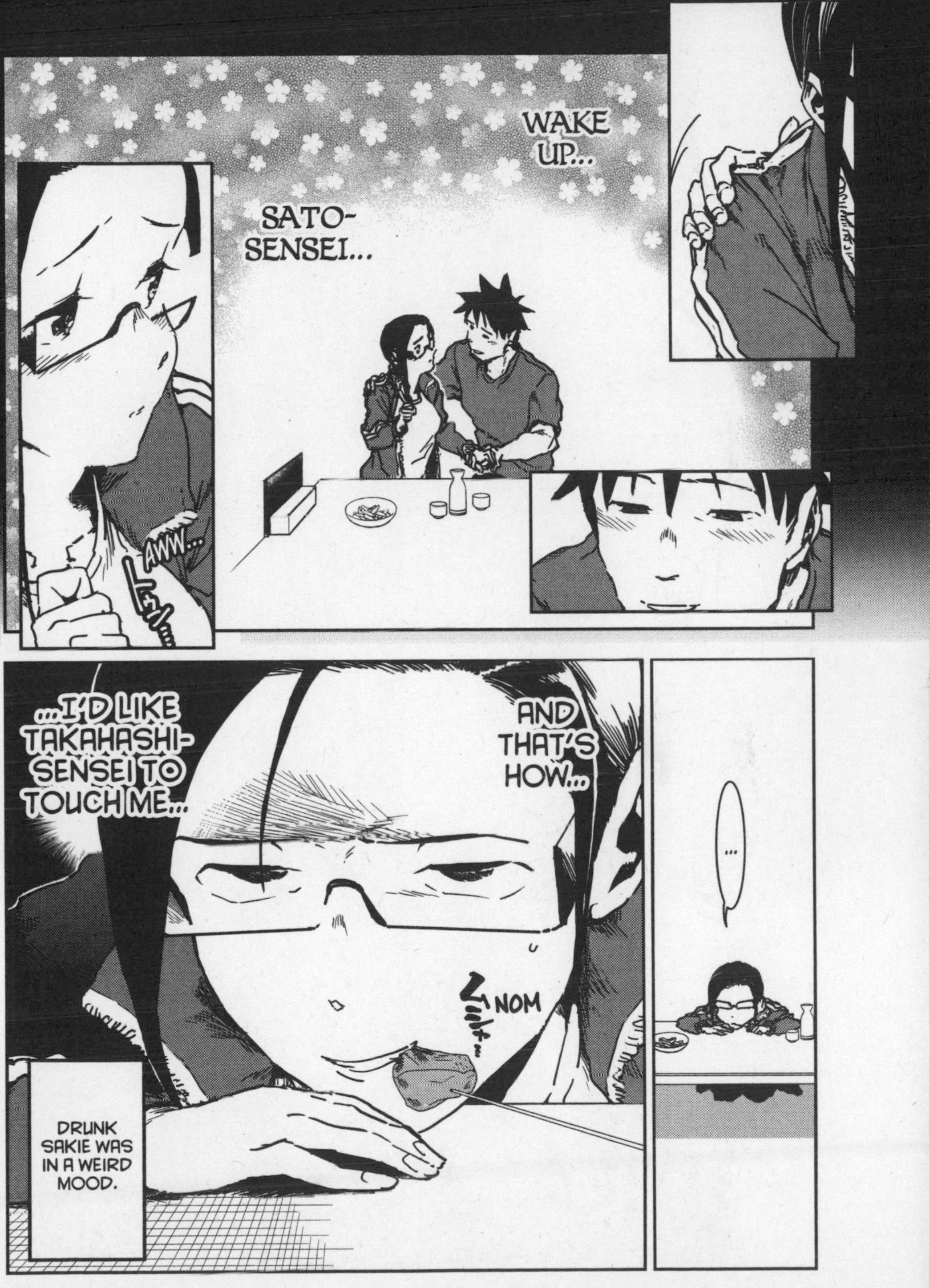
WAKE UP...
SATO-SENSEI...
AWW...
...
AND THAT'S HOW...
...I'D LIKE TAKAHASHI-SENSEI TO TOUCH ME...
NOM
DRUNK SAKIE WAS IN A WEIRD MOOD.

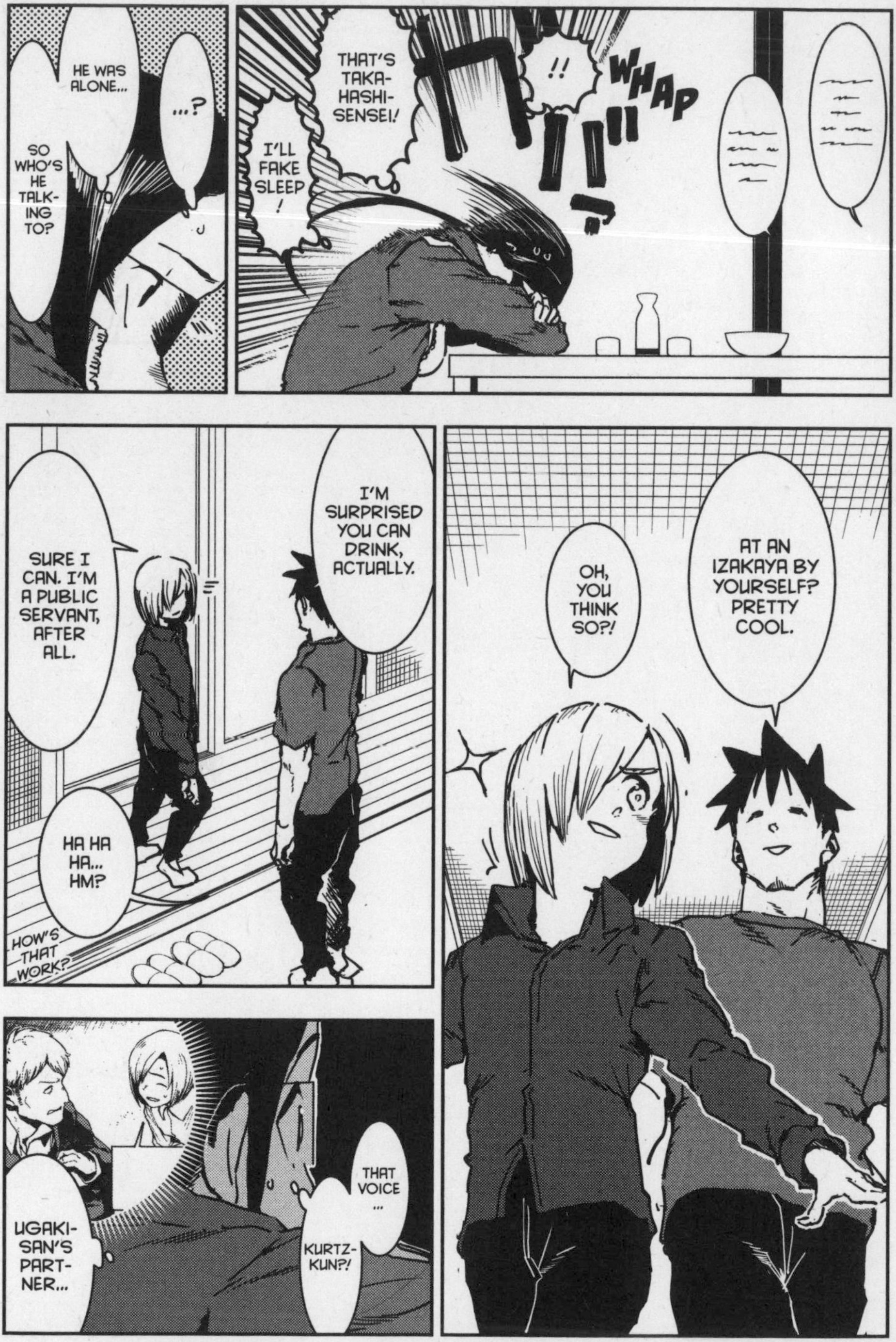
!!
WHAP
THAT'S TAKA-HASHI-SENSEI!
I'LL FAKE SLEEP!
...?
HE WAS ALONE...
SO WHO'S HE TALKING TO?
AT AN IZAKAYA BY YOURSELF? PRETTY COOL.
OH, YOU THINK SO?!
I'M SURPRISED YOU CAN DRINK, ACTUALLY.
SURE I CAN. I'M A PUBLIC SERVANT, AFTER ALL.
HA HA HA... HM?
HOW'S THAT WORK?
THAT VOICE...
KURTZ-KUN?!
UGAKI-SAN'S PARTNER...

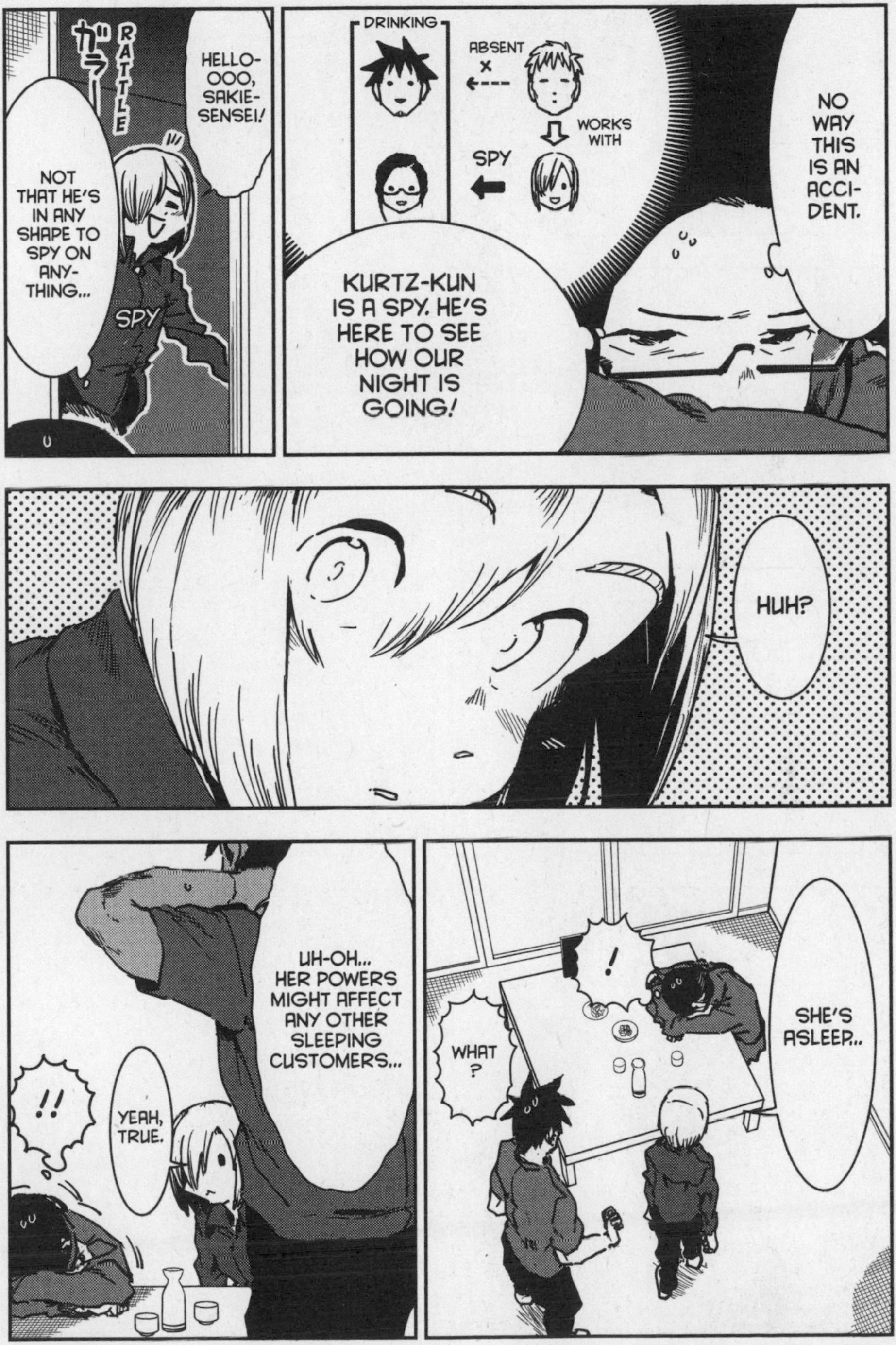
NO WAY THIS IS AN ACCI-DENT.
DRINKING
ABSENT
WORKS WITH
SPY
KURTZ-KUN IS A SPY. HE'S HERE TO SEE HOW OUR NIGHT IS GOING!
ガラー
RATTLE
HELLO-OOO, SAKIE-SENSEI!
NOT THAT HE'S IN ANY SHAPE TO SPY ON ANY-THING...
SPY
HUH?
SHE'S ASLEEP...
!
WHAT?
UH-OH... HER POWERS MIGHT AFFECT ANY OTHER SLEEPING CUSTOMERS...
YEAH, TRUE.
!!

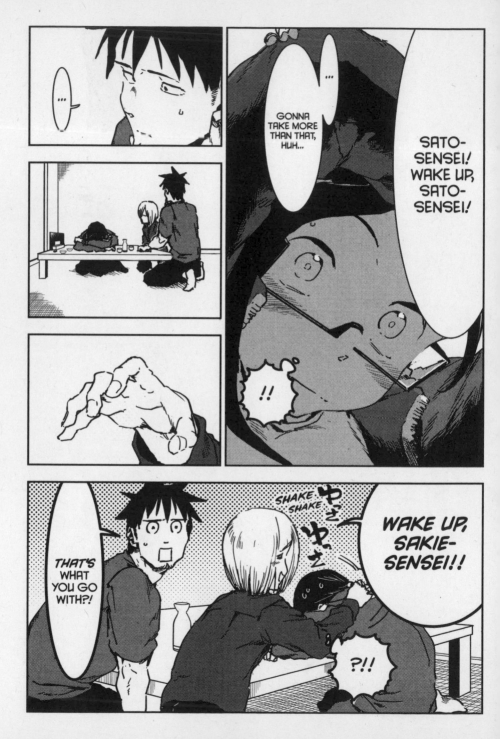

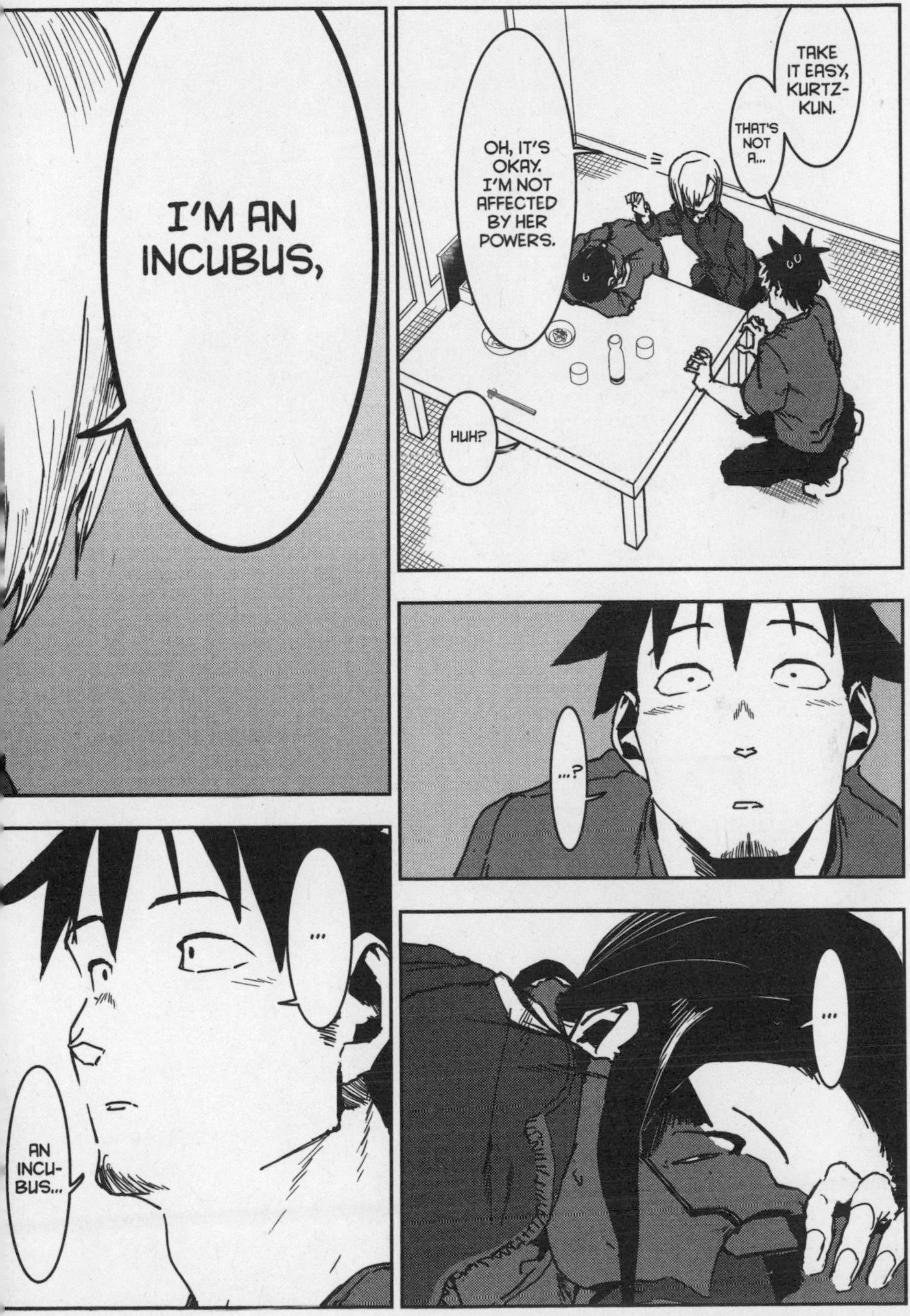
TAKE IT EASY, KURTZ-KUN.
THAT'S NOT A...
OH, IT'S OKAY. I'M NOT AFFECTED BY HER POWERS.
HUH?
I'M AN INCUBUS,
...?
...
...
AN INCUBUS...

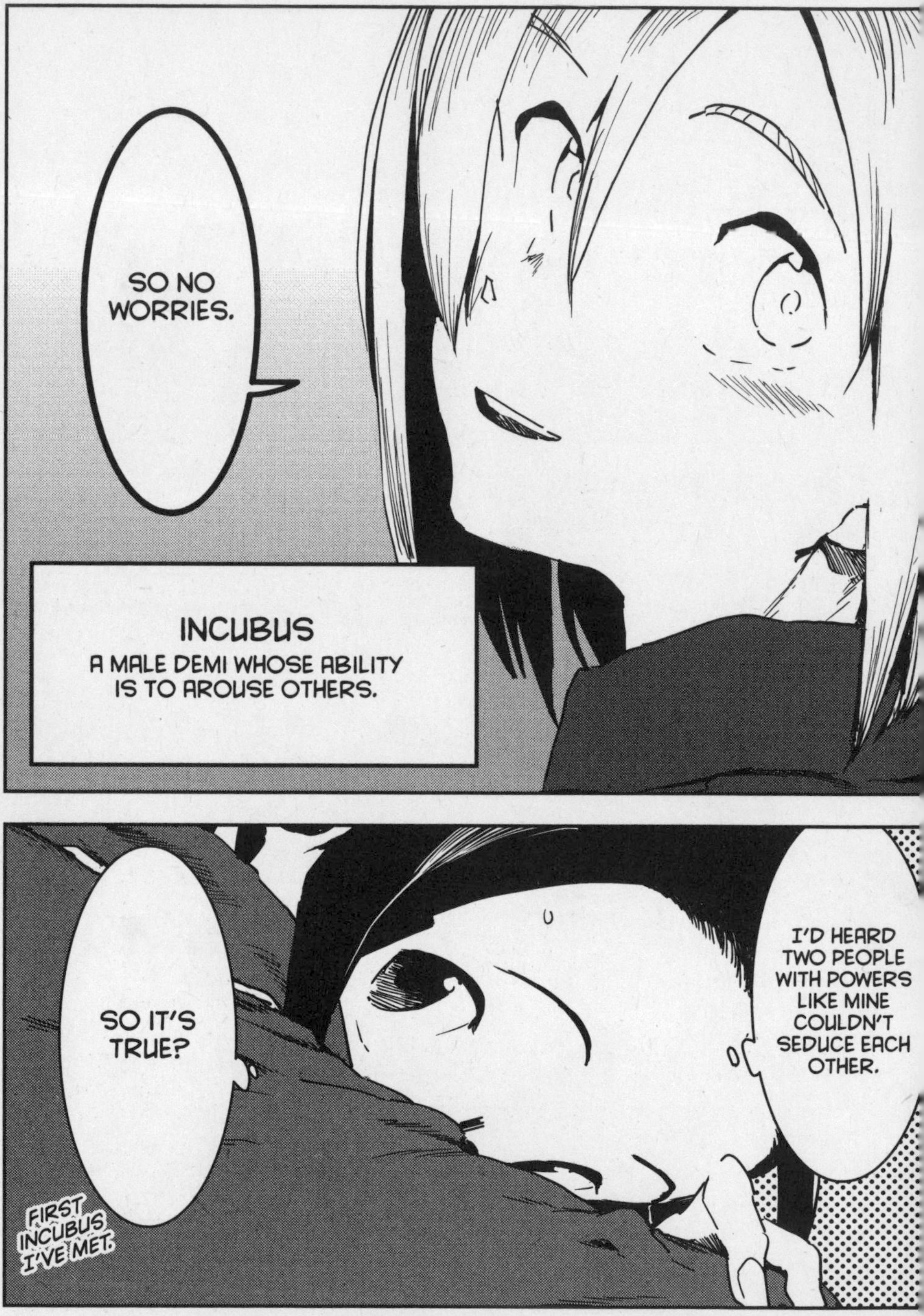
SO NO WORRIES.
INCUBUS
A MALE DEMI WHOSE ABILITY IS TO AROUSE OTHERS.
I'D HEARD TWO PEOPLE WITH POWERS LIKE MINE COULDN'T SEDUCE EACH OTHER.
SO IT'S TRUE?
FIRST INCUBUS I'VE MET.

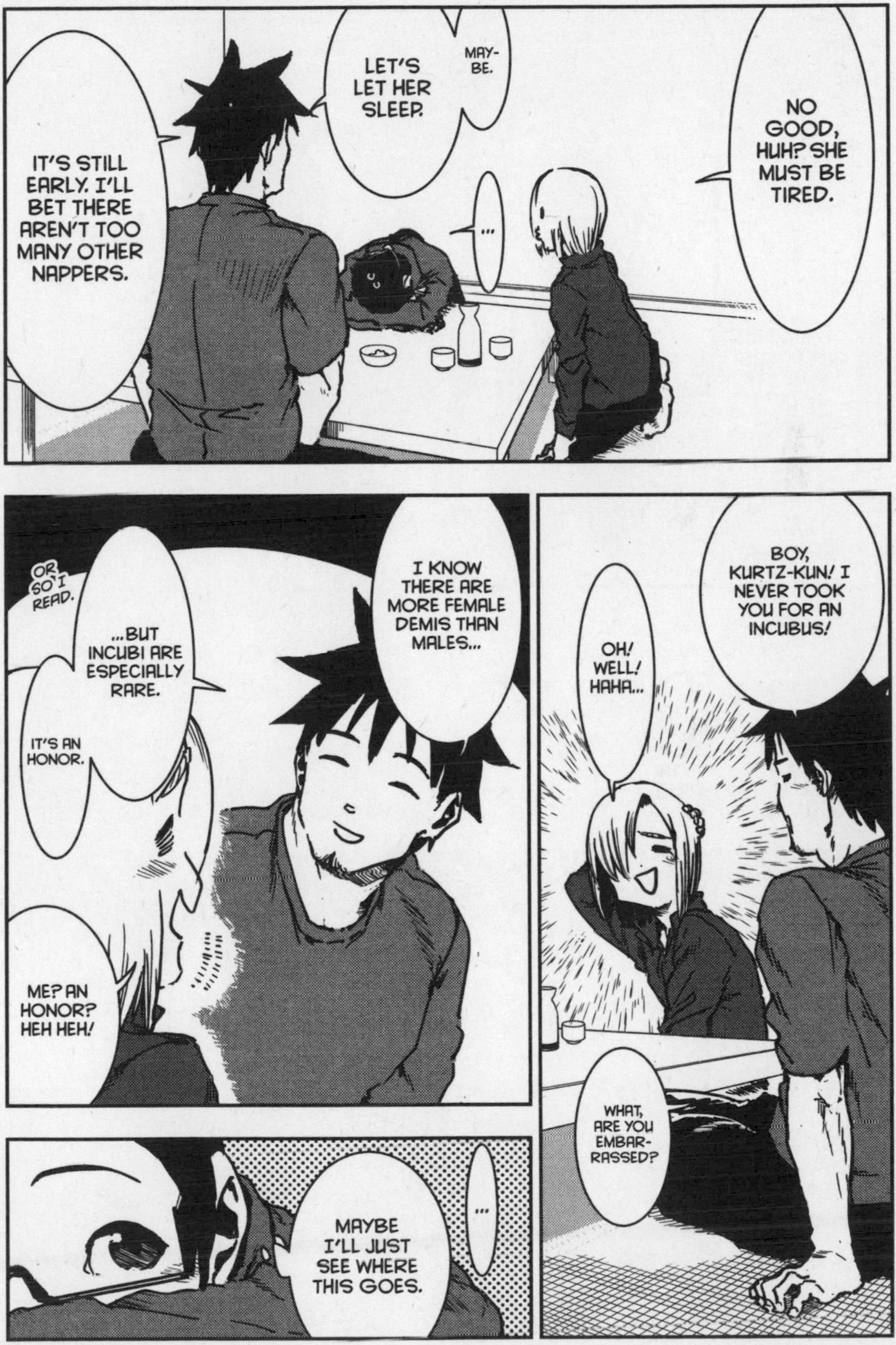
NO GOOD, HUH? SHE MUST BE TIRED.
MAY-BE.
LET'S LET HER SLEEP.
...
IT'S STILL EARLY. I'LL BET THERE AREN'T TOO MANY OTHER NAPPERS.
BOY, KURTZ-KUN! I NEVER TOOK YOU FOR AN INCUBUS!
OH! WELL! HAHA...
WHAT, ARE YOU EMBARRASSED?
I KNOW THERE ARE MORE FEMALE DEMIS THAN MALES...
...BUT INCUBI ARE ESPECIALLY RARE.
OR SO I READ.
IT'S AN HONOR.
ME? AN HONOR? HEH HEH!
...
MAYBE I'LL JUST SEE WHERE THIS GOES.

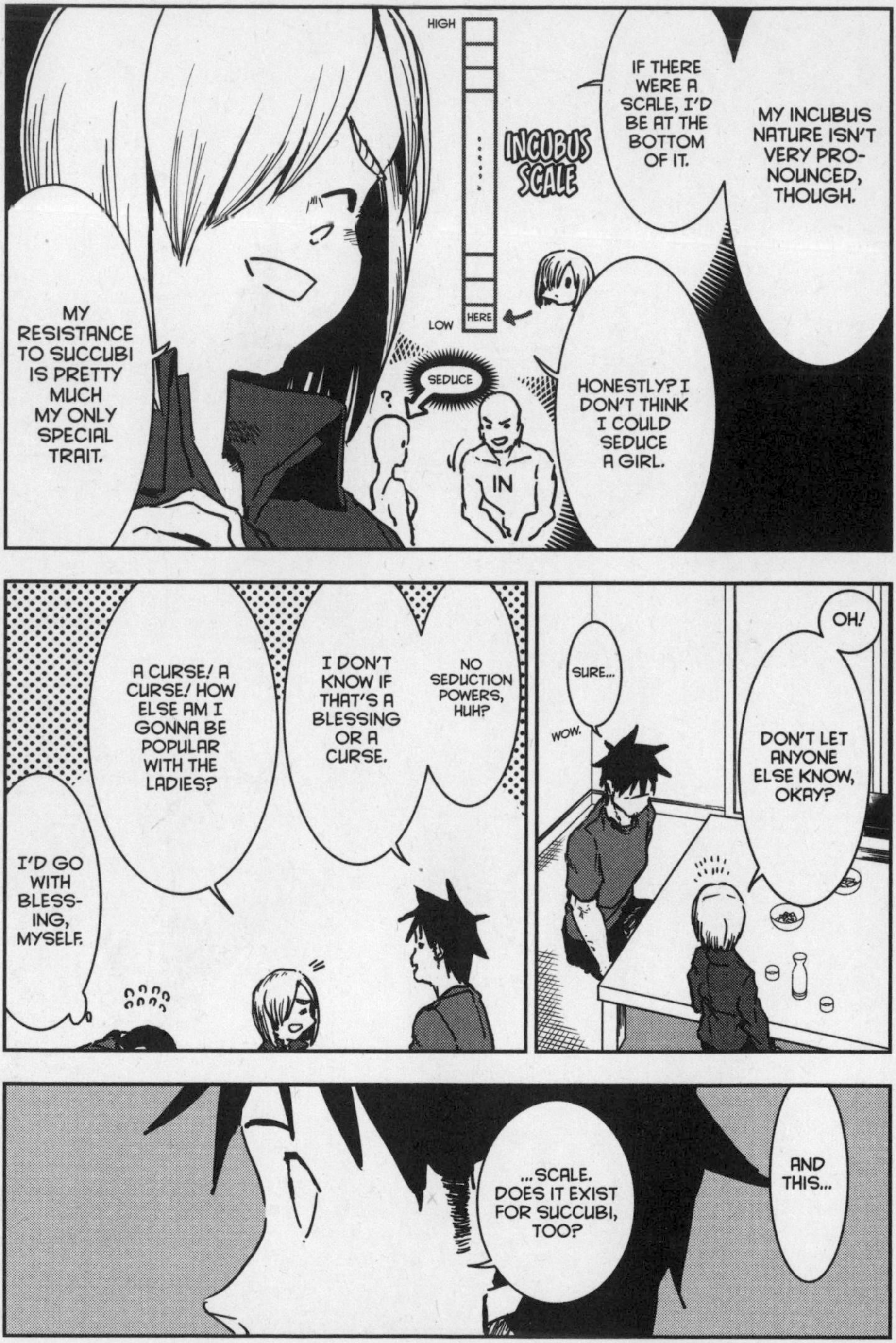
MY INCUBUS NATURE ISN'T VERY PRO-NOUNCED, THOUGH.
IF THERE WERE A SCALE, I'D BE AT THE BOTTOM OF IT.
INCUBUS SCALE
HIGH
LOW
HERE
HONESTLY? I DON'T THINK I COULD SEDUCE A GIRL.
SEDUCE
IN
MY RESISTANCE TO SUCCUBI IS PRETTY MUCH MY ONLY SPECIAL TRAIT.
OH!
DON'T LET ANYONE ELSE KNOW, OKAY?
SURE...
WOW.
NO SEDUCTION POWERS, HUH?
I DON'T KNOW IF THAT'S A BLESSING OR A CURSE.
A CURSE! A CURSE! HOW ELSE AM I GONNA BE POPULAR WITH THE LADIES?
I'D GO WITH BLESS-ING, MYSELF.
AND THIS...
...SCALE. DOES IT EXIST FOR SUCCUBI, TOO?

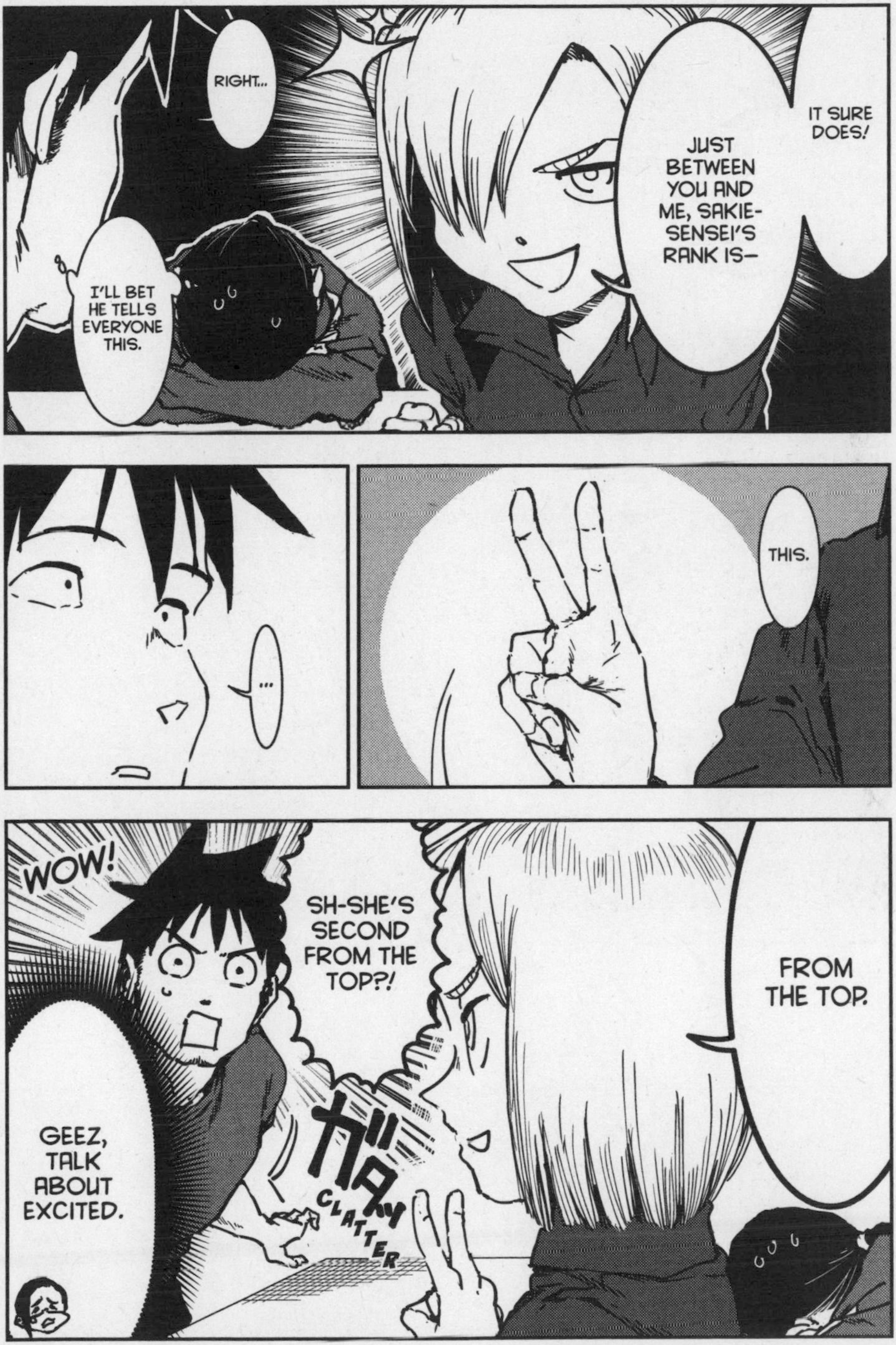
IT SURE DOES!
JUST BETWEEN YOU AND ME, SAKIE-SENSEI'S RANK IS—
RIGHT...
I'LL BET HE TELLS EVERYONE THIS.
THIS.
...
FROM THE TOP.
SH-SHE'S SECOND FROM THE TOP?!
WOW!
CLATTER
GEEZ, TALK ABOUT EXCITED.

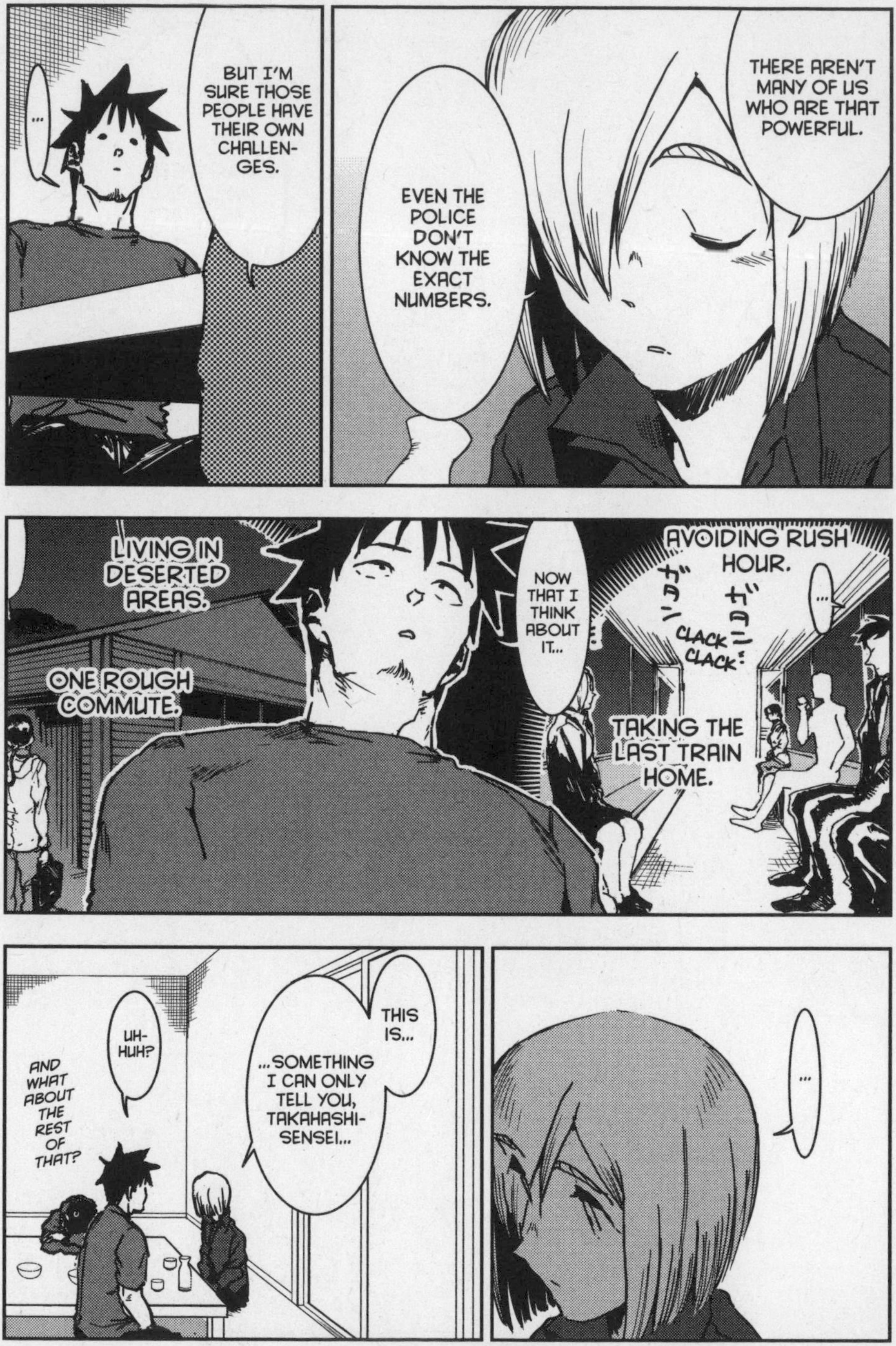
THERE AREN'T MANY OF US WHO ARE THAT POWERFUL.
EVEN THE POLICE DON'T KNOW THE EXACT NUMBERS.
BUT I'M SURE THOSE PEOPLE HAVE THEIR OWN CHALLEN-GES.
...
AVOIDING RUSH HOUR.
...
ガタン ガタン
CLACK CLACK
TAKING THE LAST TRAIN HOME.
NOW THAT I THINK ABOUT IT...
LIVING IN DESERTED AREAS.
ONE ROUGH COMMUTE.
...
THIS IS...
...SOMETHING I CAN ONLY TELL YOU, TAKAHASHI-SENSEI...
UH-HUH?
AND WHAT ABOUT THE REST OF THAT?

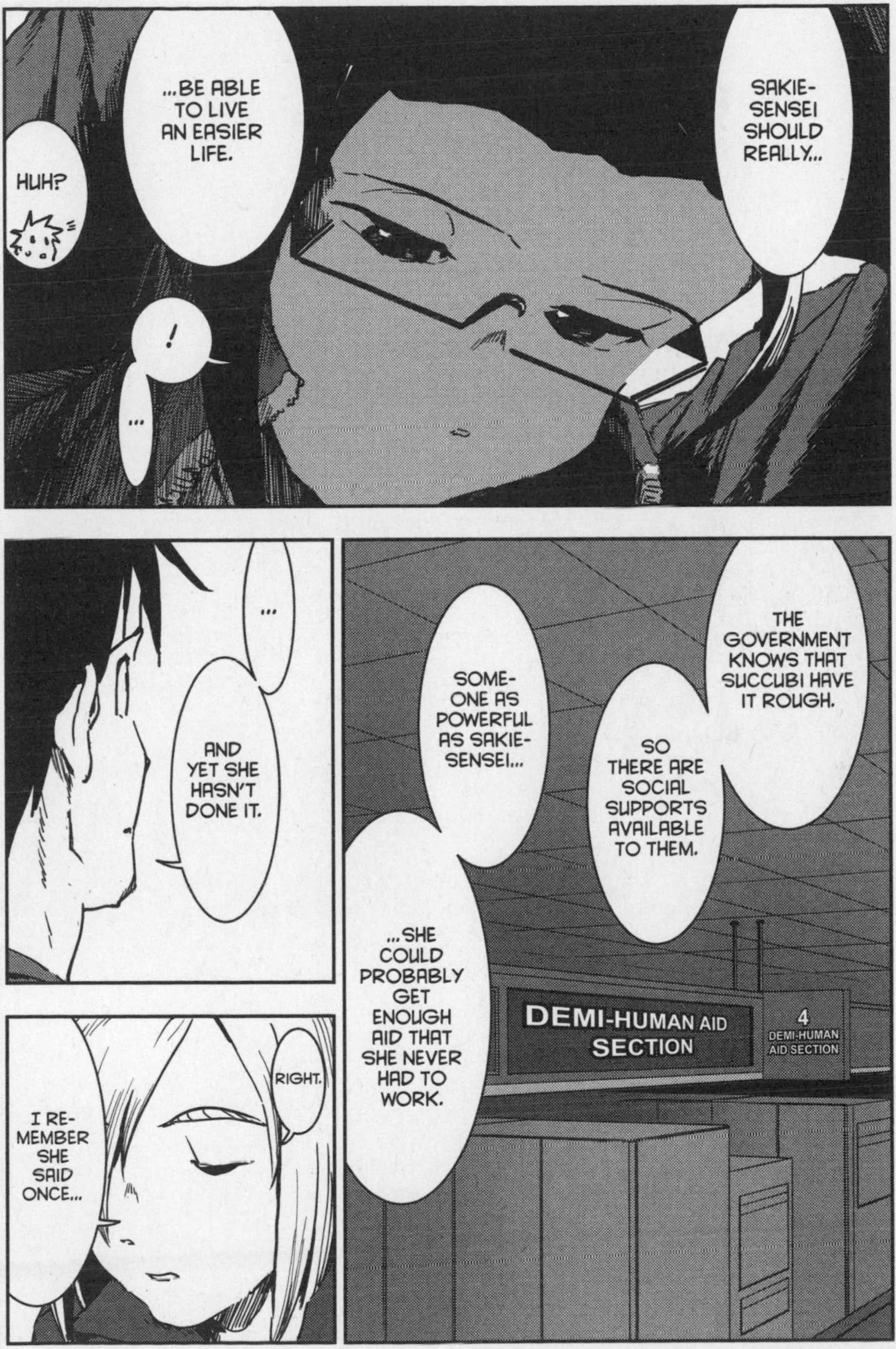
SAKIE-SENSEI SHOULD REALLY...
...BE ABLE TO LIVE AN EASIER LIFE.
HUH?
!
...
THE GOVERNMENT KNOWS THAT SUCCUBI HAVE IT ROUGH.
SO THERE ARE SOCIAL SUPPORTS AVAILABLE TO THEM.
SOME-ONE AS POWERFUL AS SAKIE-SENSEI...
...SHE COULD PROBABLY GET ENOUGH AID THAT SHE NEVER HAD TO WORK.
DEMI-HUMAN AID SECTION
4 DEMI-HUMAN AID SECTION
...
AND YET SHE HASN'T DONE IT.
RIGHT.
I RE-MEMBER SHE SAID ONCE...

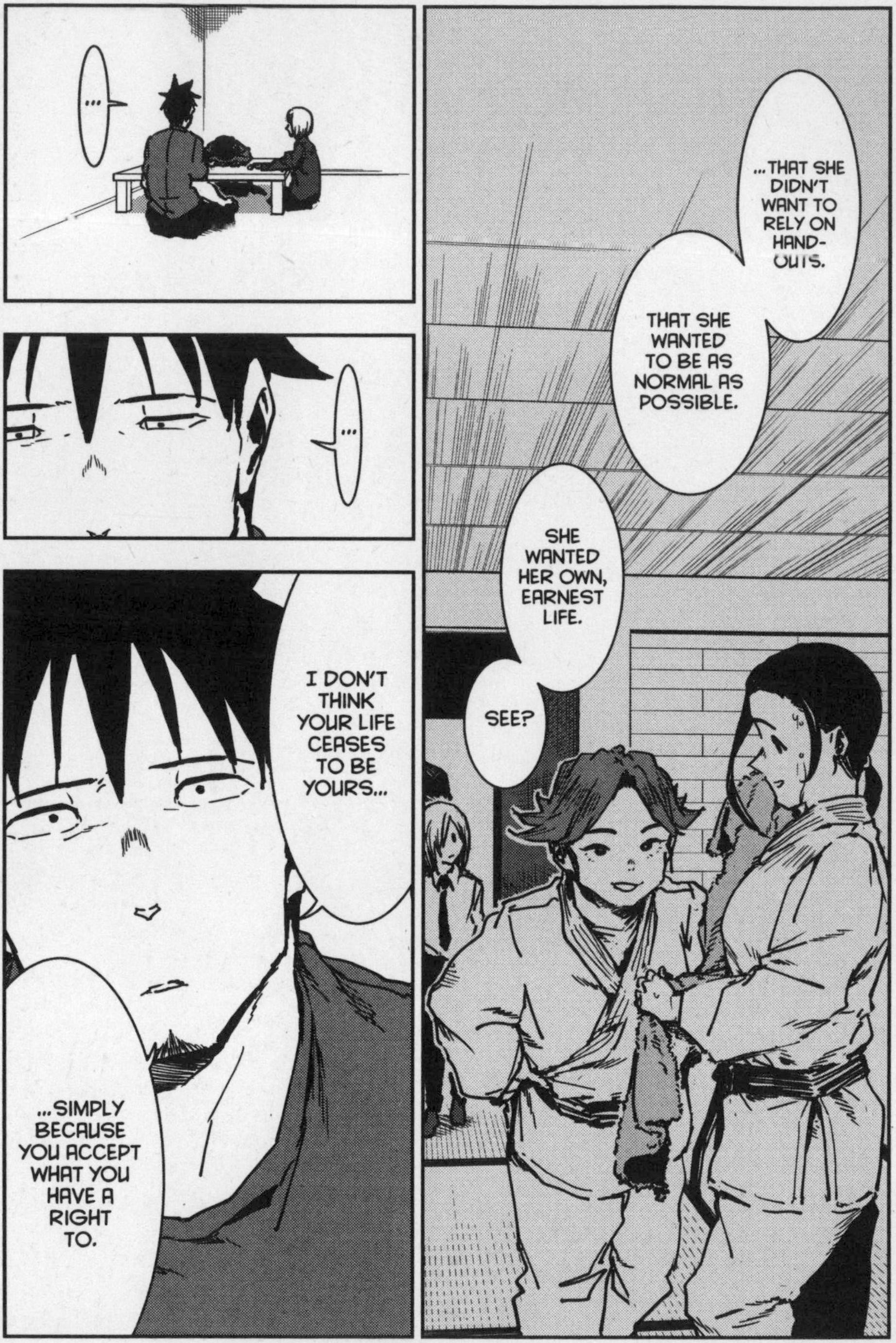
...THAT SHE DIDN'T WANT TO RELY ON HAND-OUTS.
THAT SHE WANTED TO BE AS NORMAL AS POSSIBLE.
SHE WANTED HER OWN, EARNEST LIFE.
SEE?
...
...
I DON'T THINK YOUR LIFE CEASES TO BE YOURS...
...SIMPLY BECAUSE YOU ACCEPT WHAT YOU HAVE A RIGHT TO.

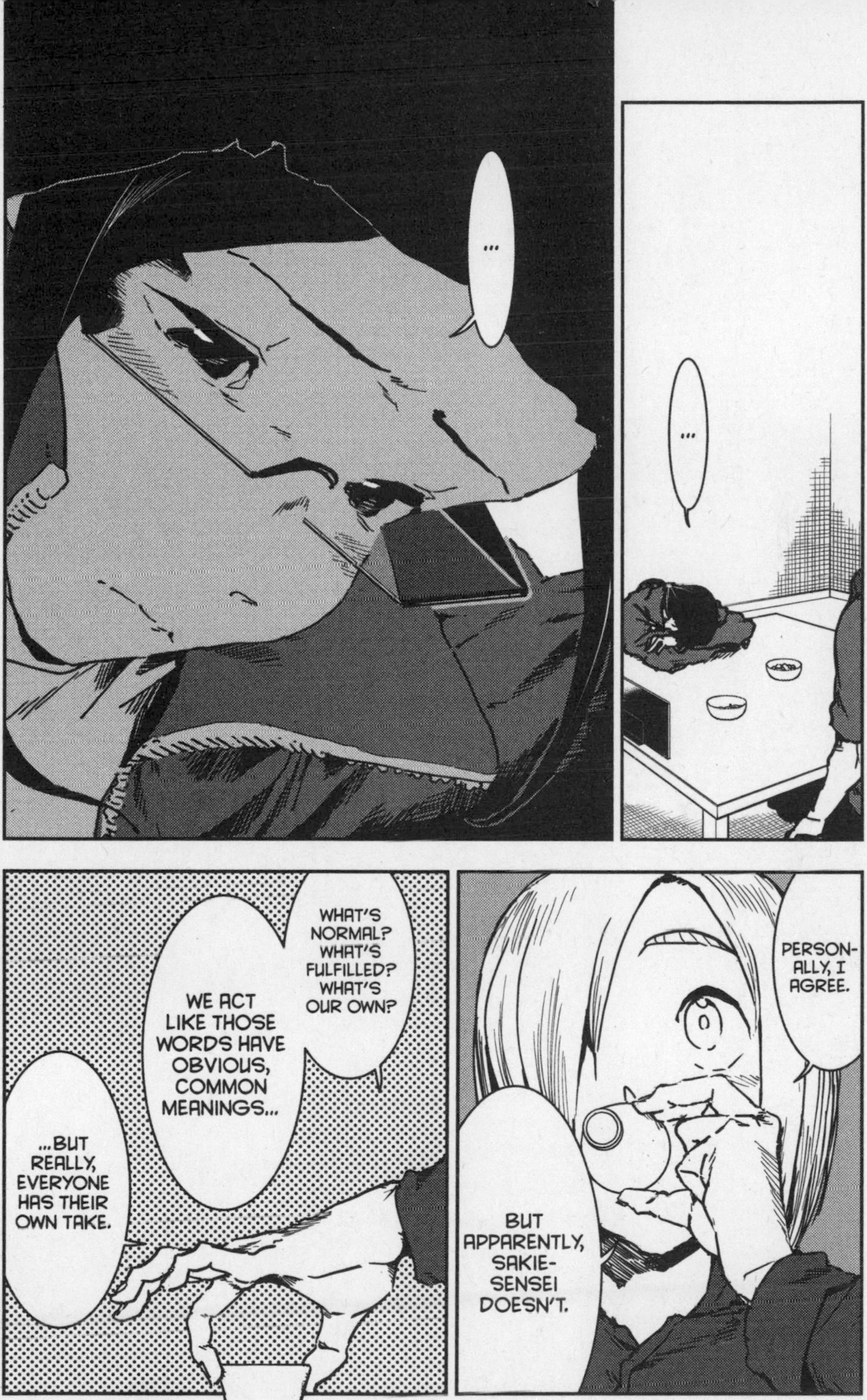
...
...
PERSONALLY, I AGREE.
BUT APPARENTLY, SAKIE-SENSEI DOESN'T.
WHAT'S NORMAL? WHAT'S FULFILLED? WHAT'S OUR OWN?
WE ACT LIKE THOSE WORDS HAVE OBVIOUS, COMMON MEANINGS...
...BUT REALLY, EVERYONE HAS THEIR OWN TAKE.

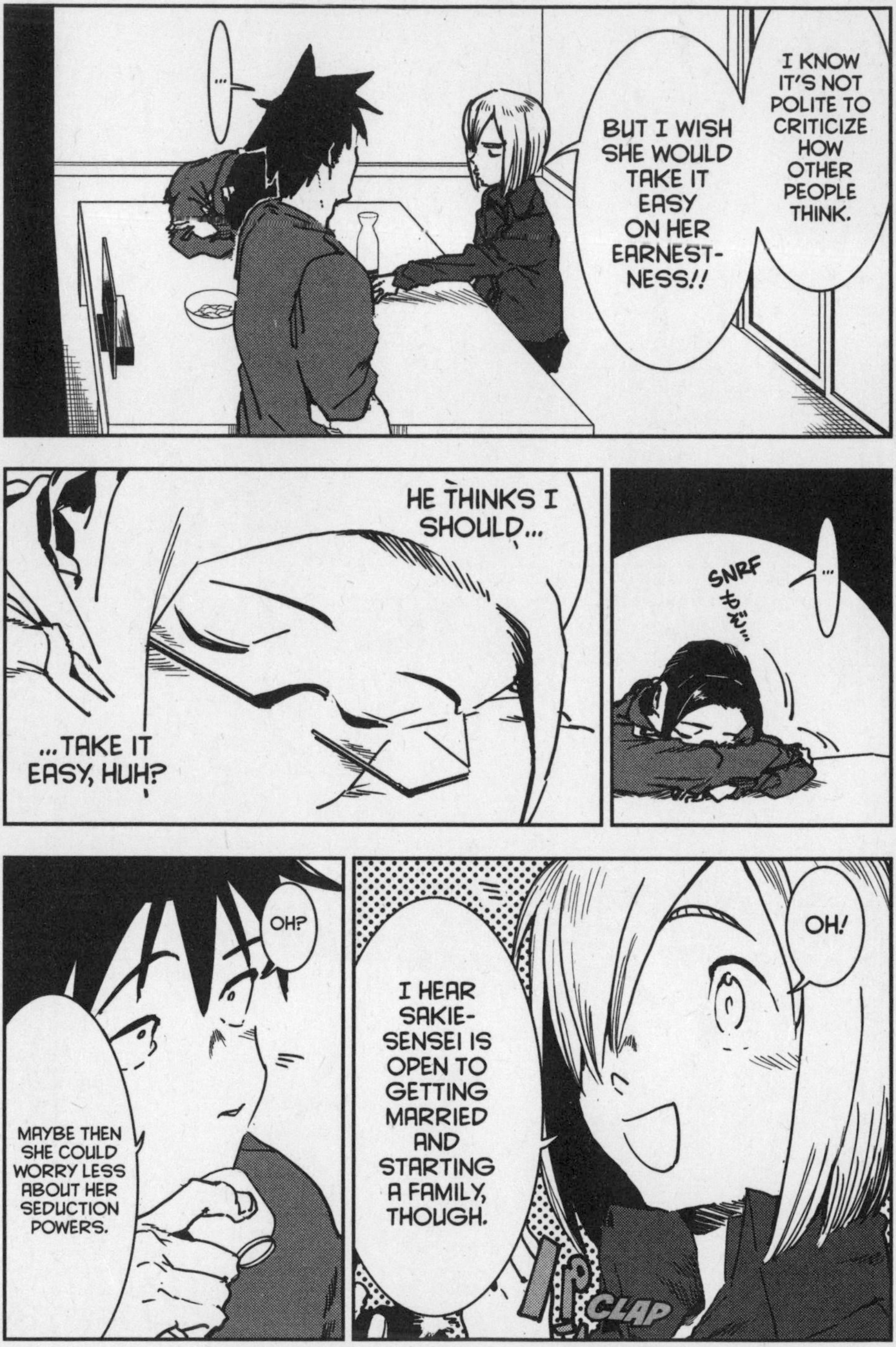
I KNOW IT'S NOT POLITE TO CRITICIZE HOW OTHER PEOPLE THINK.
BUT I WISH SHE WOULD TAKE IT EASY ON HER EARNEST-NESS!!
...
...
SNRF
もぞ...
HE THINKS I SHOULD...
...TAKE IT EASY, HUH?
OH!
I HEAR SAKIE-SENSEI IS OPEN TO GETTING MARRIED AND STARTING A FAMILY, THOUGH.
CLAP
OH?
MAYBE THEN SHE COULD WORRY LESS ABOUT HER SEDUCTION POWERS.

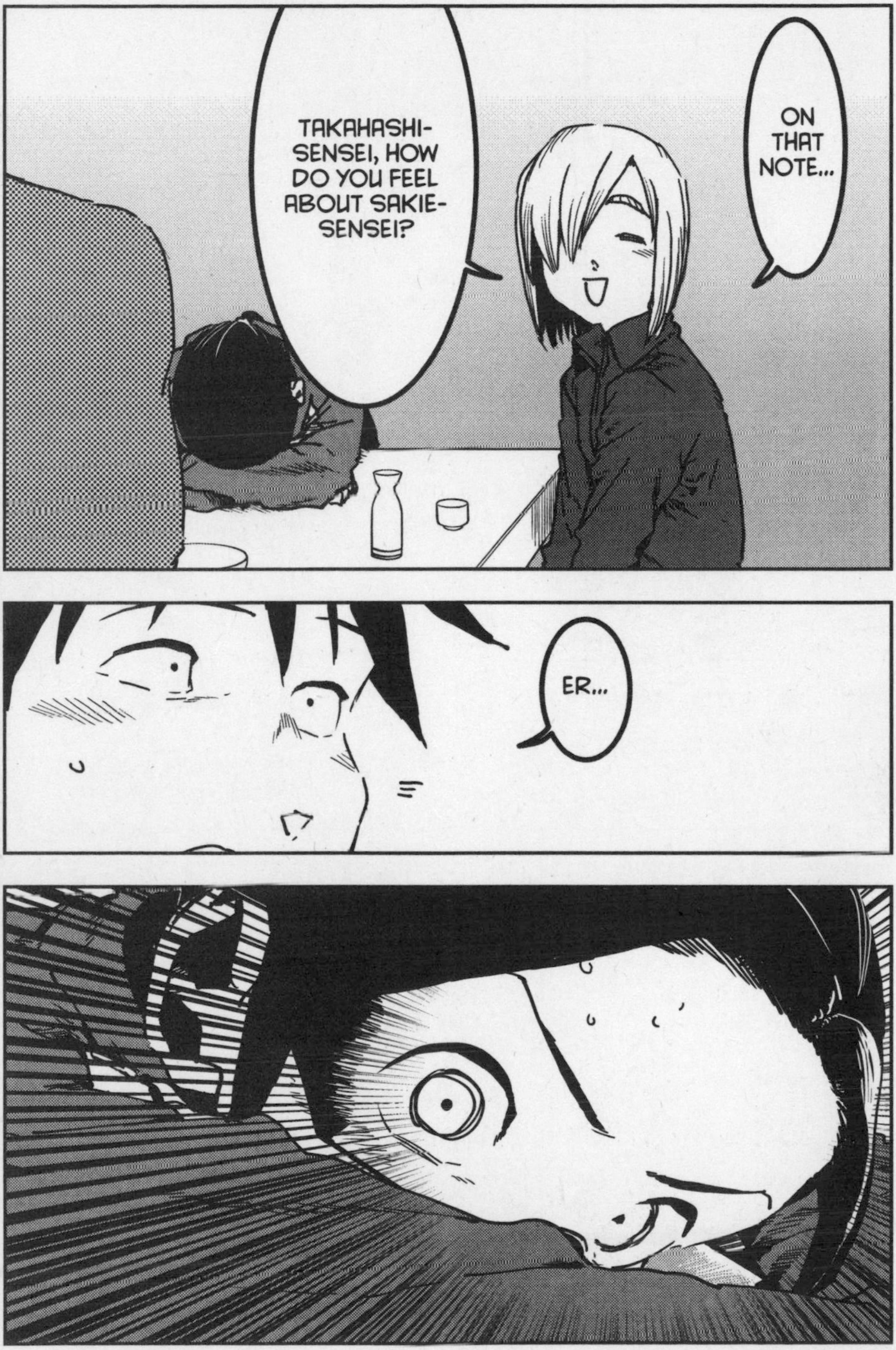
ON THAT NOTE...
TAKAHASHI-SENSEI, HOW DO YOU FEEL ABOUT SAKIE-SENSEI?
ER...

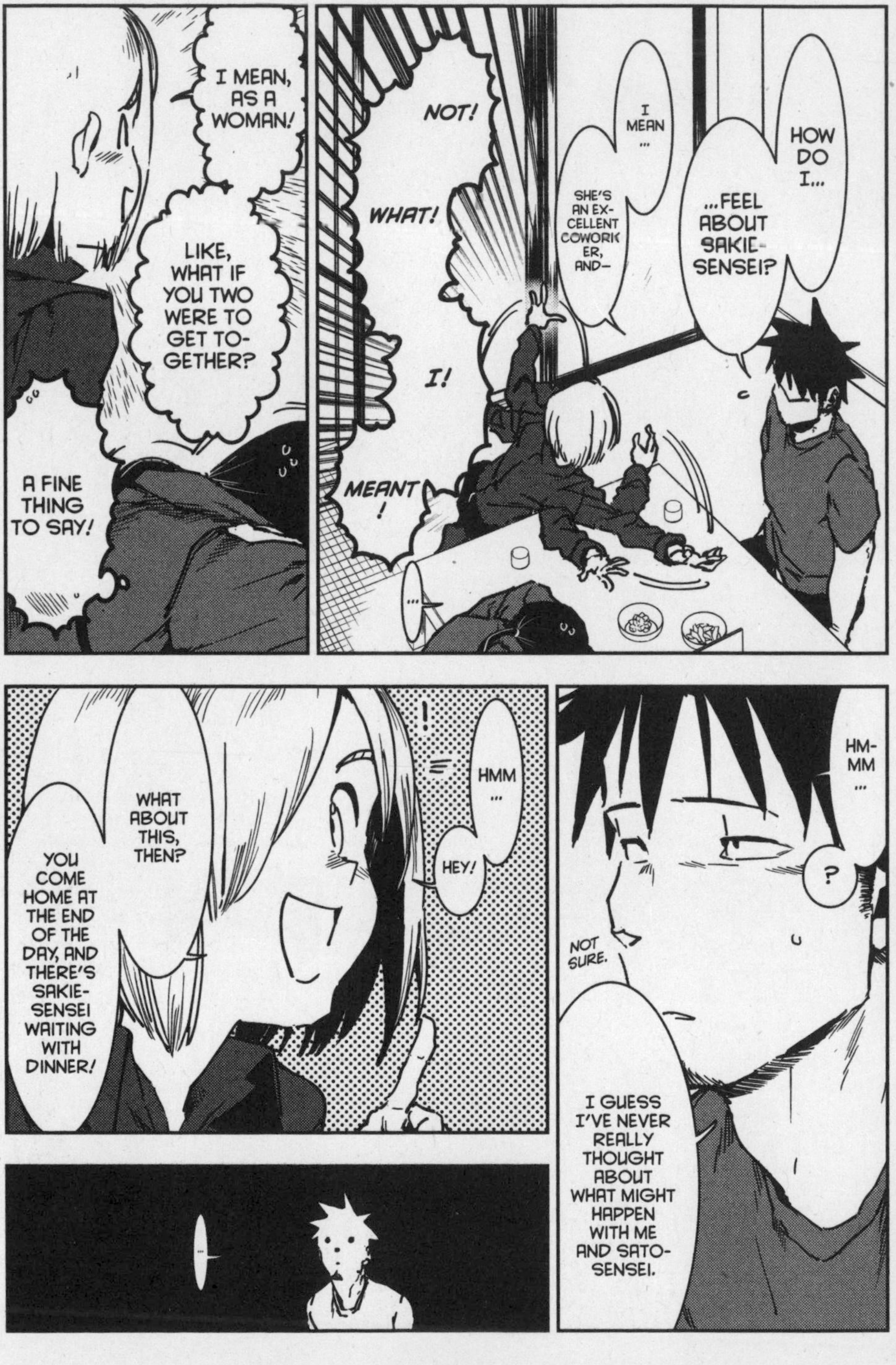
HOW DO I...
...FEEL ABOUT SAKIE-SENSEI?
I MEAN...
SHE'S AN EXCELLENT COWORKER, AND–
NOT!
WHAT!
I!
MEANT!
...
I MEAN, AS A WOMAN!
LIKE, WHAT IF YOU TWO WERE TO GET TOGETHER?
A FINE THING TO SAY!
HM-MM...
?
NOT SURE.
I GUESS I'VE NEVER REALLY THOUGHT ABOUT WHAT MIGHT HAPPEN WITH ME AND SATO-SENSEI.
!
HMM...
HEY!
WHAT ABOUT THIS, THEN?
YOU COME HOME AT THE END OF THE DAY, AND THERE'S SAKIE-SENSEI WAITING WITH DINNER!
...

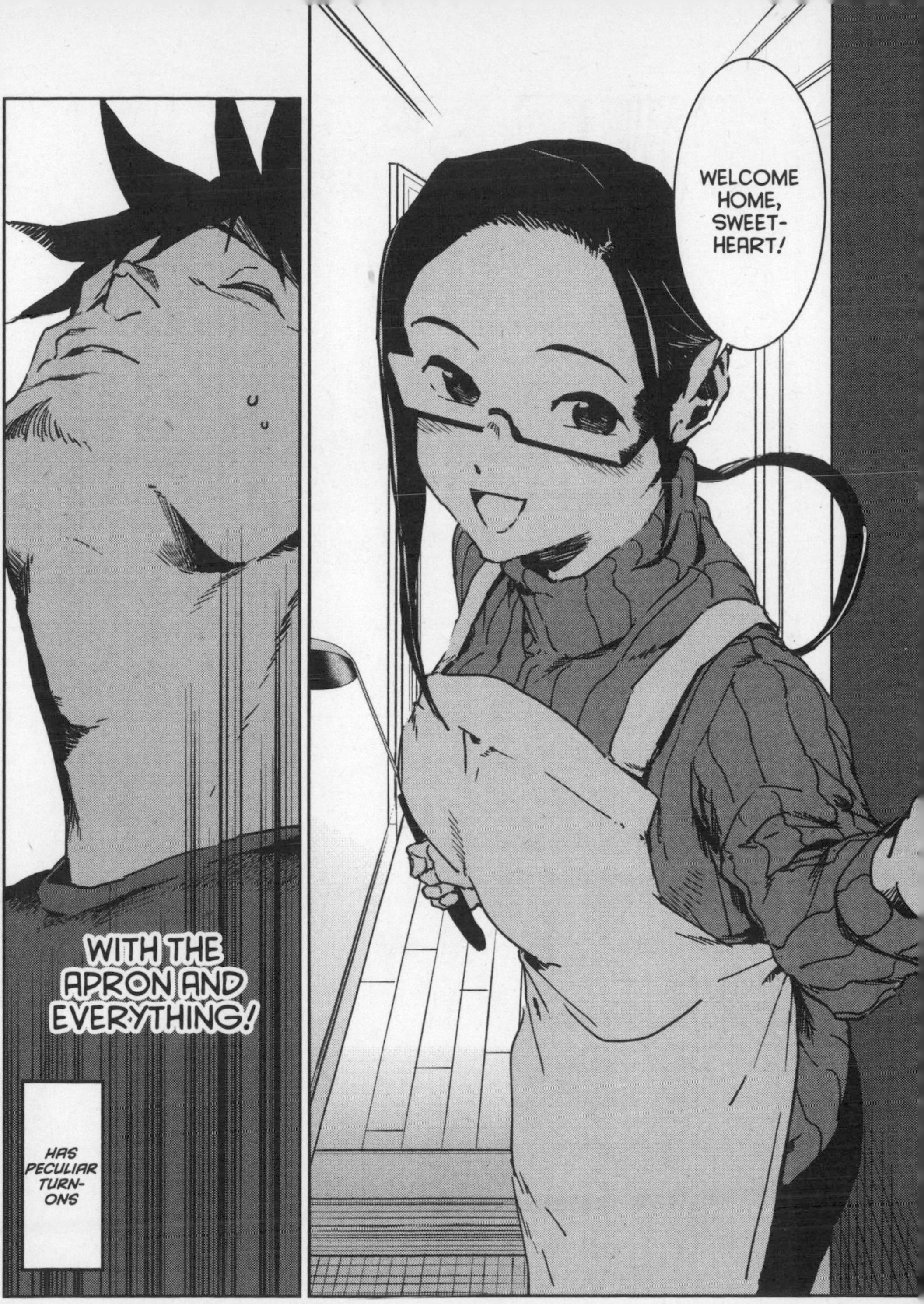
WELCOME HOME, SWEET-HEART!
WITH THE APRON AND EVERYTHING!
HAS PECULIAR TURN-ONS

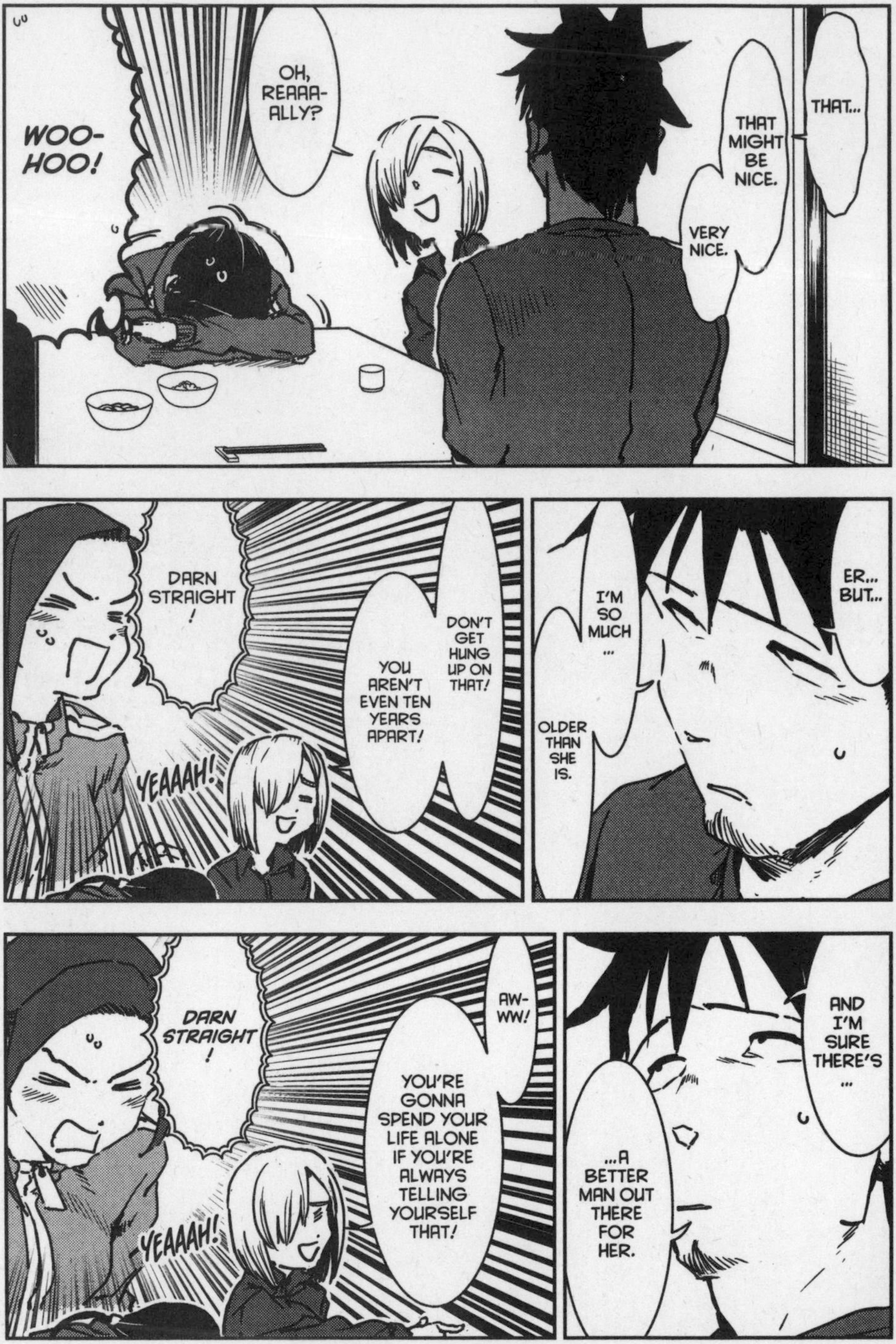
THAT...
THAT MIGHT BE NICE.
VERY NICE.
OH, REAAAA-ALLY?
WOO-HOO!
ER... BUT...
I'M SO MUCH ...
OLDER THAN SHE IS.
DON'T GET HUNG UP ON THAT!
YOU AREN'T EVEN TEN YEARS APART!
DARN STRAIGHT!
YEAAAH!
AND I'M SURE THERE'S ...
...A BETTER MAN OUT THERE FOR HER.
AWW-WW!
YOU'RE GONNA SPEND YOUR LIFE ALONE IF YOU'RE ALWAYS TELLING YOURSELF THAT!
DARN STRAIGHT!
YEAAAH!

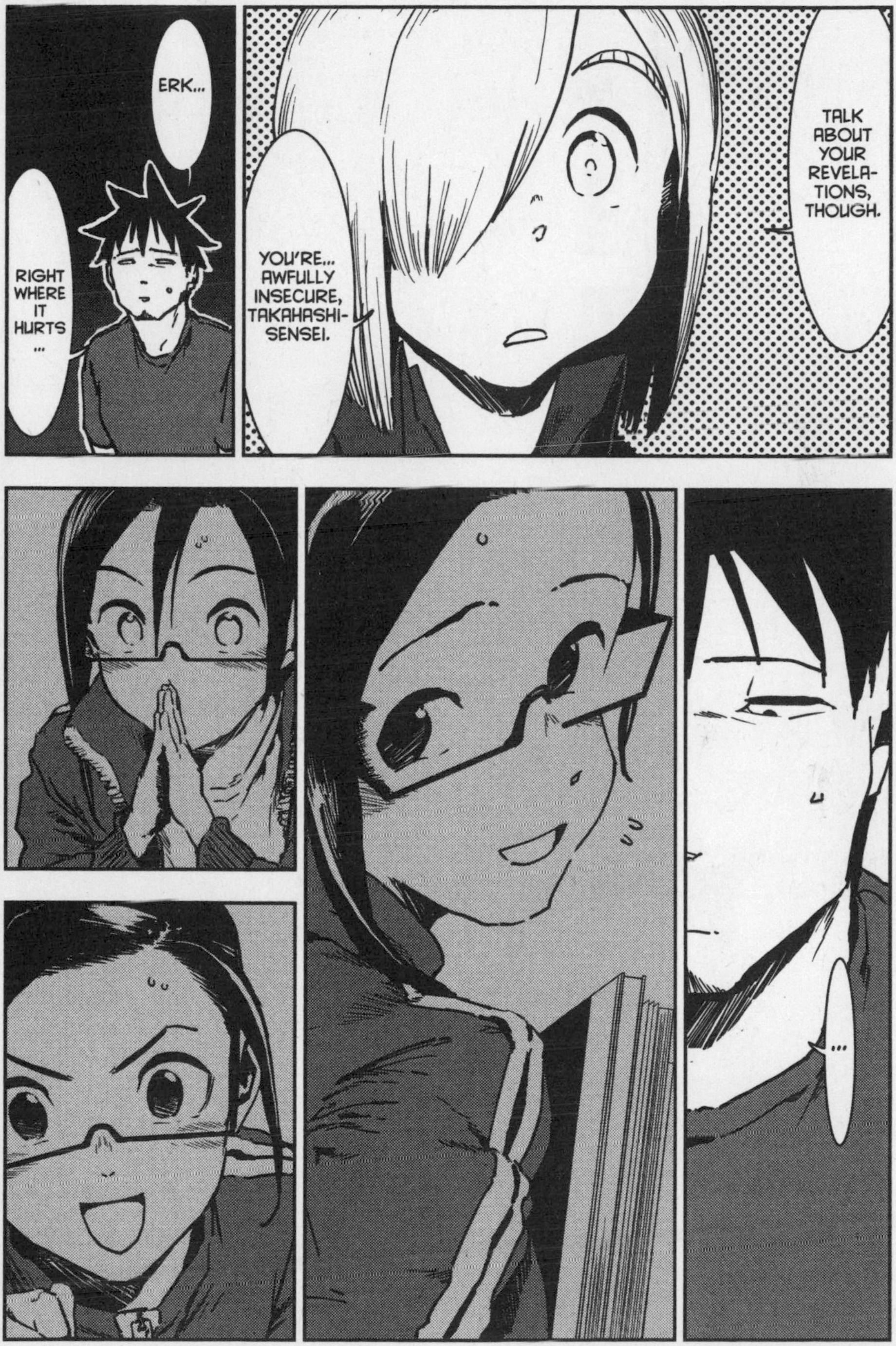

TALK ABOUT YOUR REVELATIONS, THOUGH.
YOU'RE... AWFULLY INSECURE, TAKAHASHI-SENSEI.
ERK...
RIGHT WHERE IT HURTS...
...

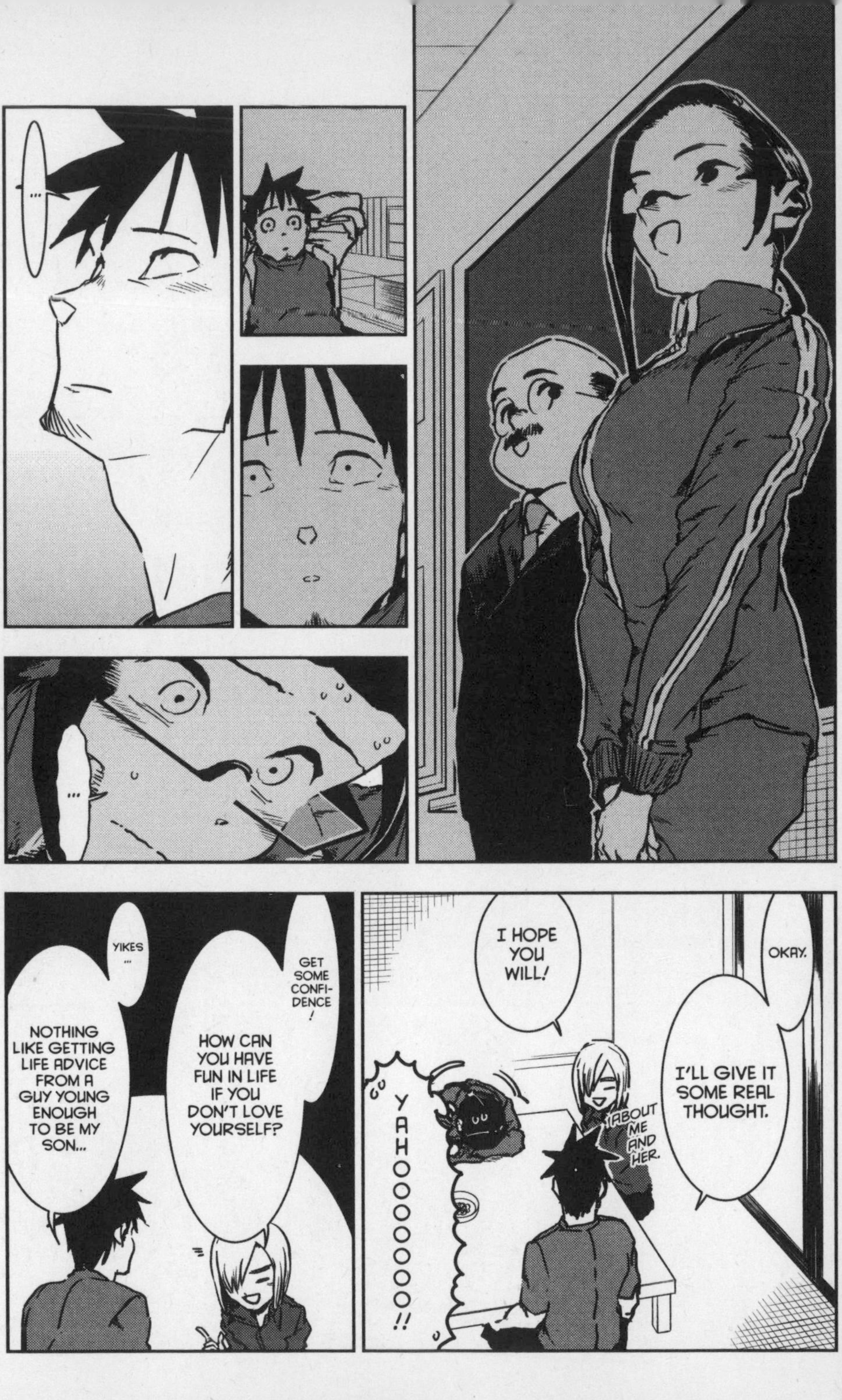
...
...
OKAY.
I'LL GIVE IT SOME REAL THOUGHT.
ABOUT ME AND HER.
I HOPE YOU WILL!
YAHOOOOOOOOO!!
GET SOME CONFI-DENCE!
HOW CAN YOU HAVE FUN IN LIFE IF YOU DON'T LOVE YOURSELF?
YIKES...
NOTHING LIKE GETTING LIFE ADVICE FROM A GUY YOUNG ENOUGH TO BE MY SON...

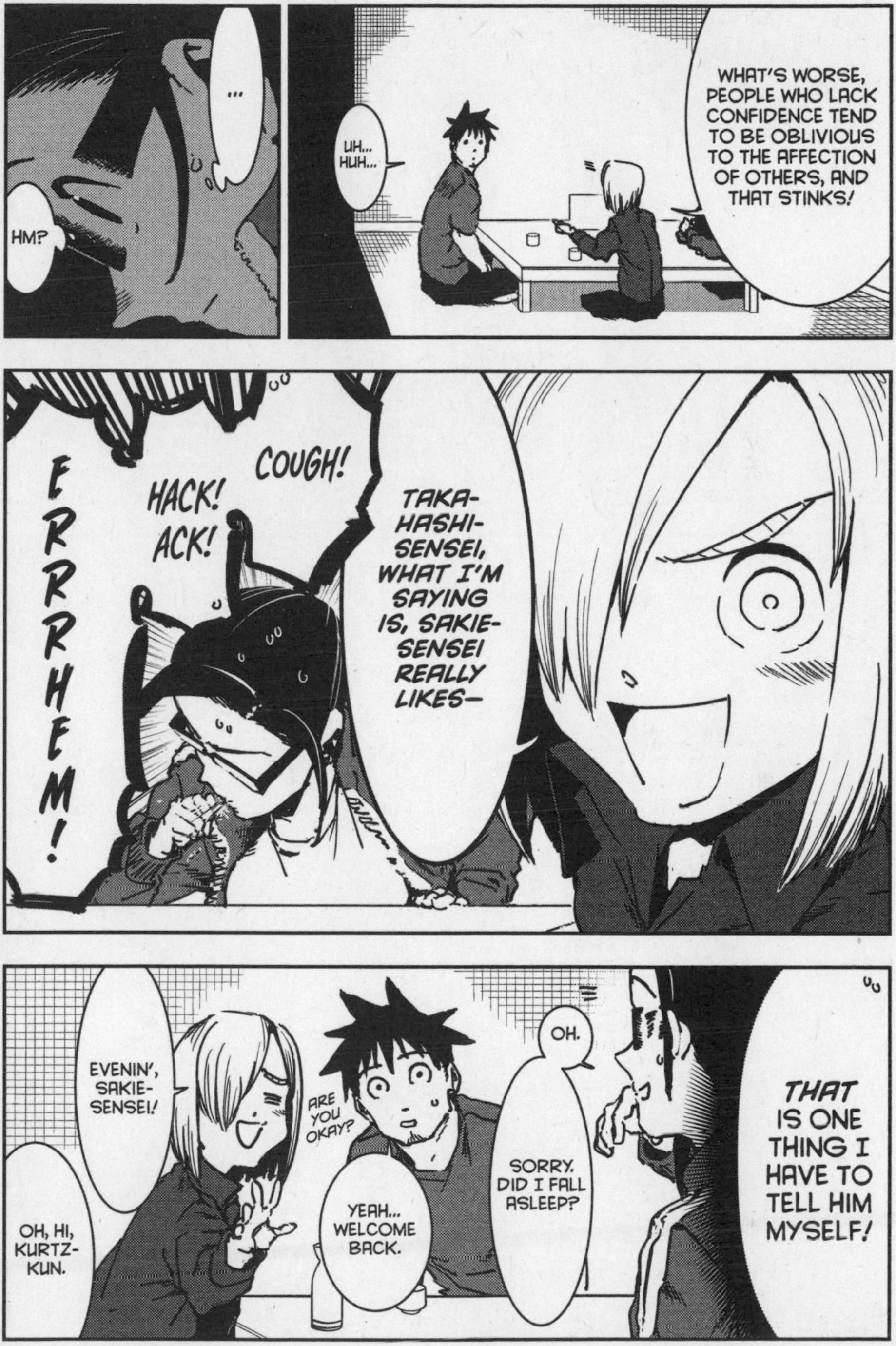
WHAT'S WORSE, PEOPLE WHO LACK CONFIDENCE TEND TO BE OBLIVIOUS TO THE AFFECTION OF OTHERS, AND THAT STINKS!
UH... HUH...
...
HM?
TAKA-HASHI-SENSEI, WHAT I'M SAYING IS, SAKIE-SENSEI REALLY LIKES—
COUGH!
HACK! ACK!
ERRRRHEM!
THAT IS ONE THING I HAVE TO TELL HIM MYSELF!
OH.
SORRY. DID I FALL ASLEEP?
ARE YOU OKAY?
YEAH... WELCOME BACK.
EVENIN', SAKIE-SENSEI!
OH, HI, KURTZ-KUN.

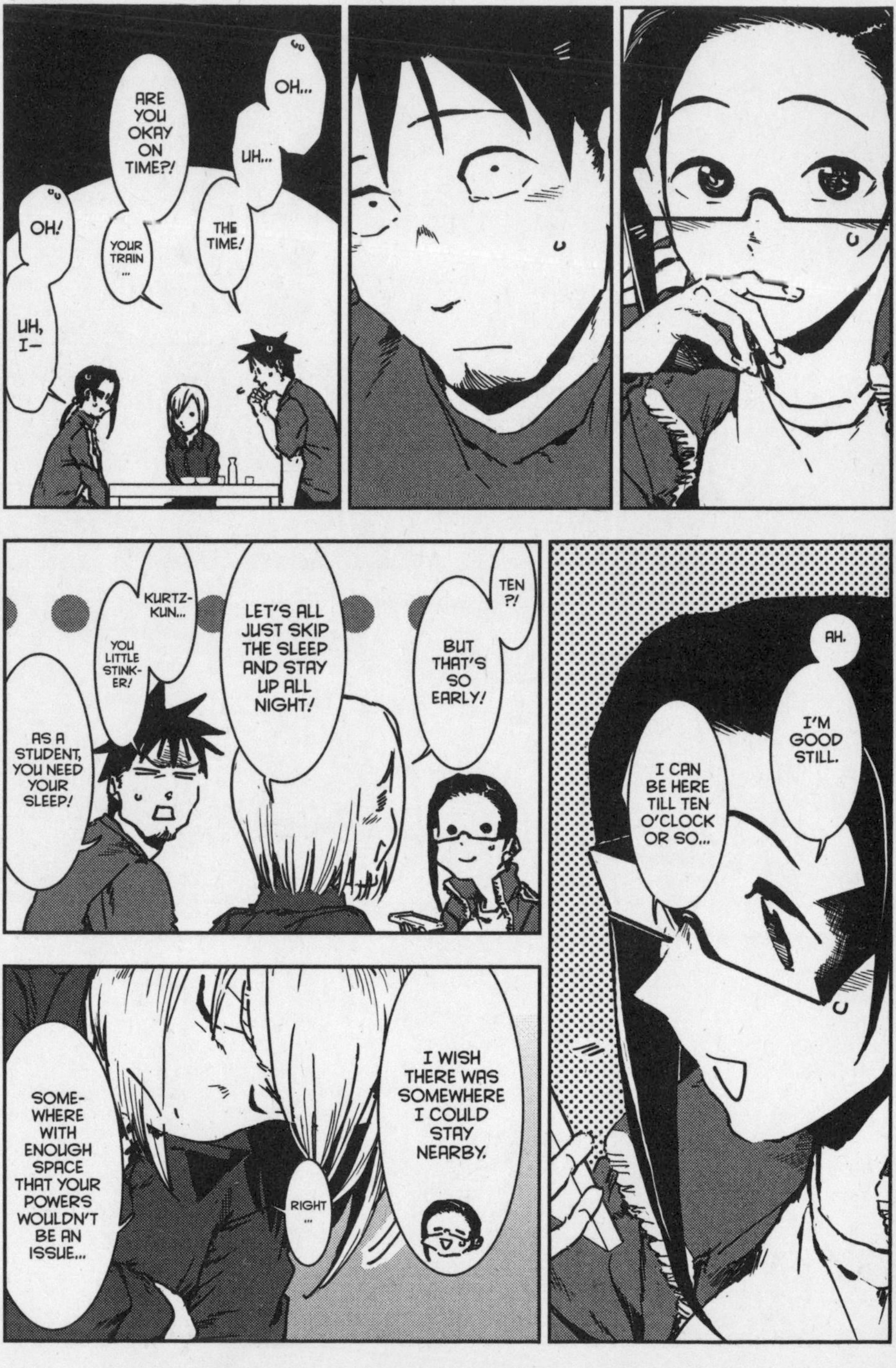
OH...
ARE YOU OKAY ON TIME?!
UH...
THE TIME!
YOUR TRAIN ...
OH!
UH, I—
AH.
I'M GOOD STILL.
I CAN BE HERE TILL TEN O'CLOCK OR SO...
TEN ?!
BUT THAT'S SO EARLY!
LET'S ALL JUST SKIP THE SLEEP AND STAY UP ALL NIGHT!
KURTZ-KUN...
YOU LITTLE STINK-ER!
AS A STUDENT, YOU NEED YOUR SLEEP!
I WISH THERE WAS SOMEWHERE I COULD STAY NEARBY.
RIGHT ...
SOME-WHERE WITH ENOUGH SPACE THAT YOUR POWERS WOULDN'T BE AN ISSUE...

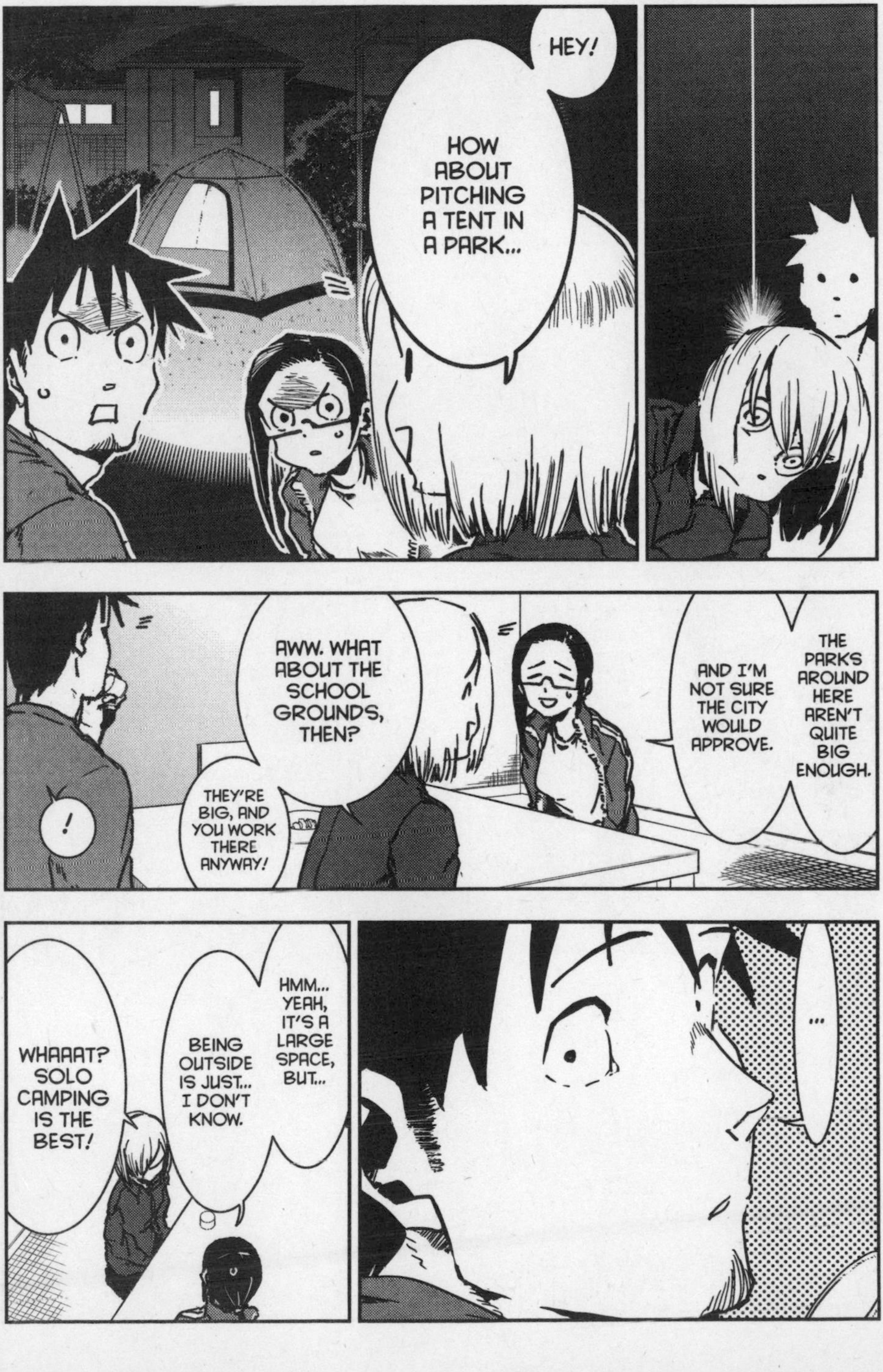
HEY!
HOW ABOUT PITCHING A TENT IN A PARK...
THE PARKS AROUND HERE AREN'T QUITE BIG ENOUGH.
AND I'M NOT SURE THE CITY WOULD APPROVE.
AWW. WHAT ABOUT THE SCHOOL GROUNDS, THEN?
THEY'RE BIG, AND YOU WORK THERE ANYWAY!
!
...
HMM... YEAH, IT'S A LARGE SPACE, BUT...
BEING OUTSIDE IS JUST... I DON'T KNOW.
WHAAAT? SOLO CAMPING IS THE BEST!

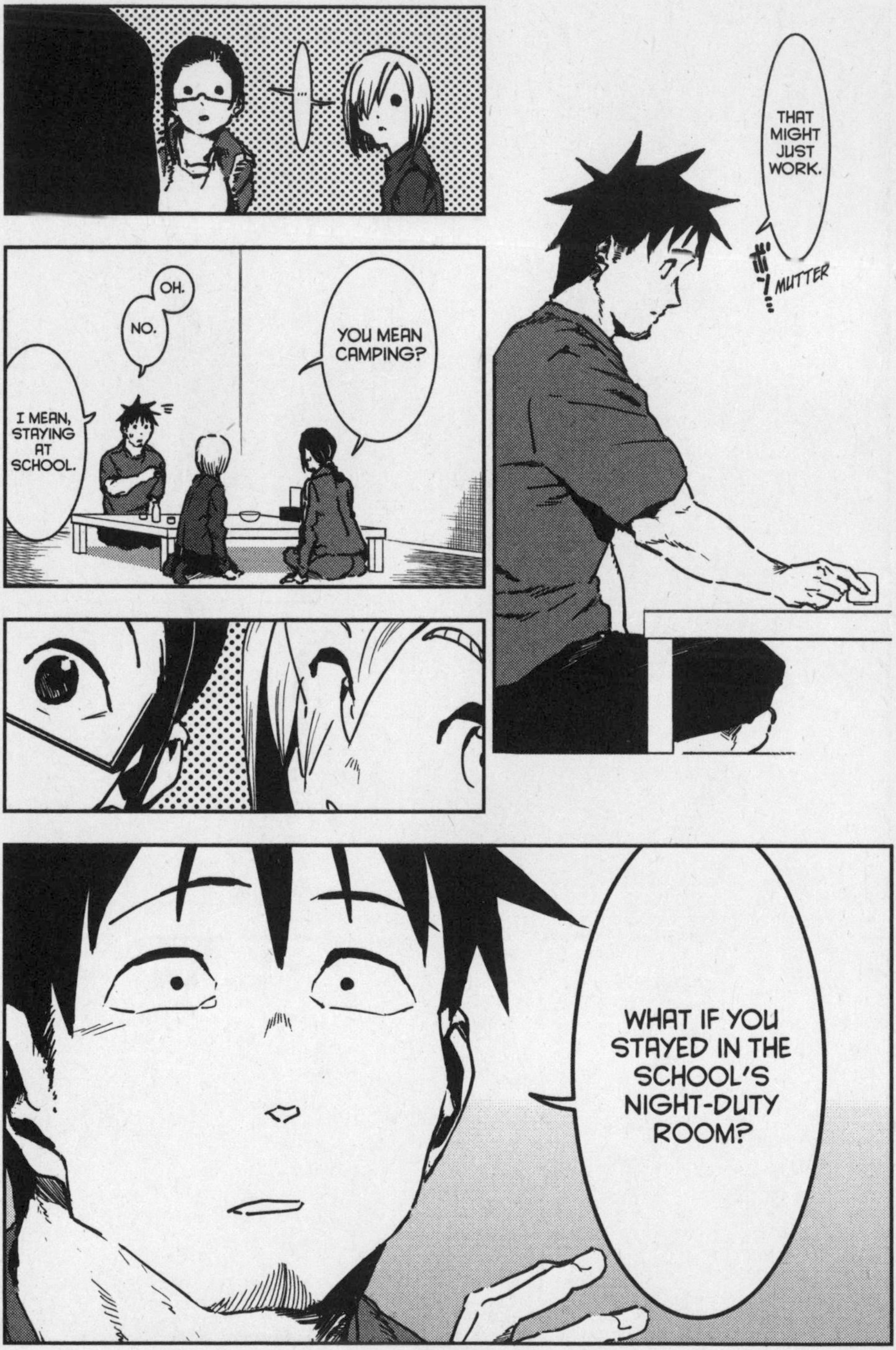
THAT MIGHT JUST WORK.
MUTTER
...
YOU MEAN CAMPING?
OH.
NO.
I MEAN, STAYING AT SCHOOL.
WHAT IF YOU STAYED IN THE SCHOOL'S NIGHT-DUTY ROOM?

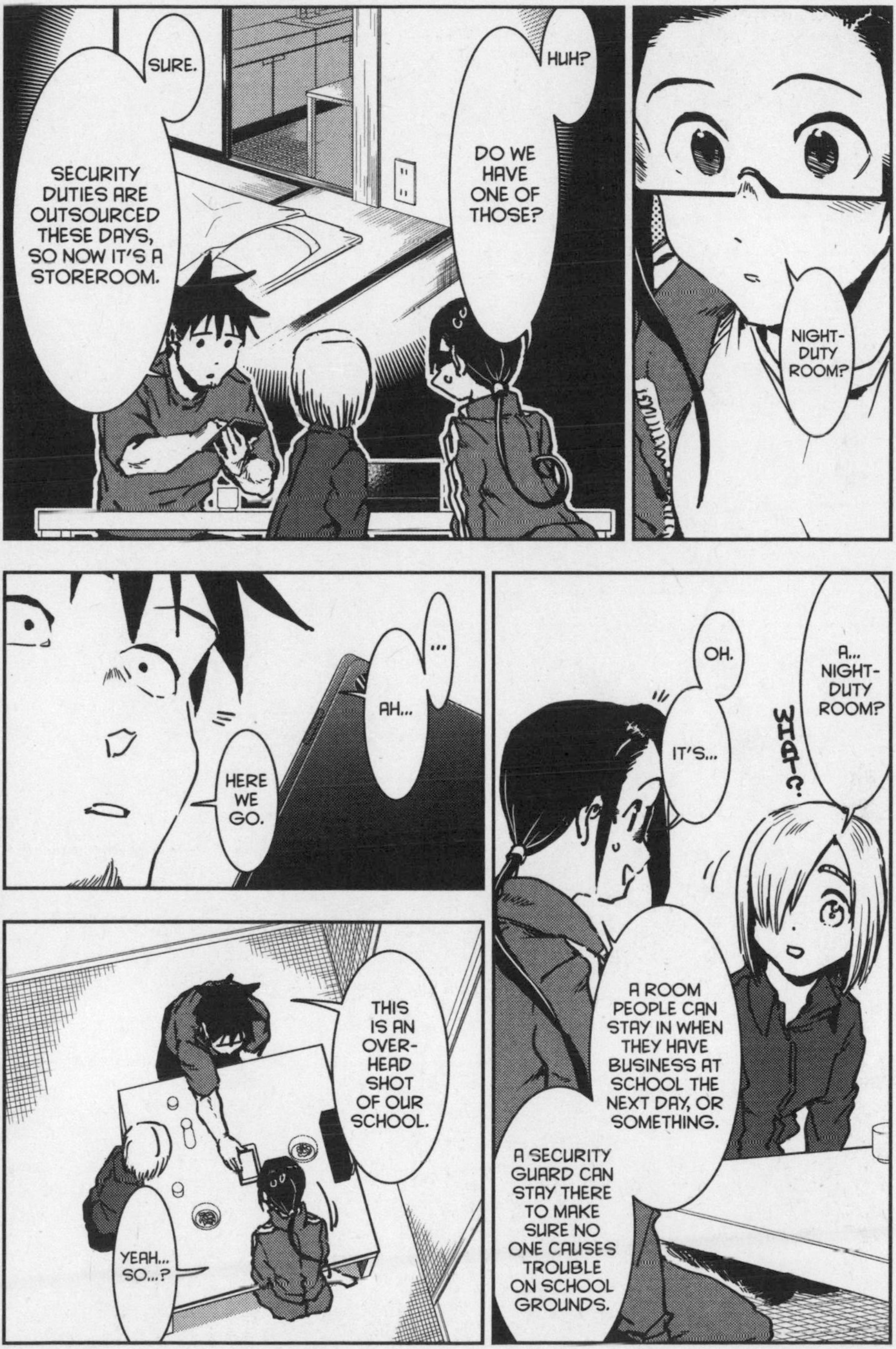
NIGHT-DUTY ROOM?
HUH?
DO WE HAVE ONE OF THOSE?
SURE.
SECURITY DUTIES ARE OUTSOURCED THESE DAYS, SO NOW IT'S A STOREROOM.
A... NIGHT-DUTY ROOM?
WHAT?
OH.
IT'S...
A ROOM PEOPLE CAN STAY IN WHEN THEY HAVE BUSINESS AT SCHOOL THE NEXT DAY, OR SOMETHING.
A SECURITY GUARD CAN STAY THERE TO MAKE SURE NO ONE CAUSES TROUBLE ON SCHOOL GROUNDS.
...
AH...
HERE WE GO.
THIS IS AN OVERHEAD SHOT OF OUR SCHOOL.
YEAH... SO...?

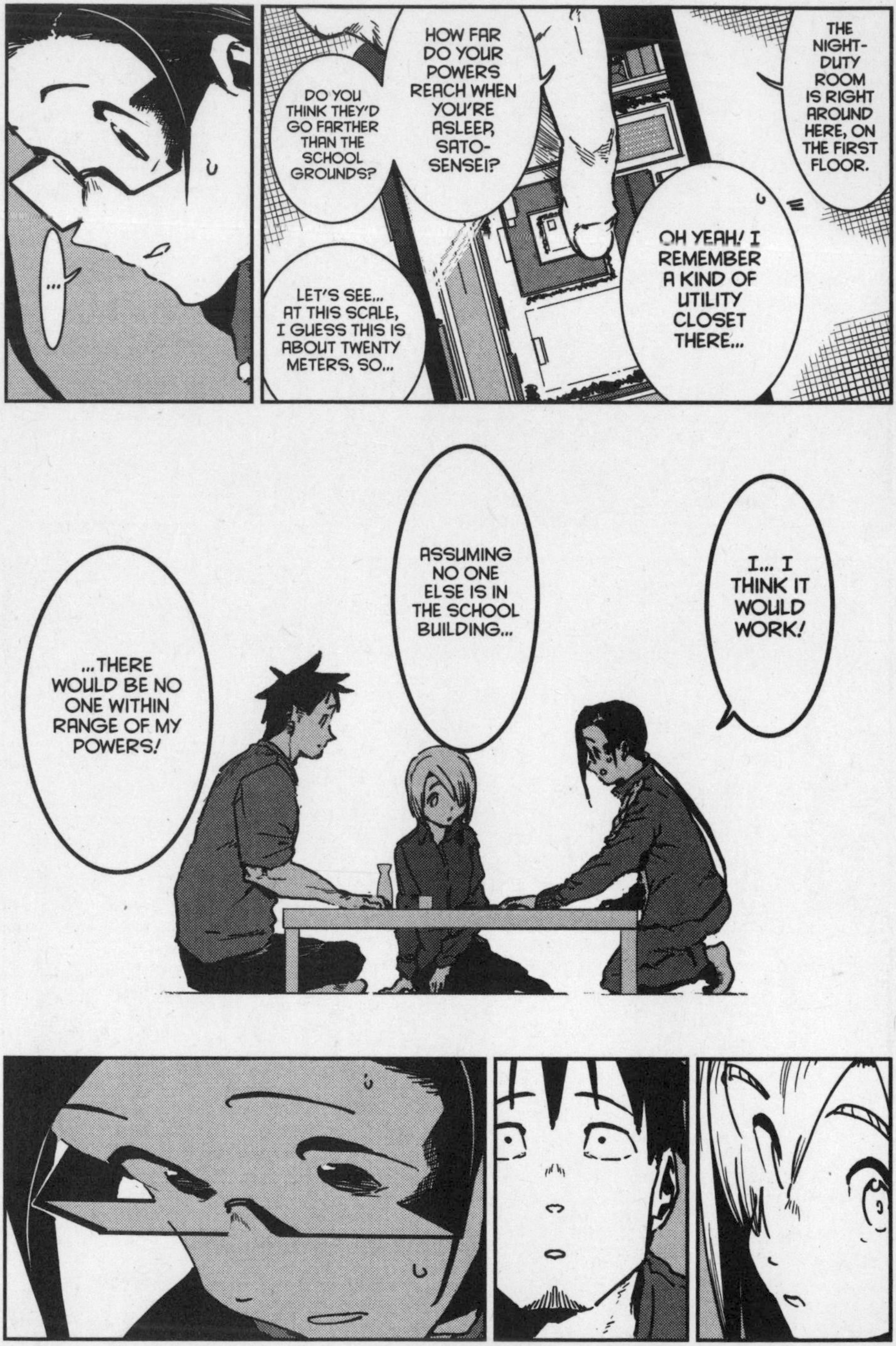
THE NIGHT-DUTY ROOM IS RIGHT AROUND HERE, ON THE FIRST FLOOR.
OH YEAH! I REMEMBER A KIND OF UTILITY CLOSET THERE...
HOW FAR DO YOUR POWERS REACH WHEN YOU'RE ASLEEP, SATO-SENSEI?
DO YOU THINK THEY'D GO FARTHER THAN THE SCHOOL GROUNDS?
LET'S SEE... AT THIS SCALE, I GUESS THIS IS ABOUT TWENTY METERS, SO...
...
I... I THINK IT WOULD WORK!
ASSUMING NO ONE ELSE IS IN THE SCHOOL BUILDING...
...THERE WOULD BE NO ONE WITHIN RANGE OF MY POWERS!

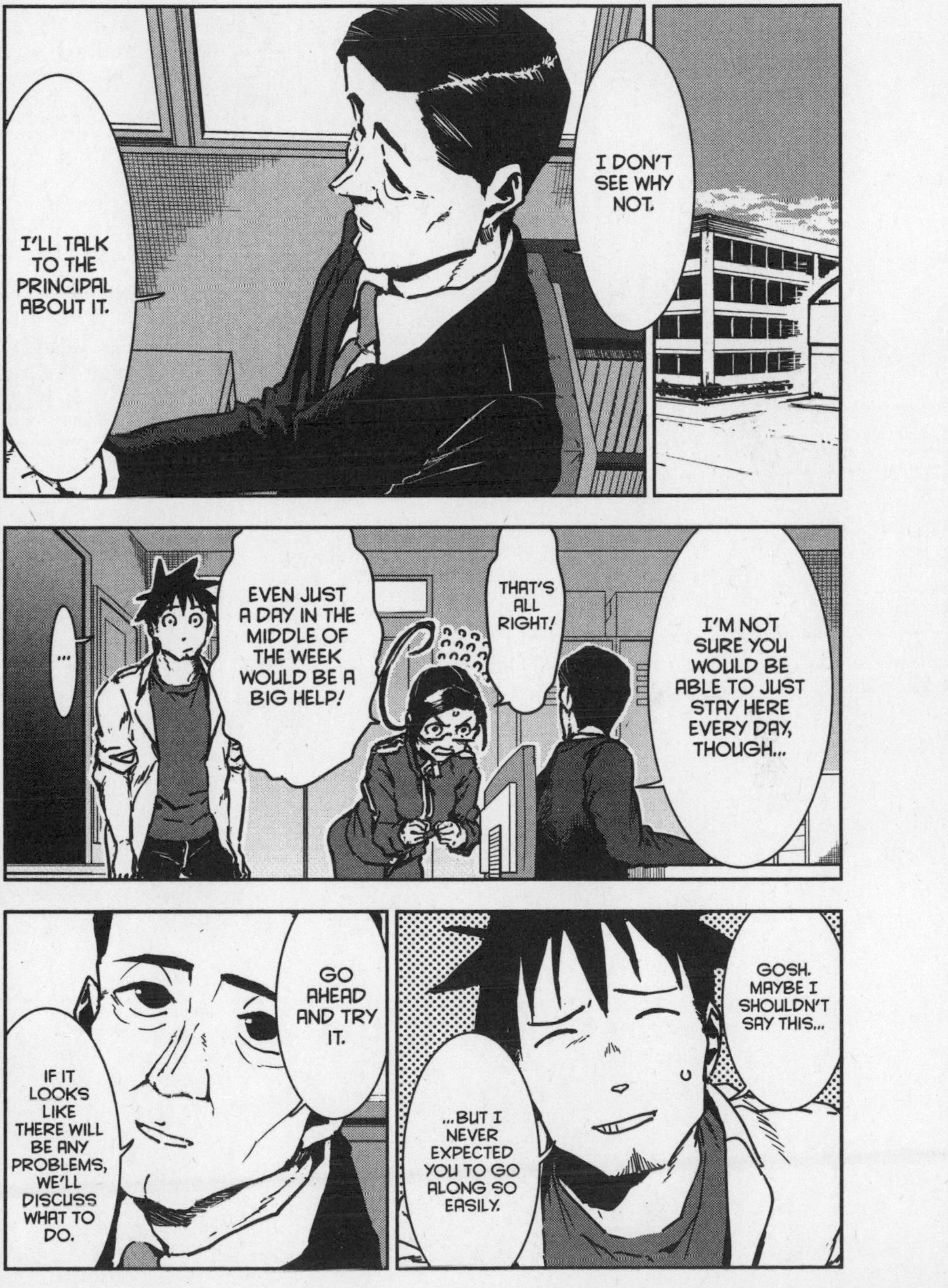
I DON'T SEE WHY NOT.
I'LL TALK TO THE PRINCIPAL ABOUT IT.
I'M NOT SURE YOU WOULD BE ABLE TO JUST STAY HERE EVERY DAY, THOUGH...
THAT'S ALL RIGHT!
EVEN JUST A DAY IN THE MIDDLE OF THE WEEK WOULD BE A BIG HELP!
...
GOSH. MAYBE I SHOULDN'T SAY THIS...
...BUT I NEVER EXPECTED YOU TO GO ALONG SO EASILY.
GO AHEAD AND TRY IT.
IF IT LOOKS LIKE THERE WILL BE ANY PROBLEMS, WE'LL DISCUSS WHAT TO DO.

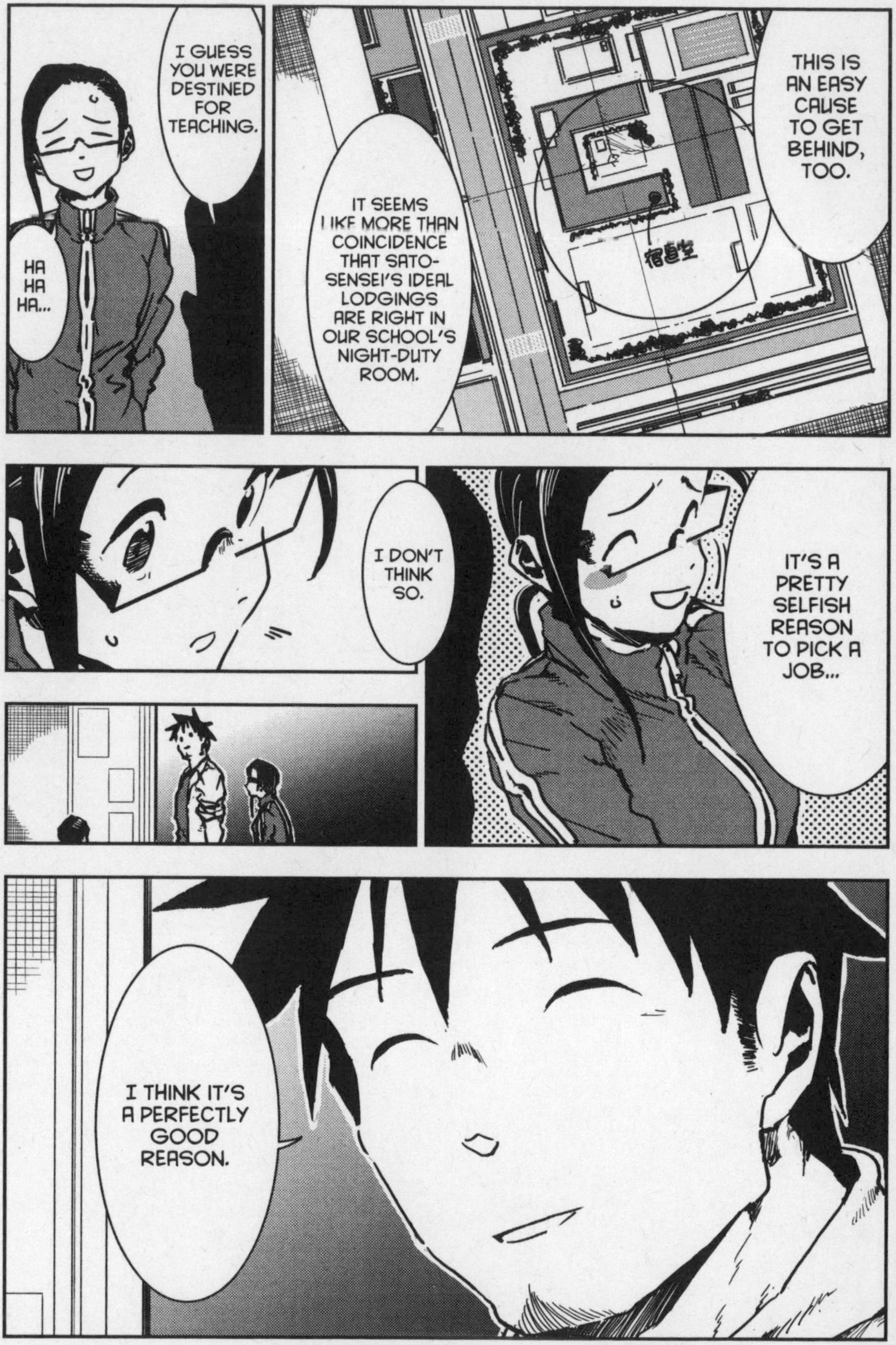
THIS IS AN EASY CAUSE TO GET BEHIND, TOO.
IT SEEMS LIKE MORE THAN COINCIDENCE THAT SATO-SENSEI'S IDEAL LODGINGS ARE RIGHT IN OUR SCHOOL'S NIGHT-DUTY ROOM.
宿直室
I GUESS YOU WERE DESTINED FOR TEACHING.
HA HA HA...
IT'S A PRETTY SELFISH REASON TO PICK A JOB...
I DON'T THINK SO.
I THINK IT'S A PERFECTLY GOOD REASON.

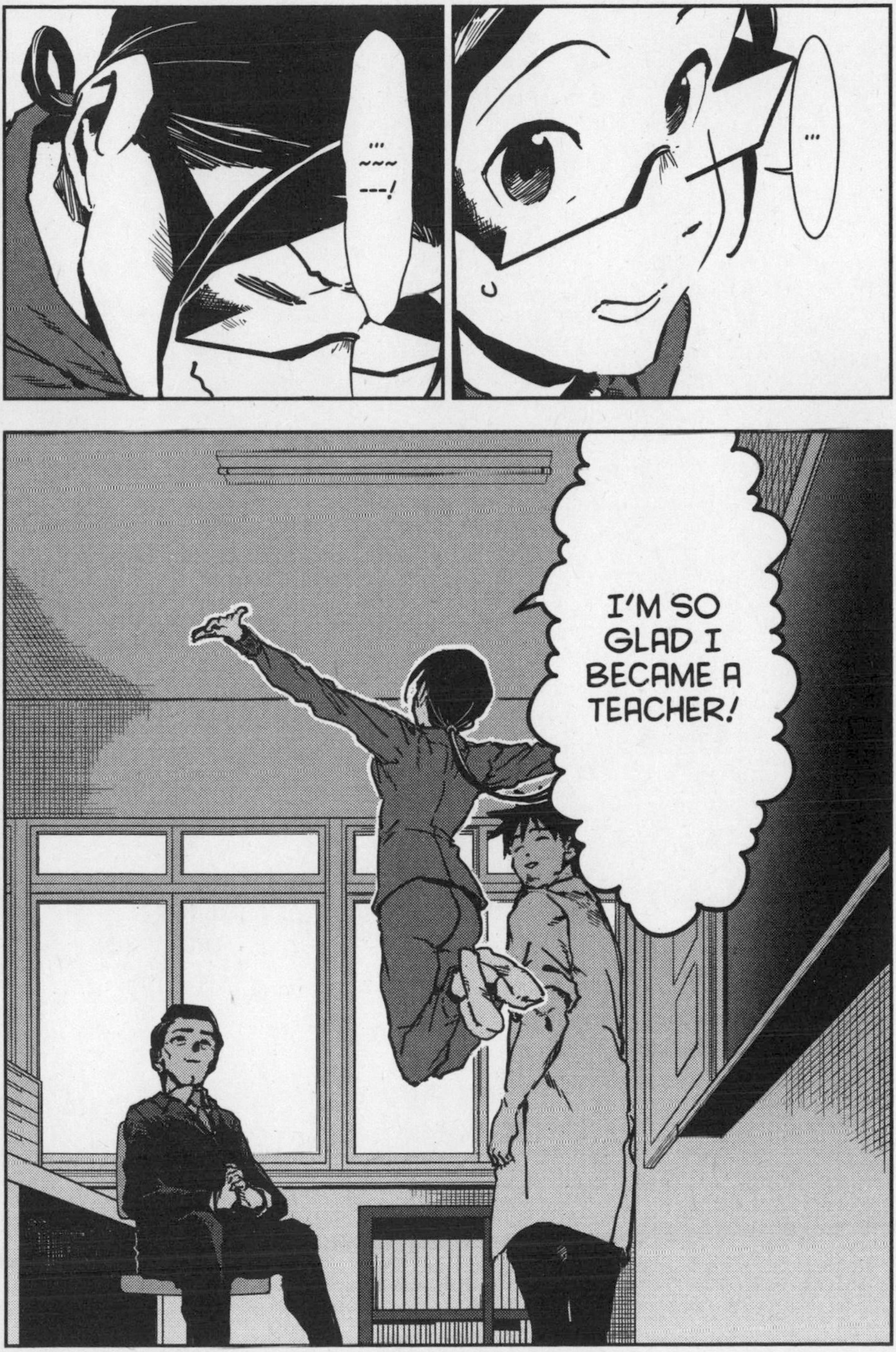
...
...
~~~
---!
I'M SO GLAD I BECAME A TEACHER!
~~~

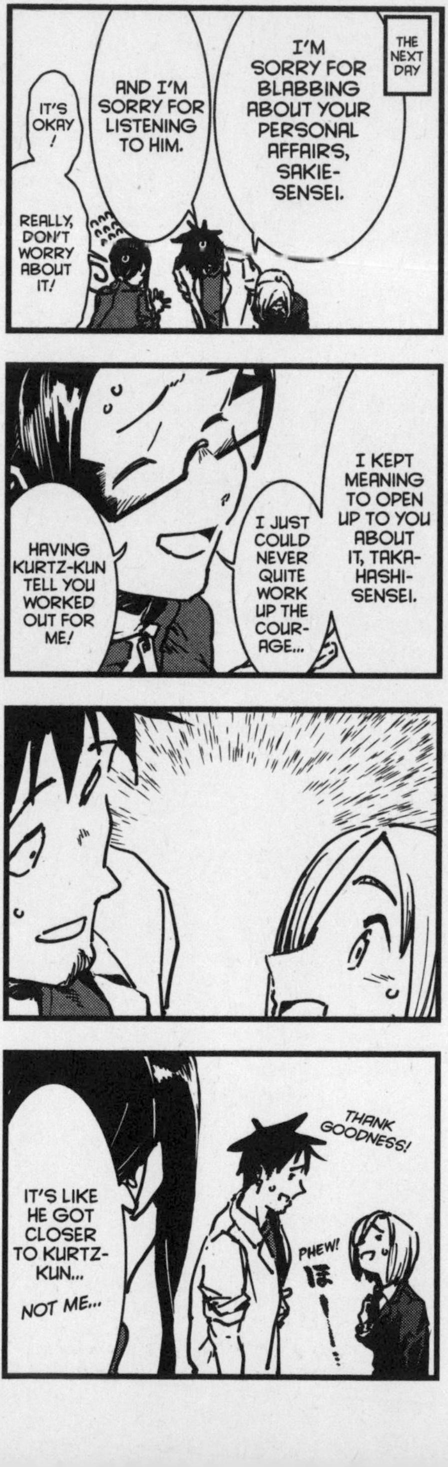
THE NEXT DAY
I'M SORRY FOR BLABBING ABOUT YOUR PERSONAL AFFAIRS, SAKIE-SENSEI.
AND I'M SORRY FOR LISTENING TO HIM.
IT'S OKAY!
REALLY, DON'T WORRY ABOUT IT!
I KEPT MEANING TO OPEN UP TO YOU ABOUT IT, TAKA-HASHI-SENSEI.
I JUST COULD NEVER QUITE WORK UP THE COUR-AGE...
HAVING KURTZ-KUN TELL YOU WORKED OUT FOR ME!
THANK GOODNESS!
PHEW!
IT'S LIKE HE GOT CLOSER TO KURTZ-KUN...
NOT ME...

INTERVIEWS WITH MONSTER GIRLS

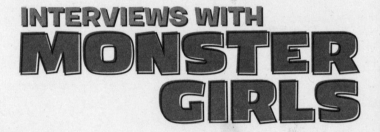

Chapter 43: The Succubus in the Night-Duty Room

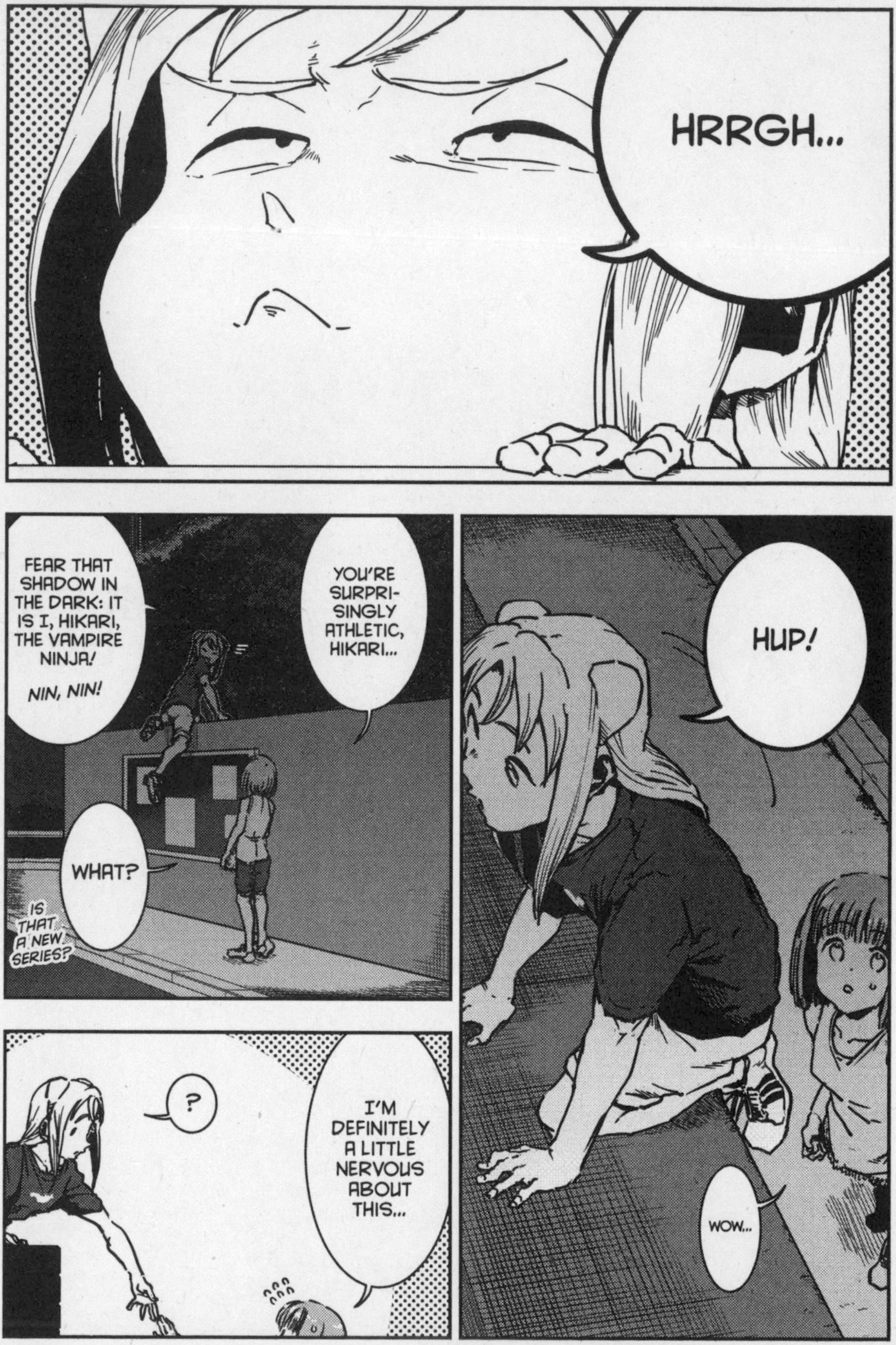
HRRGH...
HUP!
WOW...
YOU'RE SURPRISINGLY ATHLETIC, HIKARI...
FEAR THAT SHADOW IN THE DARK: IT IS I, HIKARI, THE VAMPIRE NINJA!
NIN, NIN!
WHAT?
IS THAT A NEW SERIES?
I'M DEFINITELY A LITTLE NERVOUS ABOUT THIS...
?

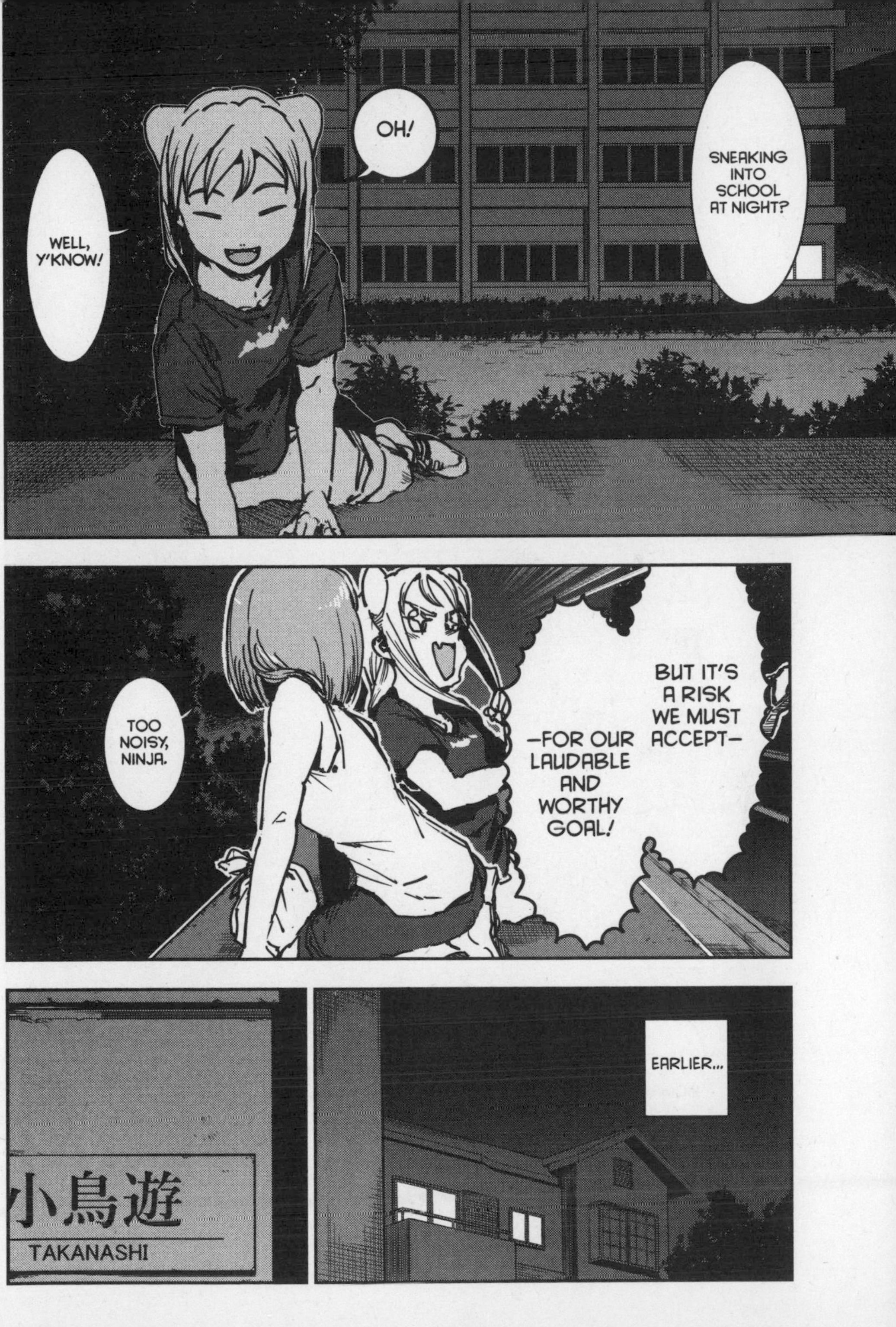
SNEAKING INTO SCHOOL AT NIGHT?
OH!
WELL, Y'KNOW!
BUT IT'S A RISK WE MUST ACCEPT—
—FOR OUR LAUDABLE AND WORTHY GOAL!
TOO NOISY, NINJA.
EARLIER...
小鳥遊
TAKANASHI

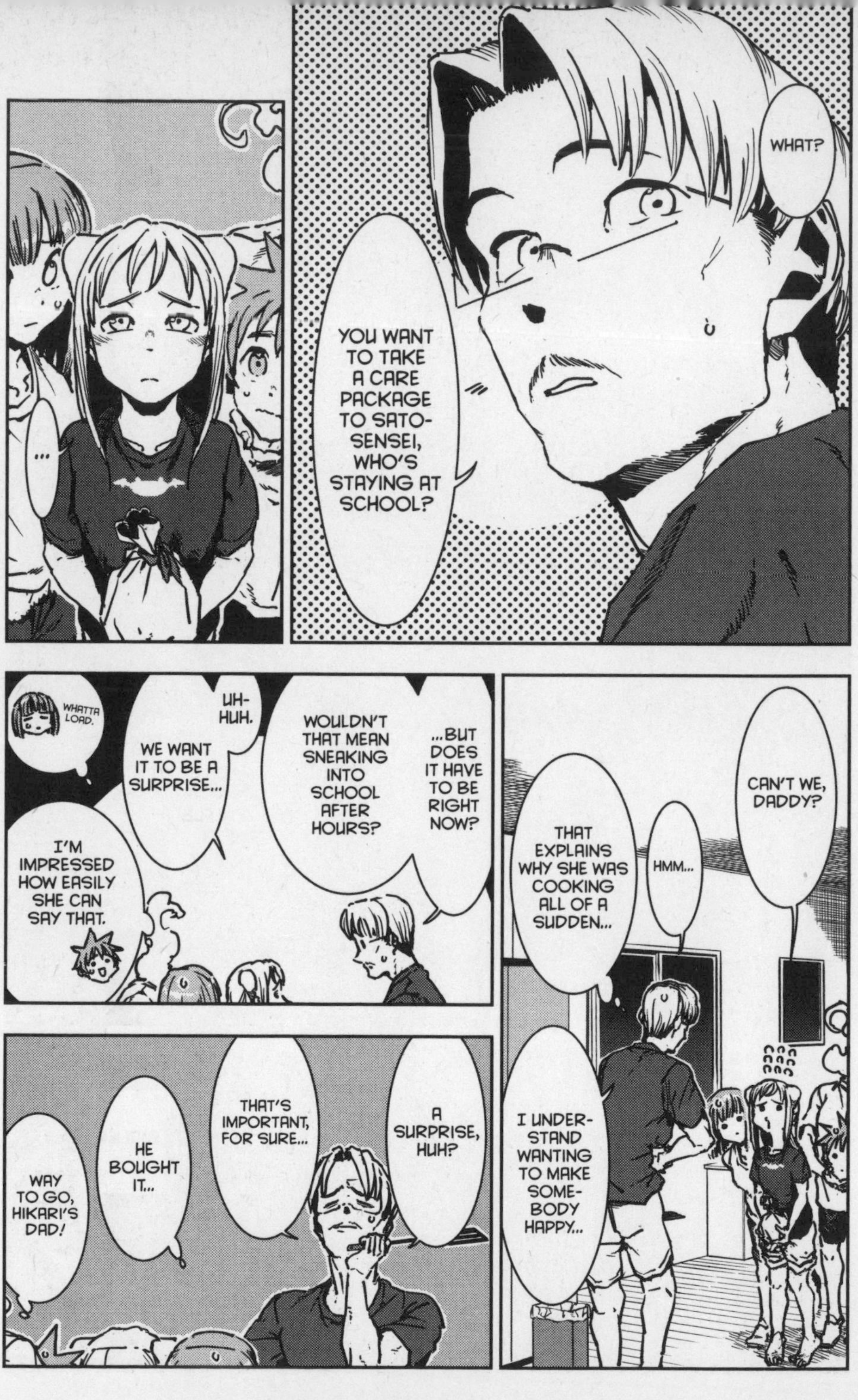
WHAT?
YOU WANT TO TAKE A CARE PACKAGE TO SATO-SENSEI, WHO'S STAYING AT SCHOOL?
...
CAN'T WE, DADDY?
HMM...
THAT EXPLAINS WHY SHE WAS COOKING ALL OF A SUDDEN...
I UNDER-STAND WANTING TO MAKE SOME-BODY HAPPY...
...BUT DOES IT HAVE TO BE RIGHT NOW?
WOULDN'T THAT MEAN SNEAKING INTO SCHOOL AFTER HOURS?
UH-HUH.
WE WANT IT TO BE A SURPRISE...
WHATTA LOAD.
I'M IMPRESSED HOW EASILY SHE CAN SAY THAT.
A SURPRISE, HUH?
THAT'S IMPORTANT, FOR SURE...
HE BOUGHT IT...
WAY TO GO, HIKARI'S DAD!

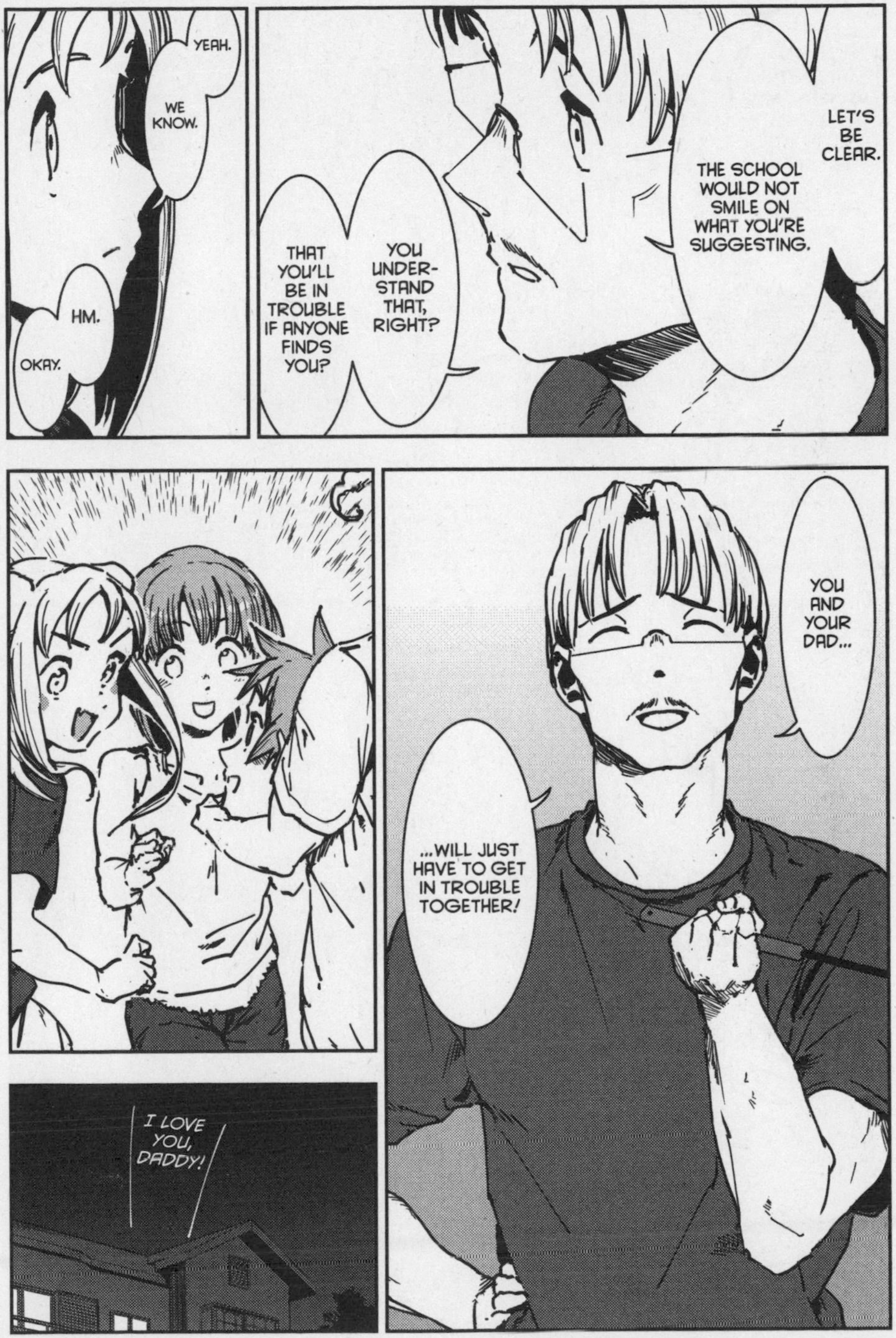
LET'S BE CLEAR.
THE SCHOOL WOULD NOT SMILE ON WHAT YOU'RE SUGGESTING.
YOU UNDERSTAND THAT, RIGHT?
THAT YOU'LL BE IN TROUBLE IF ANYONE FINDS YOU?
YEAH.
WE KNOW.
HM.
OKAY.
YOU AND YOUR DAD...
...WILL JUST HAVE TO GET IN TROUBLE TOGETHER!
I LOVE YOU, DADDY!

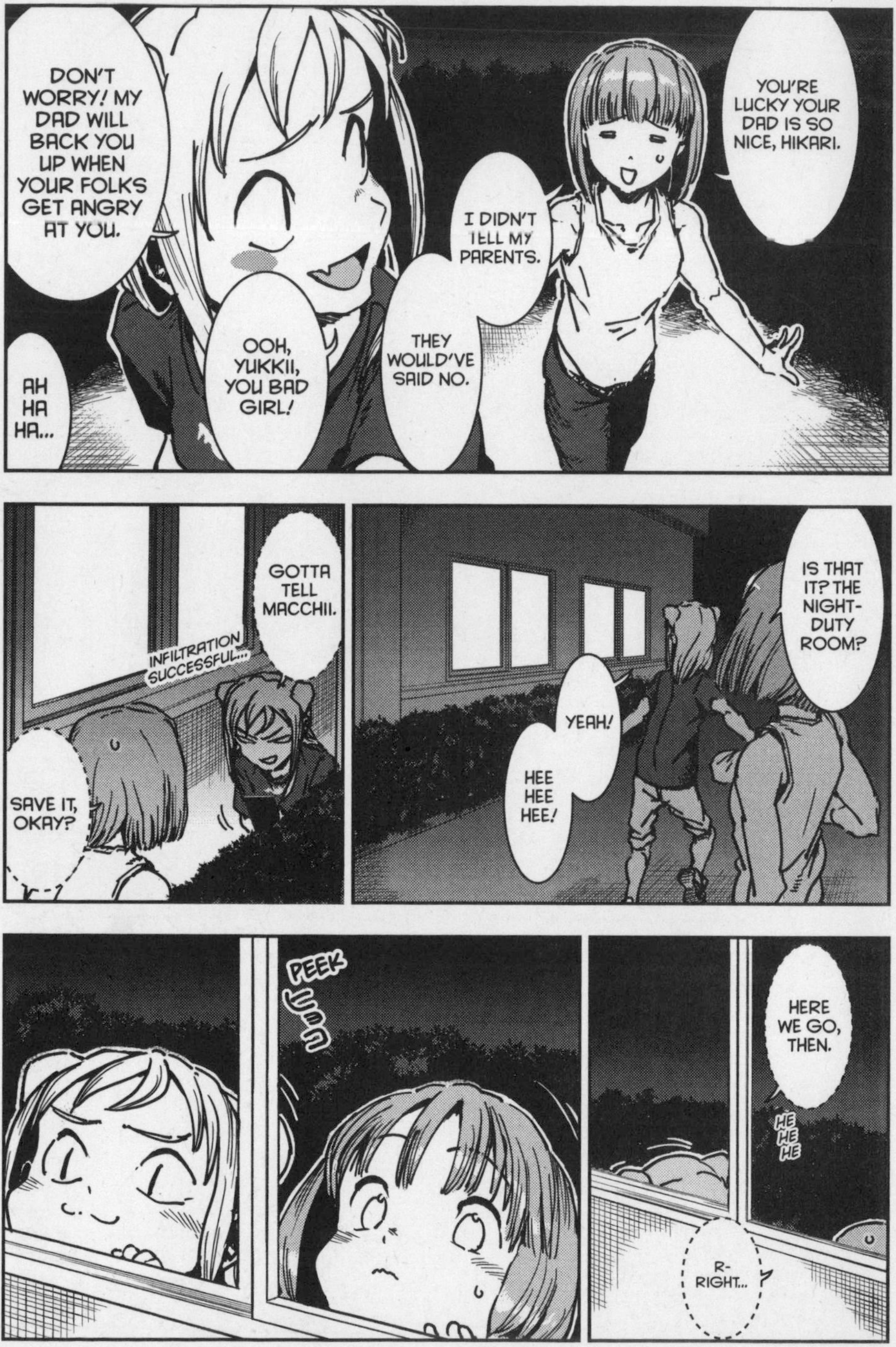

YOU'RE LUCKY YOUR DAD IS SO NICE, HIKARI.
I DIDN'T TELL MY PARENTS.
THEY WOULD'VE SAID NO.
DON'T WORRY! MY DAD WILL BACK YOU UP WHEN YOUR FOLKS GET ANGRY AT YOU.
OOH, YUKKII, YOU BAD GIRL!
AH HA HA...
IS THAT IT? THE NIGHT-DUTY ROOM?
YEAH!
HEE HEE HEE!
GOTTA TELL MACCHII.
INFILTRATION SUCCESSFUL...
SAVE IT, OKAY?
HERE WE GO, THEN.
HE HE HE
R-RIGHT...
PEEK

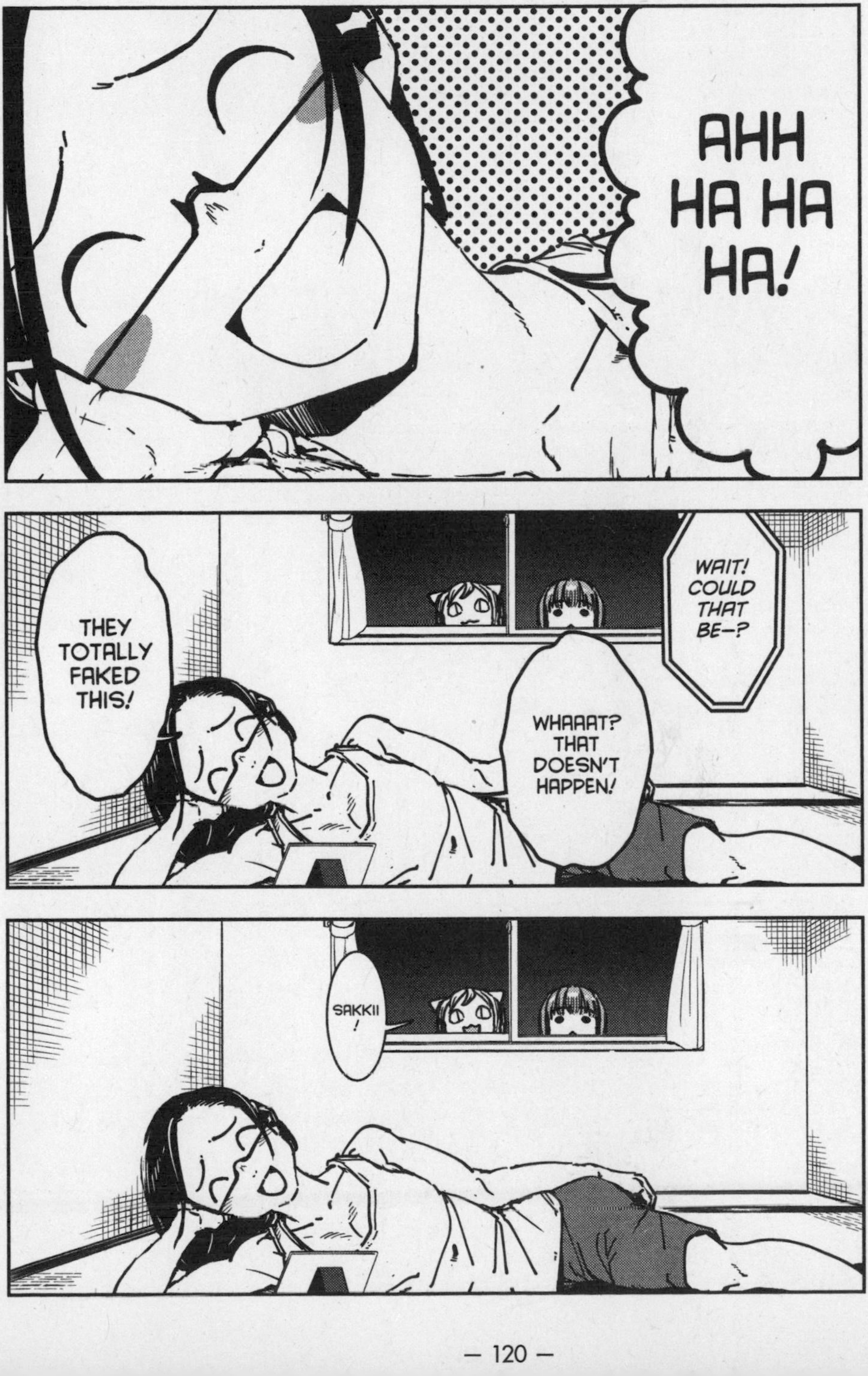
AHH HA HA HA!
WAIT! COULD THAT BE–?
WHAAAT? THAT DOESN'T HAPPEN!
THEY TOTALLY FAKED THIS!
SAKKII!

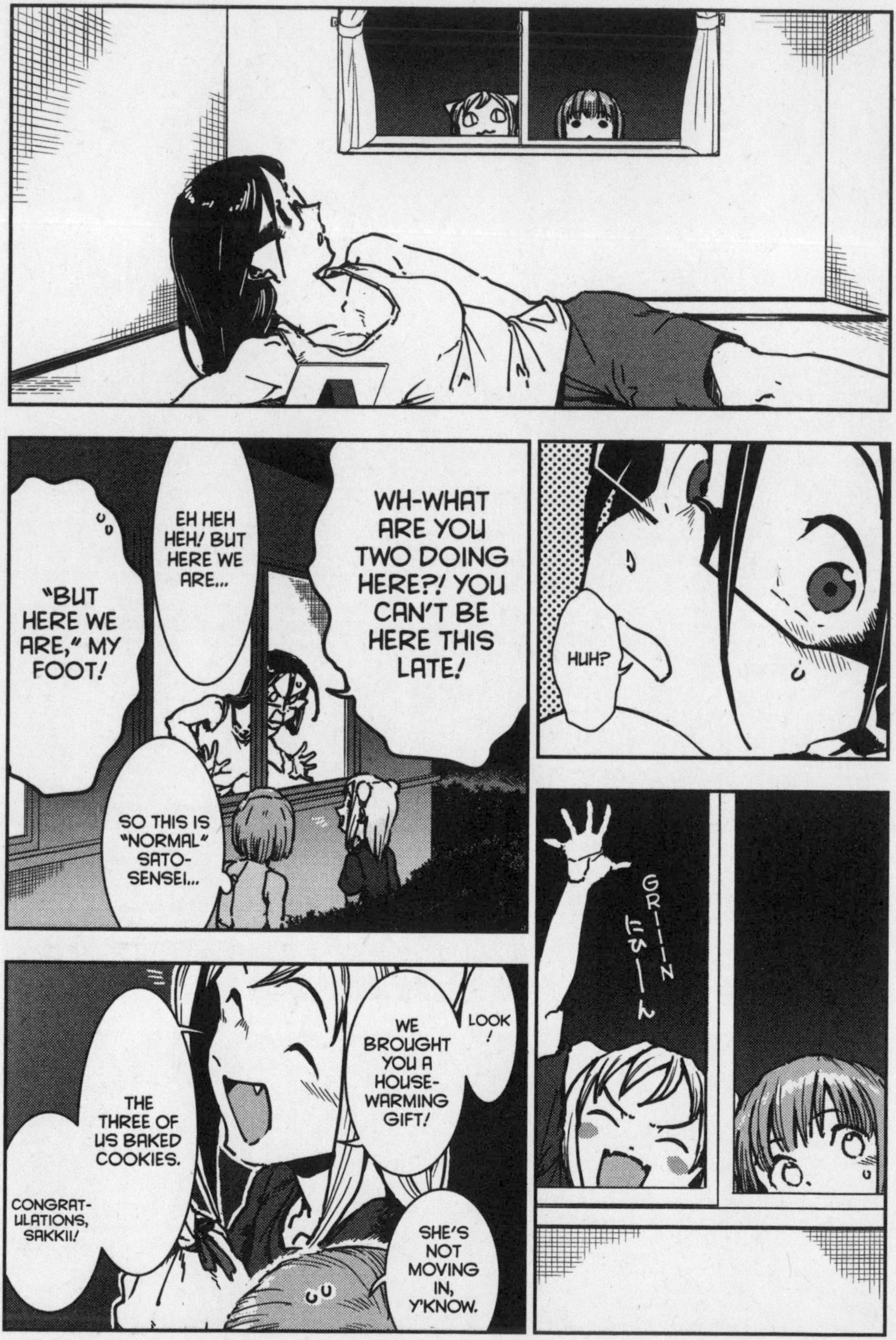
HUH?
WH-WHAT ARE YOU TWO DOING HERE?! YOU CAN'T BE HERE THIS LATE!
EH HEH HEH! BUT HERE WE ARE...
"BUT HERE WE ARE," MY FOOT!
SO THIS IS "NORMAL" SATO-SENSEI...
GRIIIN
LOOK!
WE BROUGHT YOU A HOUSE-WARMING GIFT!
THE THREE OF US BAKED COOKIES.
CONGRAT-ULATIONS, SAKKII!
SHE'S NOT MOVING IN, Y'KNOW.

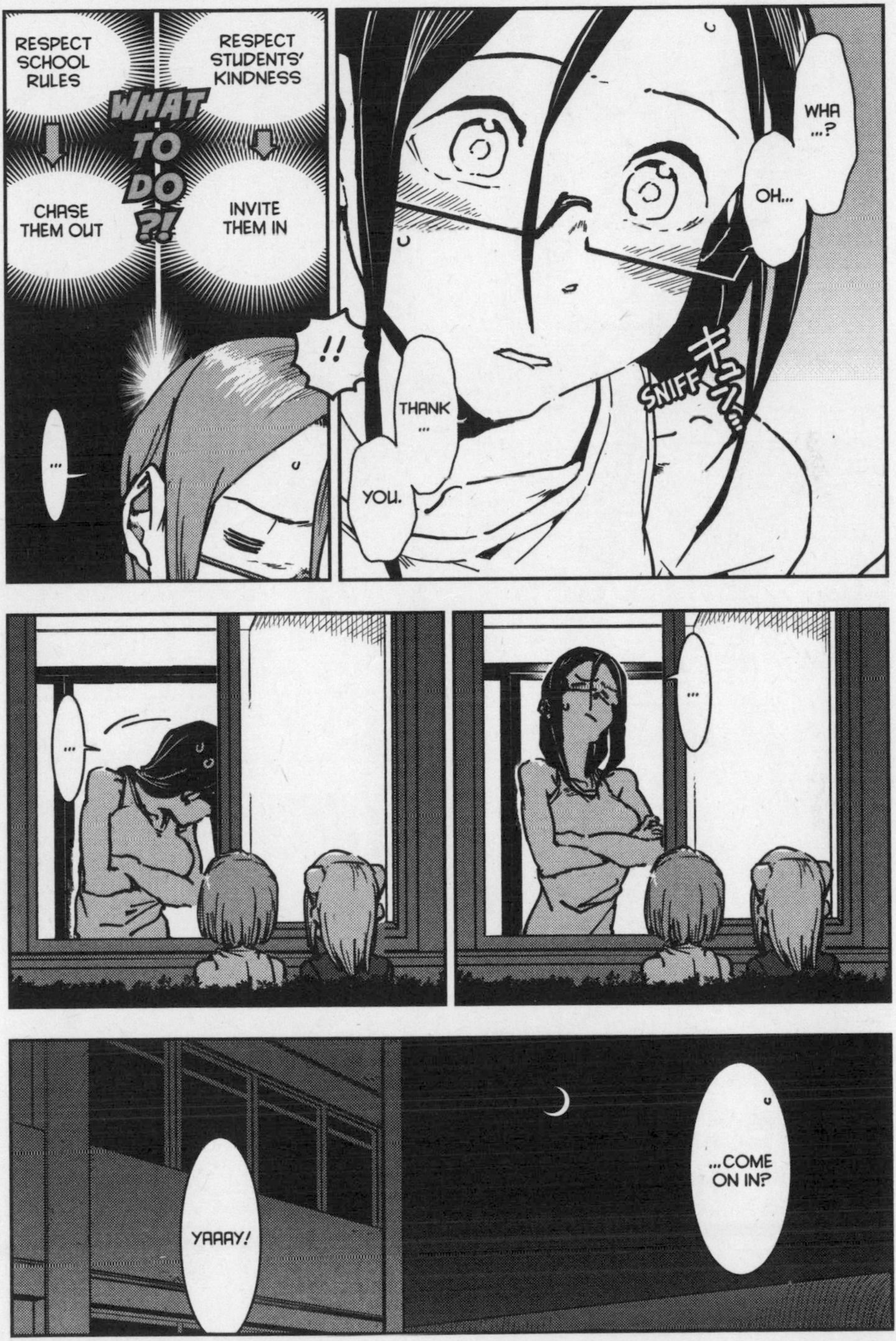
WHA ...?
OH...
THANK ...
YOU.
SNIFF
RESPECT STUDENTS' KINDNESS
RESPECT SCHOOL RULES
WHAT TO DO?!
INVITE THEM IN
CHASE THEM OUT
!!
...
...
...
...COME ON IN?
YAAAY!

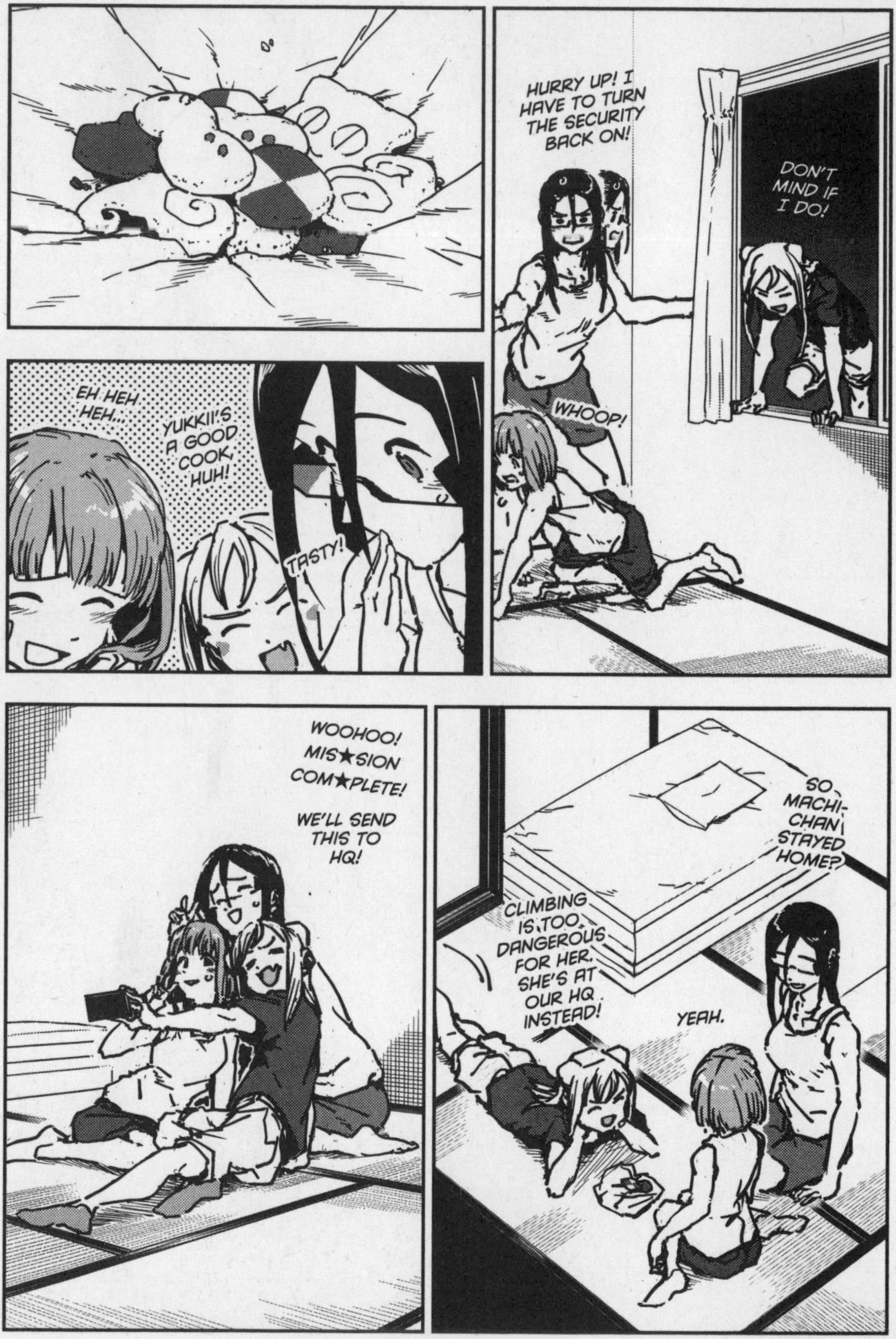
HURRY UP! I HAVE TO TURN THE SECURITY BACK ON!
DON'T MIND IF I DO!
WHOOP!
EH HEH HEH...
YUKKII'S A GOOD COOK, HUH!
TASTY!
SO MACHI-CHAN STAYED HOME?
CLIMBING IS TOO DANGEROUS FOR HER. SHE'S AT OUR HQ INSTEAD!
YEAH.
WOOHOO! MIS★SION COM★PLETE!
WE'LL SEND THIS TO HQ!

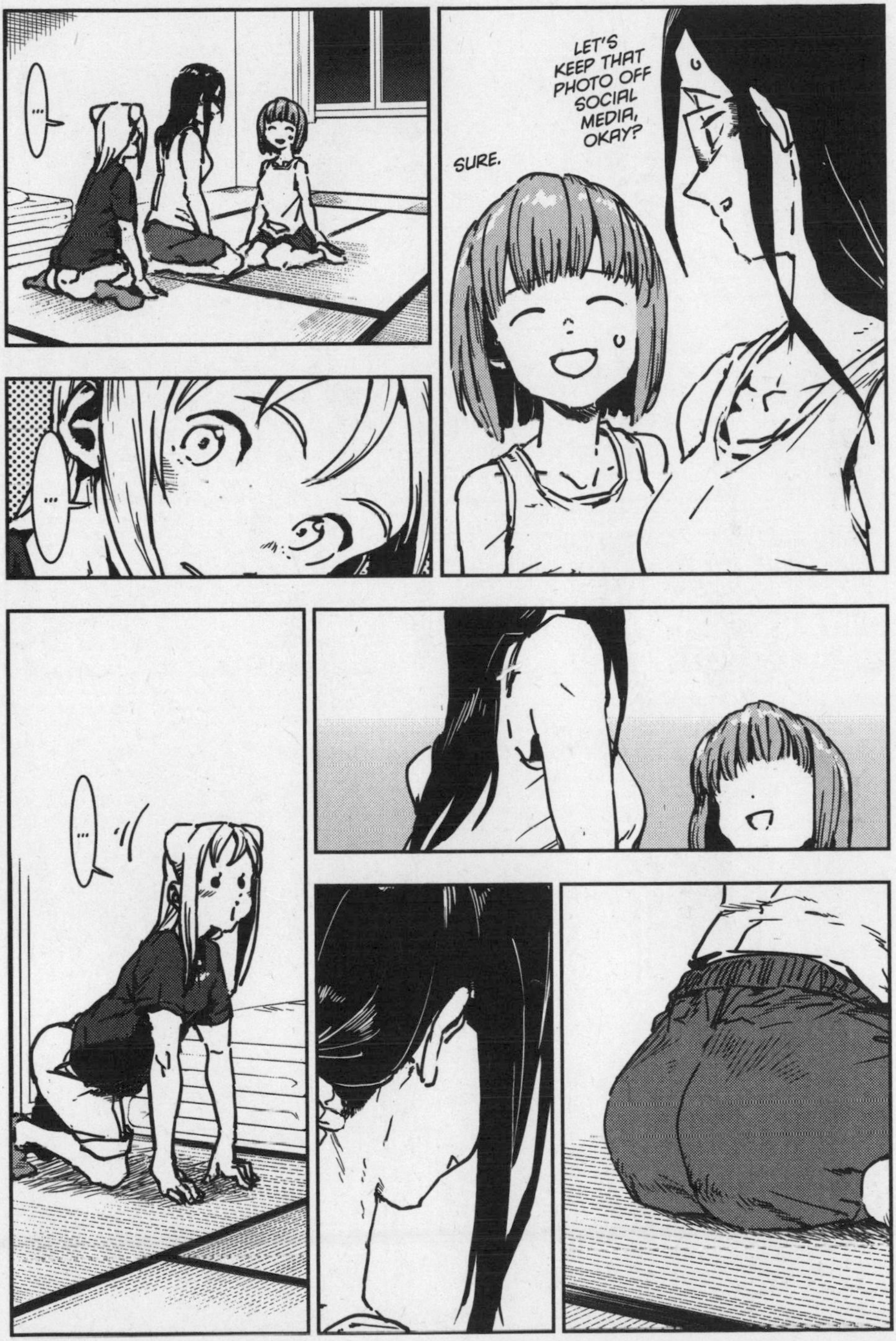
LET'S KEEP THAT PHOTO OFF SOCIAL MEDIA, OKAY?
SURE.
...
...
...

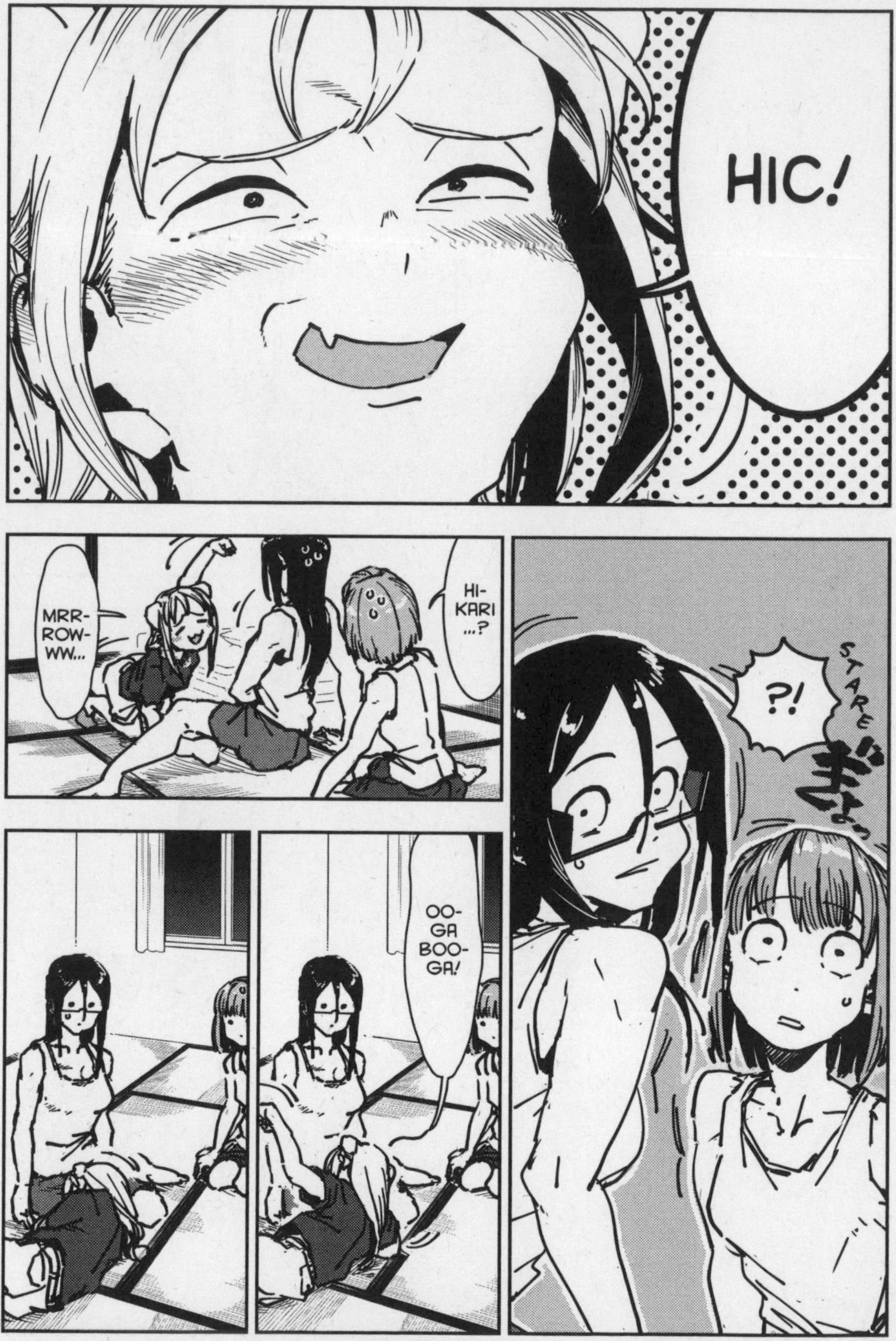
HIC!
?!
STARE
ぎょっ
HI-KARI ...?
MRR-ROW-WW...
OO-GA BOO-GA!

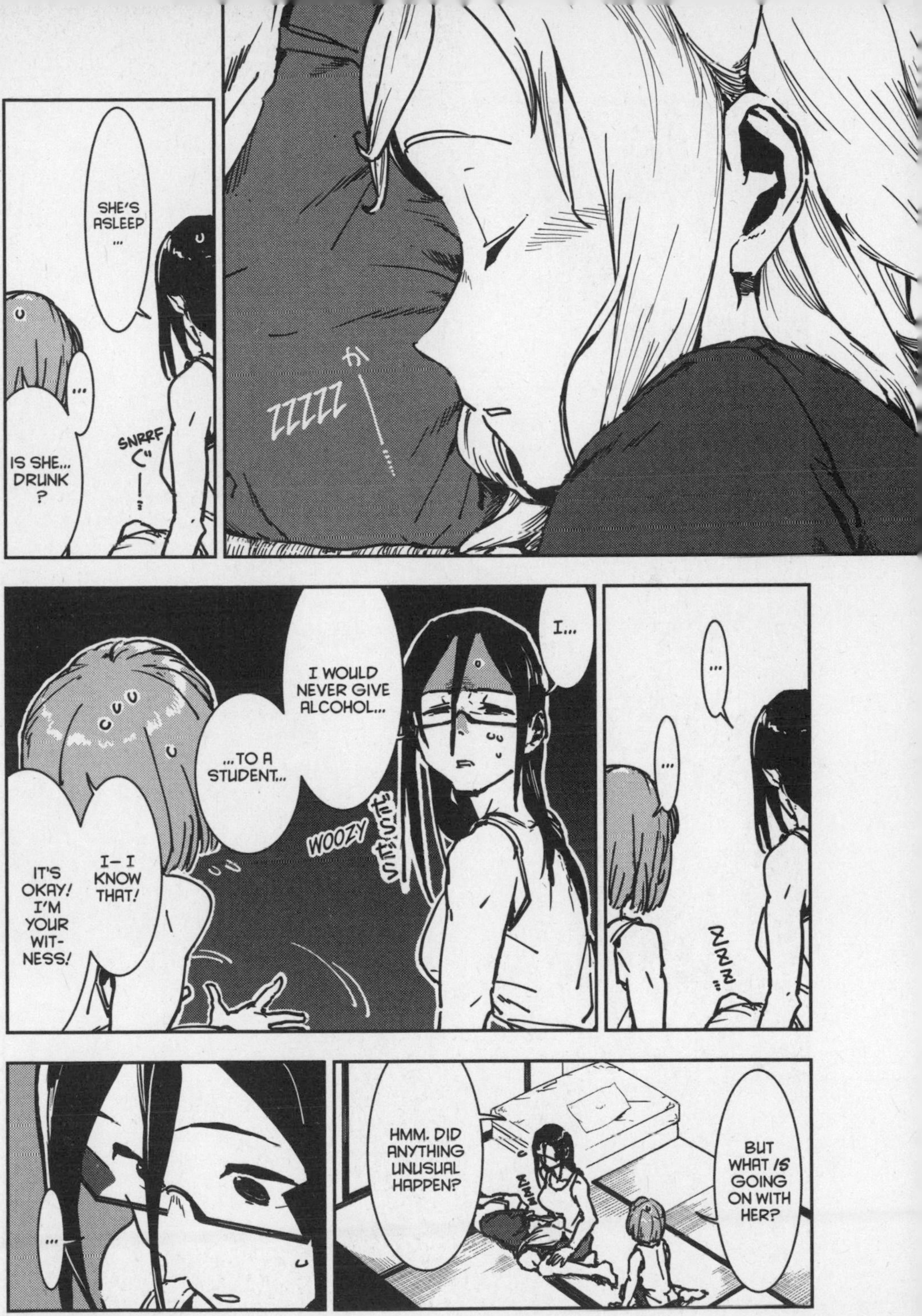
ZZZZZ
SHE'S ASLEEP ...
SNRRF
...
IS SHE... DRUNK?
...
...
ZNNN...
I...
I WOULD NEVER GIVE ALCOHOL...
...TO A STUDENT...
WOOZY
I— I KNOW THAT!
IT'S OKAY! I'M YOUR WITNESS!
BUT WHAT IS GOING ON WITH HER?
HMM. DID ANYTHING UNUSUAL HAPPEN?
ZNNN
...

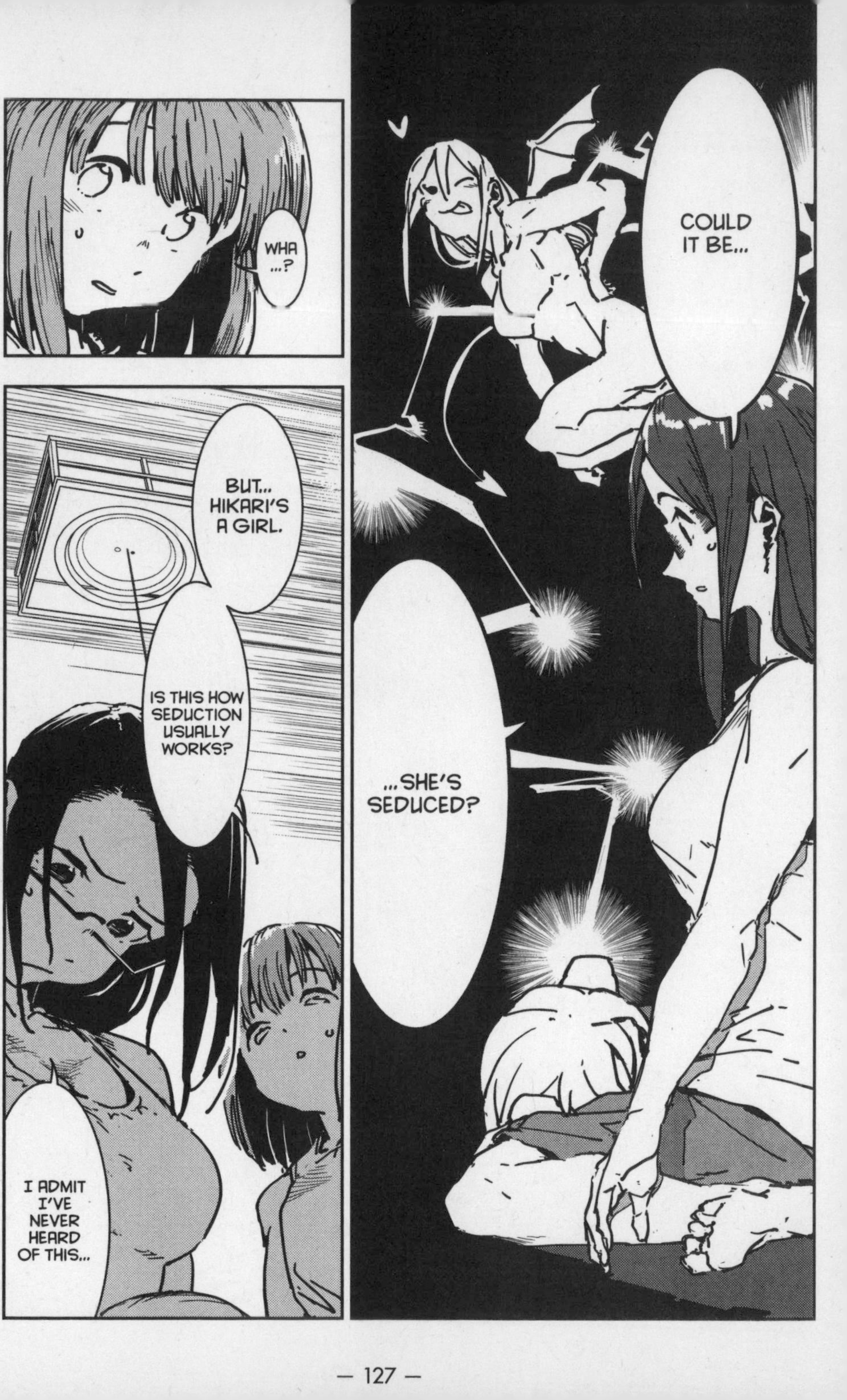
COULD IT BE...
...SHE'S SEDUCED?
WHA ...?
BUT... HIKARI'S A GIRL.
IS THIS HOW SEDUCTION USUALLY WORKS?
I ADMIT I'VE NEVER HEARD OF THIS...

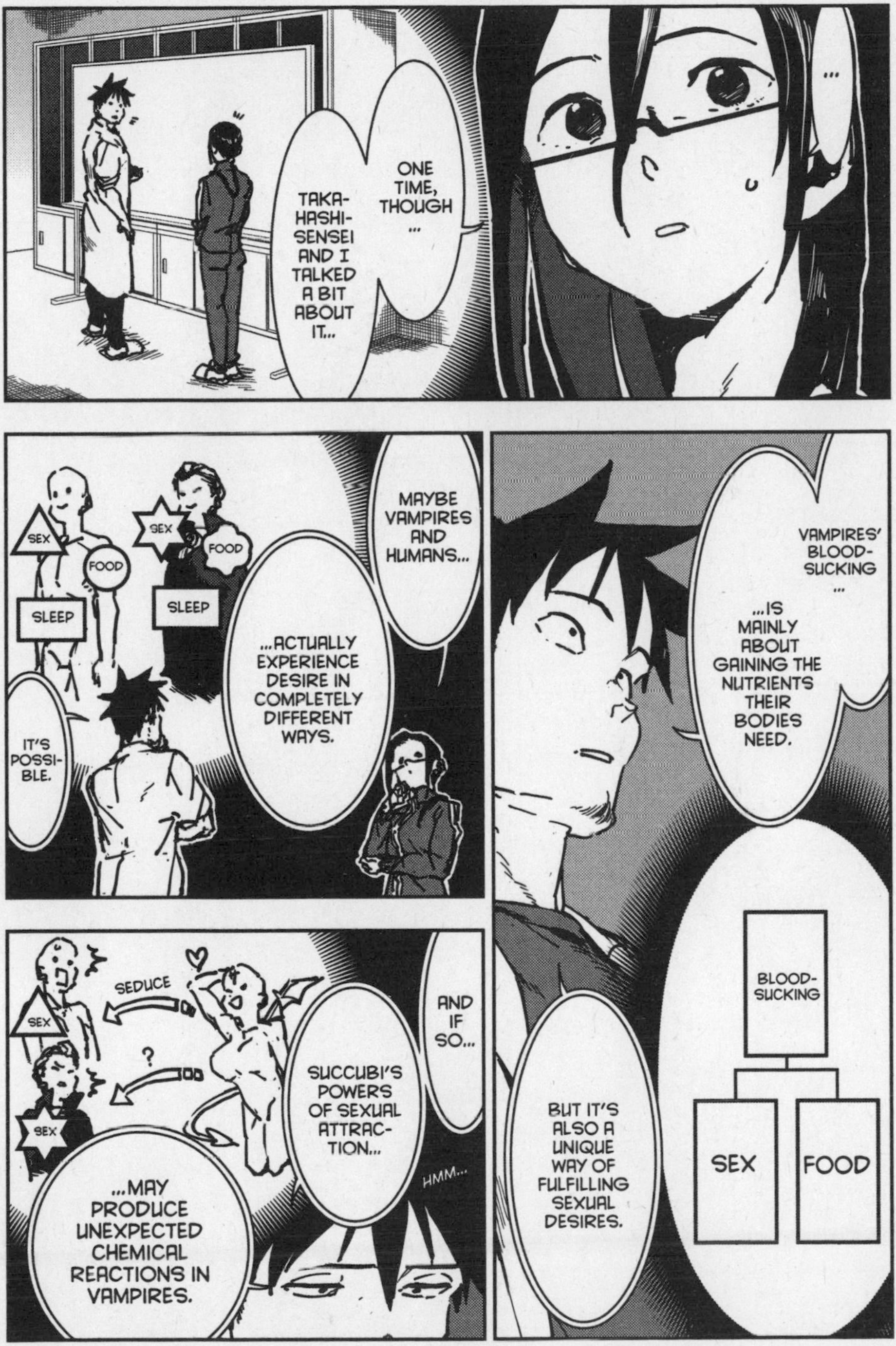
...
ONE TIME, THOUGH...
TAKAHASHI-SENSEI AND I TALKED A BIT ABOUT IT...
VAMPIRES' BLOOD-SUCKING...
...IS MAINLY ABOUT GAINING THE NUTRIENTS THEIR BODIES NEED.
BLOOD-SUCKING
SEX
FOOD
BUT IT'S ALSO A UNIQUE WAY OF FULFILLING SEXUAL DESIRES.
MAYBE VAMPIRES AND HUMANS...
...ACTUALLY EXPERIENCE DESIRE IN COMPLETELY DIFFERENT WAYS.
SEX
FOOD
SLEEP
SEX
FOOD
SLEEP
IT'S POSSIBLE.
AND IF SO...
SUCCUBI'S POWERS OF SEXUAL ATTRACTION...
SEDUCE
SEX
?
SEX
HMM...
...MAY PRODUCE UNEXPECTED CHEMICAL REACTIONS IN VAMPIRES.

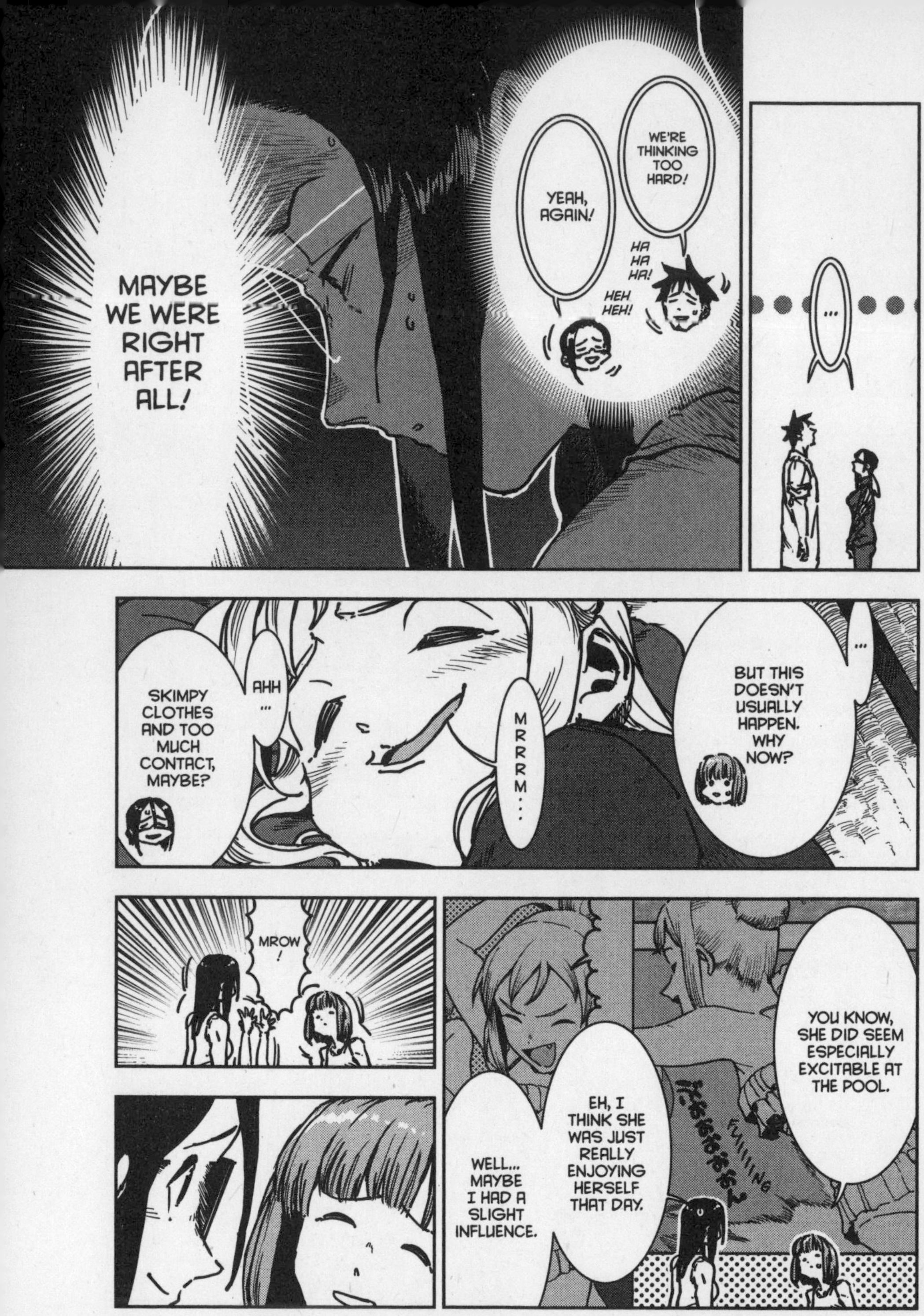
...
WE'RE THINKING TOO HARD!
HA HA HA!
YEAH, AGAIN!
HEH HEH!
MAYBE WE WERE RIGHT AFTER ALL!
...
BUT THIS DOESN'T USUALLY HAPPEN. WHY NOW?
MRRRM...
AHH...
SKIMPY CLOTHES AND TOO MUCH CONTACT, MAYBE?
YOU KNOW, SHE DID SEEM ESPECIALLY EXCITABLE AT THE POOL.
EH, I THINK SHE WAS JUST REALLY ENJOYING HERSELF THAT DAY.
WELL... MAYBE I HAD A SLIGHT INFLUENCE.
MROW!

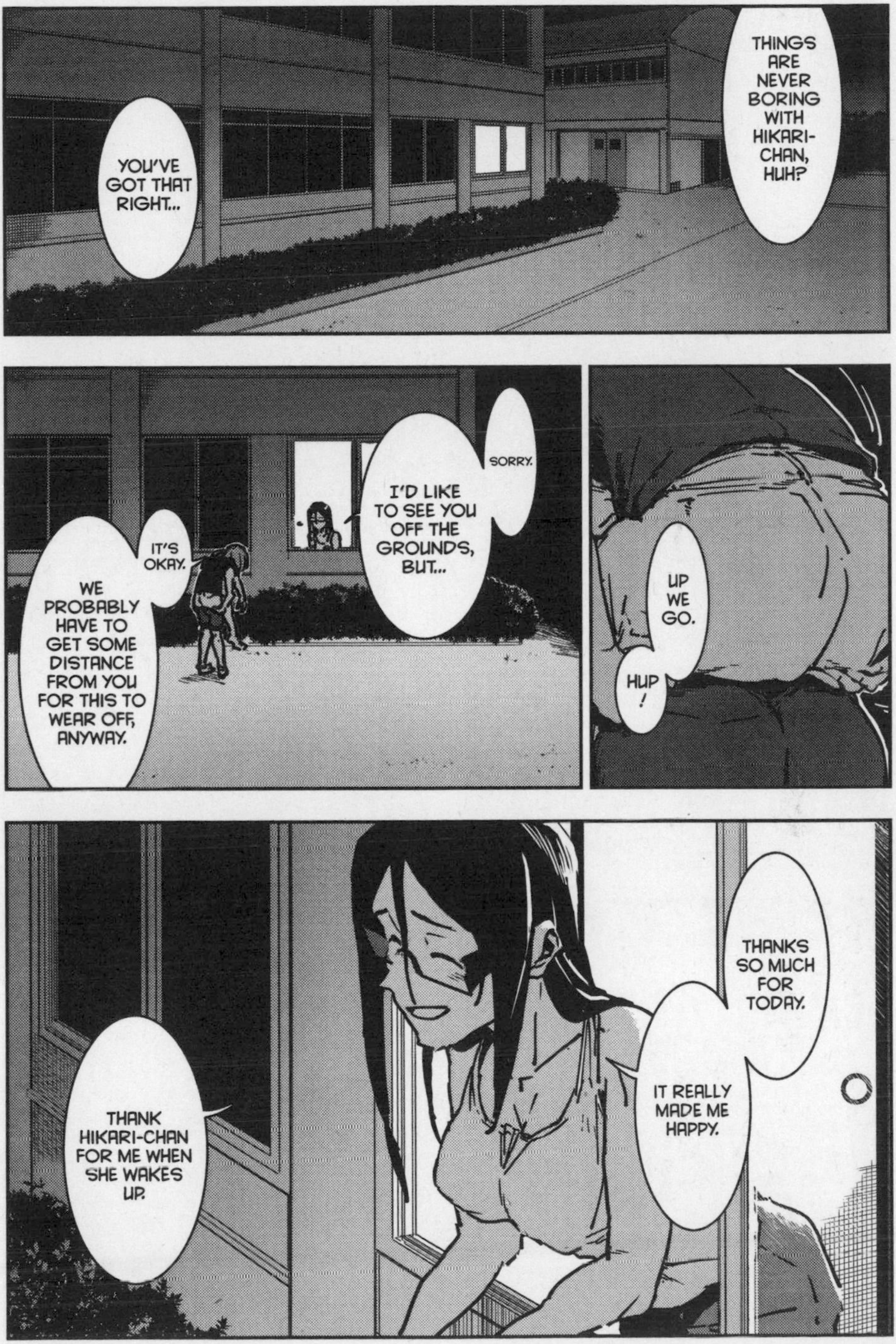
THINGS ARE NEVER BORING WITH HIKARI-CHAN, HUH?
YOU'VE GOT THAT RIGHT...
UP WE GO.
HUP!
SORRY.
I'D LIKE TO SEE YOU OFF THE GROUNDS, BUT...
IT'S OKAY.
WE PROBABLY HAVE TO GET SOME DISTANCE FROM YOU FOR THIS TO WEAR OFF, ANYWAY.
THANKS SO MUCH FOR TODAY.
IT REALLY MADE ME HAPPY.
THANK HIKARI-CHAN FOR ME WHEN SHE WAKES UP.

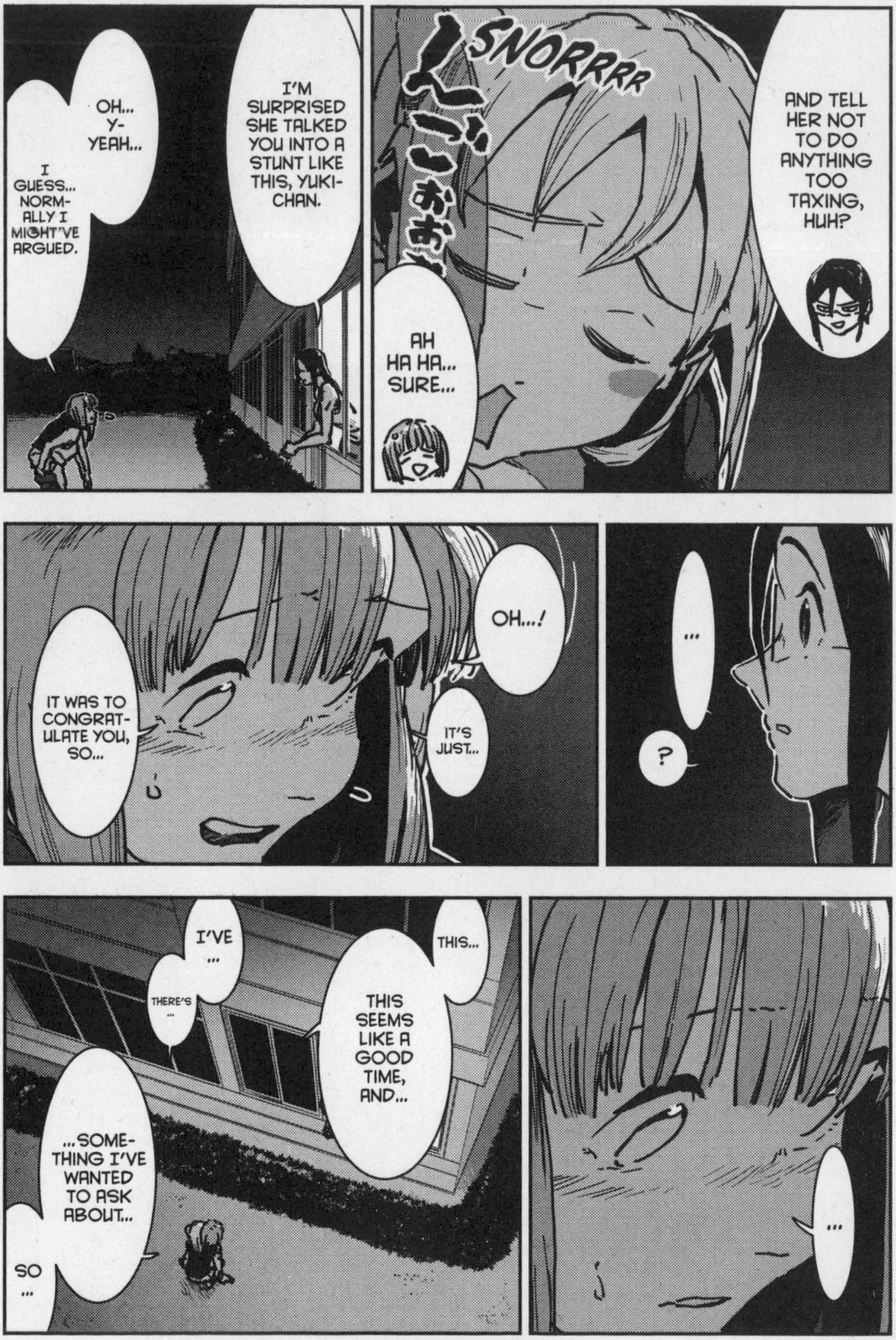
AND TELL HER NOT TO DO ANYTHING TOO TAXING, HUH?
SNORRRR
AH HA HA... SURE...
I'M SURPRISED SHE TALKED YOU INTO A STUNT LIKE THIS, YUKI-CHAN.
OH... Y-YEAH...
I GUESS... NORMALLY I MIGHT'VE ARGUED.
...
?
OH...!
IT'S JUST...
IT WAS TO CONGRATULATE YOU, SO...
...
THIS...
THIS SEEMS LIKE A GOOD TIME, AND...
I'VE ...
THERE'S ...
...SOMETHING I'VE WANTED TO ASK ABOUT...
SO ...

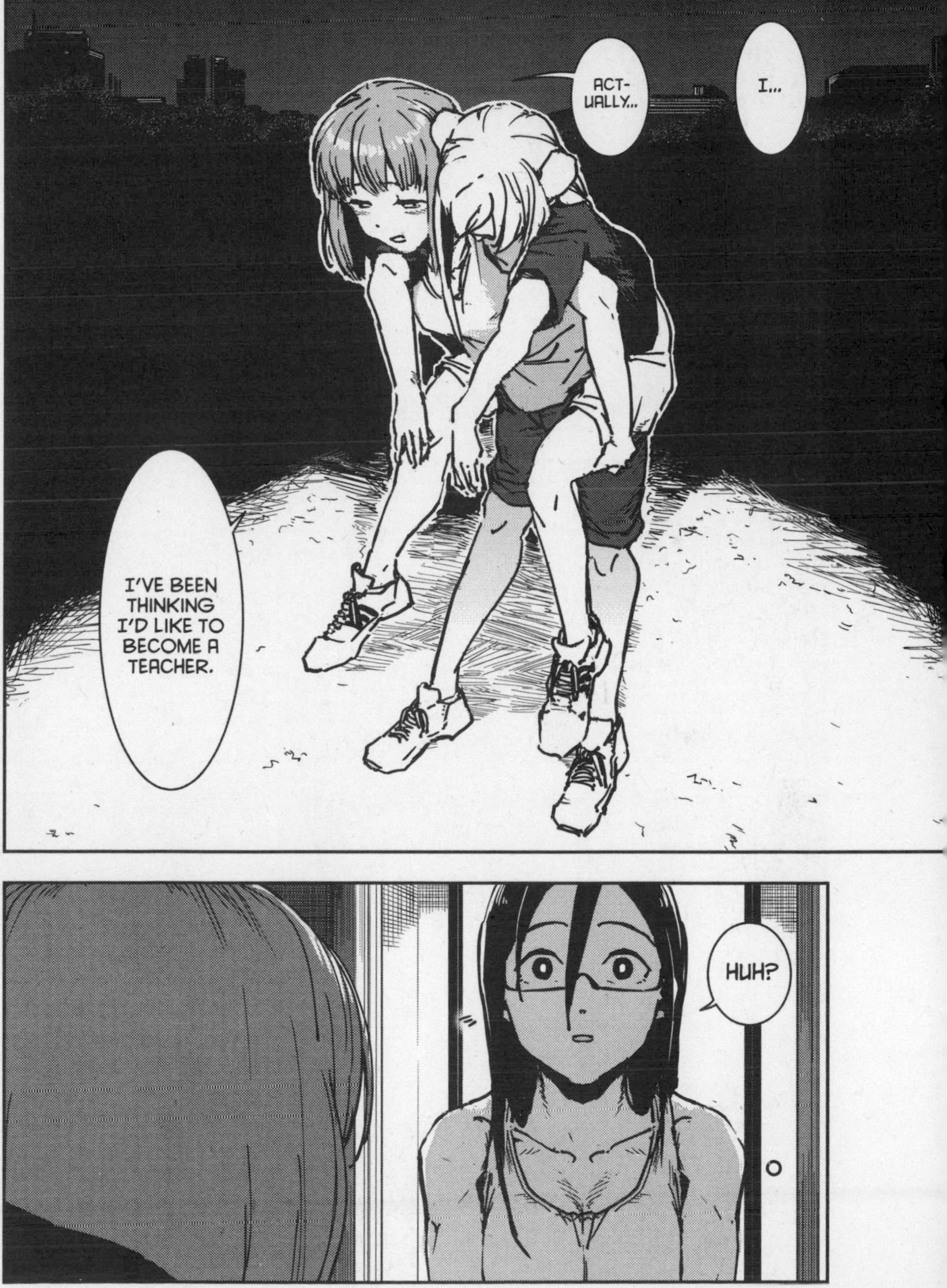
I...
ACT-UALLY...
I'VE BEEN THINKING I'D LIKE TO BECOME A TEACHER.
HUH?

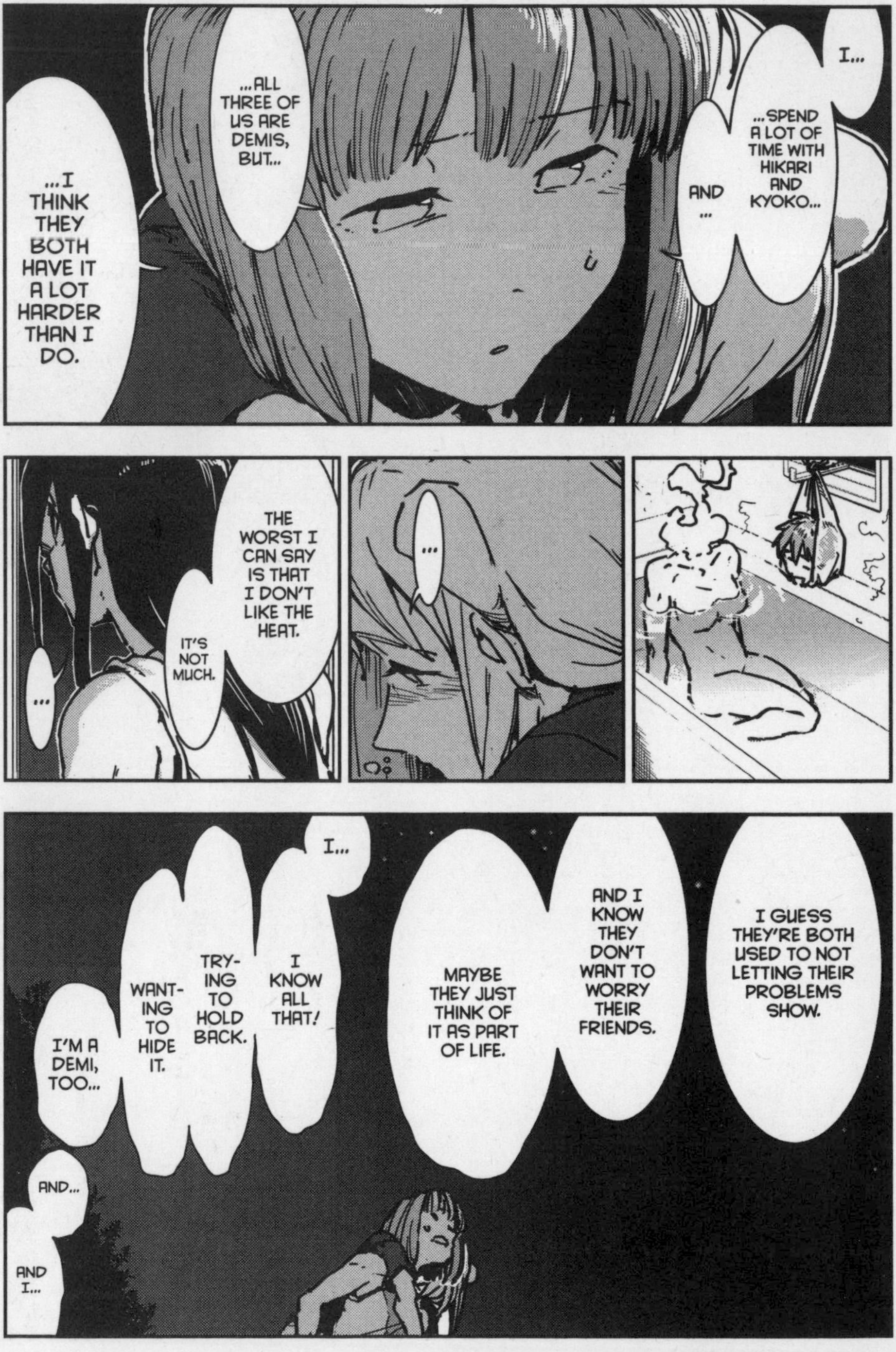
I...
...SPEND A LOT OF TIME WITH HIKARI AND KYOKO...
AND ...
...ALL THREE OF US ARE DEMIS, BUT...
...I THINK THEY BOTH HAVE IT A LOT HARDER THAN I DO.
...
THE WORST I CAN SAY IS THAT I DON'T LIKE THE HEAT.
IT'S NOT MUCH.
...
I GUESS THEY'RE BOTH USED TO NOT LETTING THEIR PROBLEMS SHOW.
AND I KNOW THEY DON'T WANT TO WORRY THEIR FRIENDS.
MAYBE THEY JUST THINK OF IT AS PART OF LIFE.
I...
I KNOW ALL THAT!
TRYING TO HOLD BACK.
WANTING TO HIDE IT.
I'M A DEMI, TOO...
AND...
AND I...

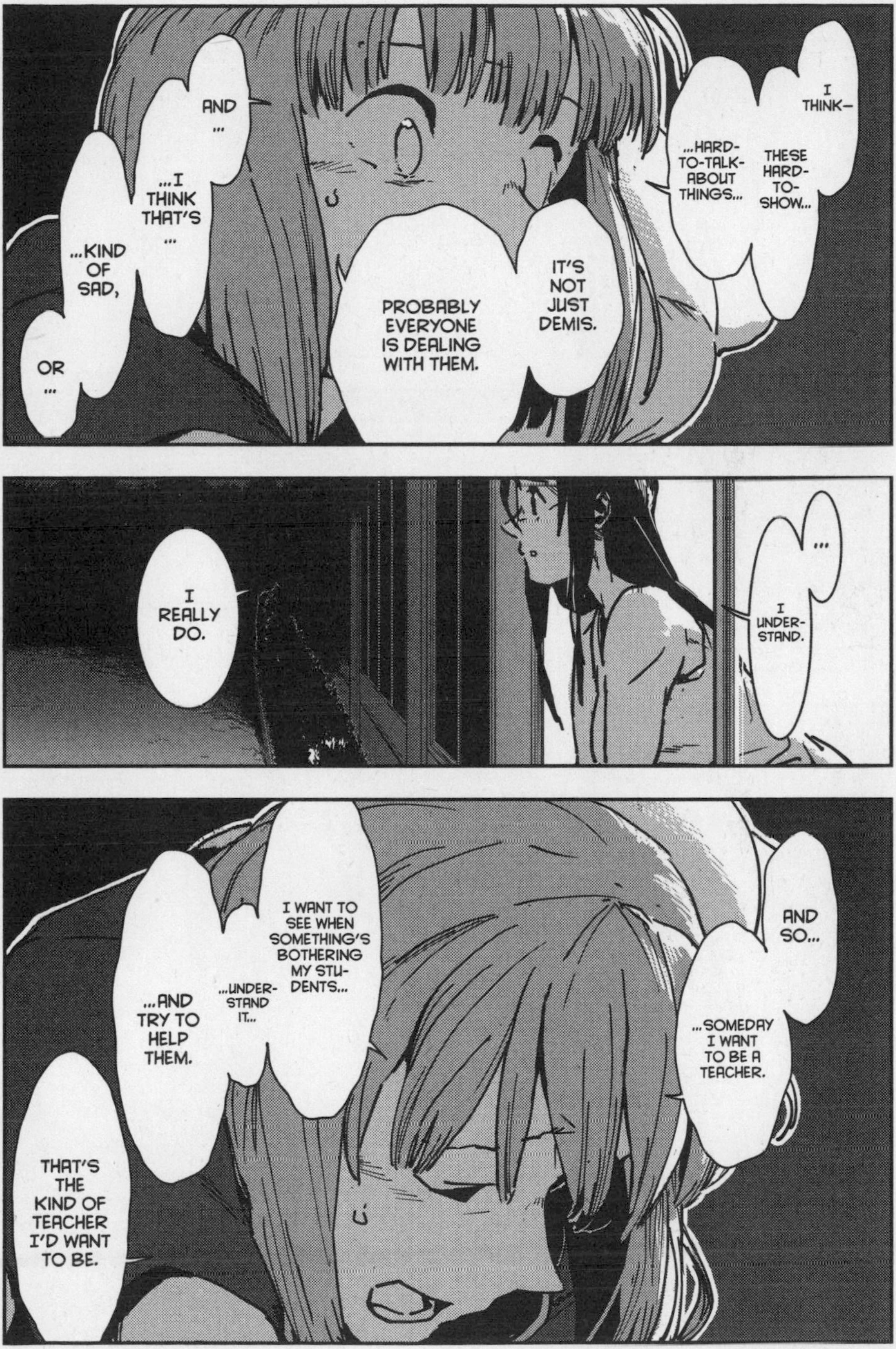
I THINK—
THESE HARD-TO-SHOW...
...HARD-TO-TALK-ABOUT THINGS...
IT'S NOT JUST DEMIS.
PROBABLY EVERYONE IS DEALING WITH THEM.
AND ...
...I THINK THAT'S ...
...KIND OF SAD,
OR ...
...
I UNDER-STAND.
I REALLY DO.
AND SO...
...SOMEDAY I WANT TO BE A TEACHER.
I WANT TO SEE WHEN SOMETHING'S BOTHERING MY STU-DENTS...
...UNDER-STAND IT...
...AND TRY TO HELP THEM.
THAT'S THE KIND OF TEACHER I'D WANT TO BE.

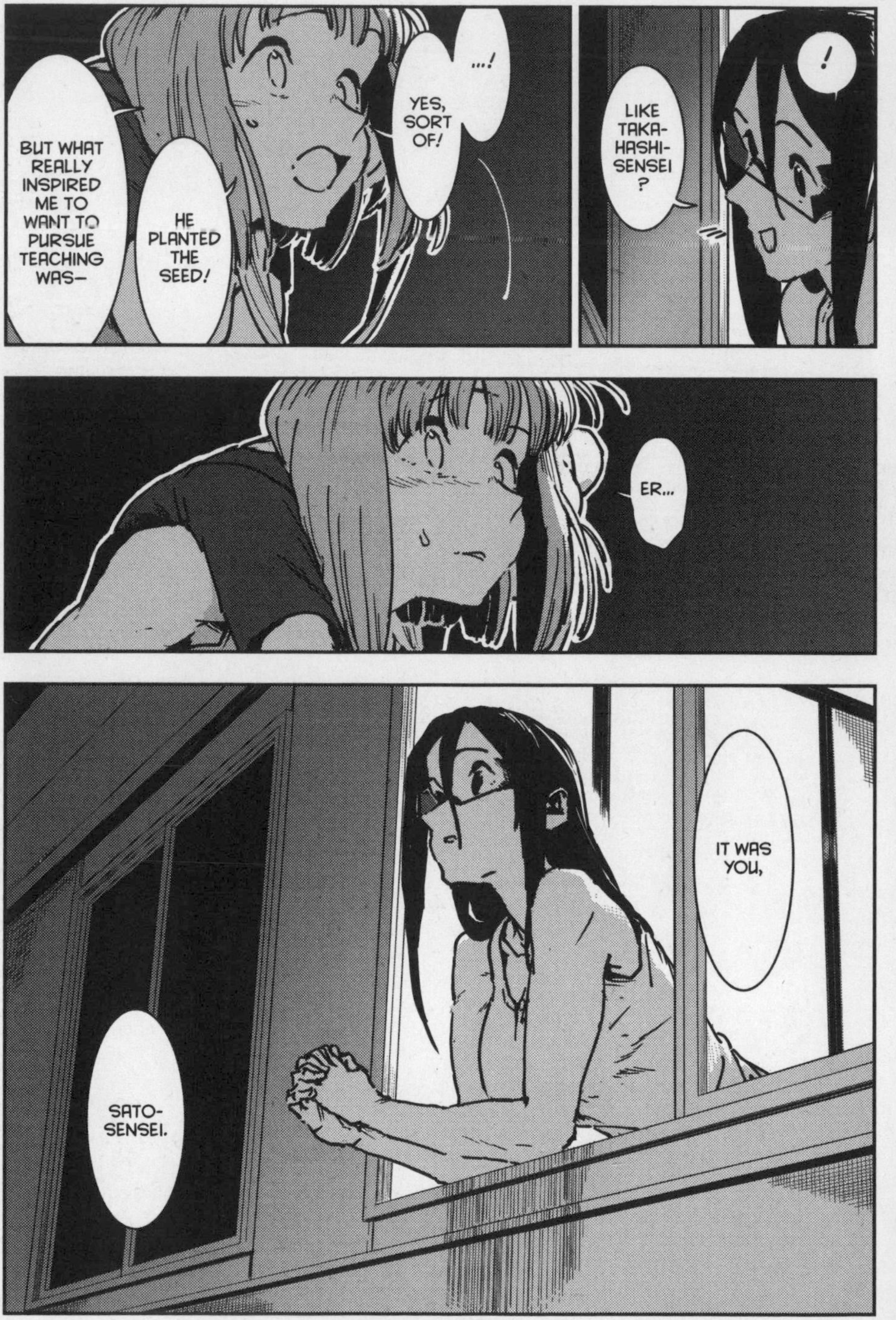
!
LIKE TAKA-HASHI-SENSEI?
...!
YES, SORT OF!
HE PLANTED THE SEED!
BUT WHAT REALLY INSPIRED ME TO WANT TO PURSUE TEACHING WAS—
ER...
IT WAS YOU,
SATO-SENSEI.

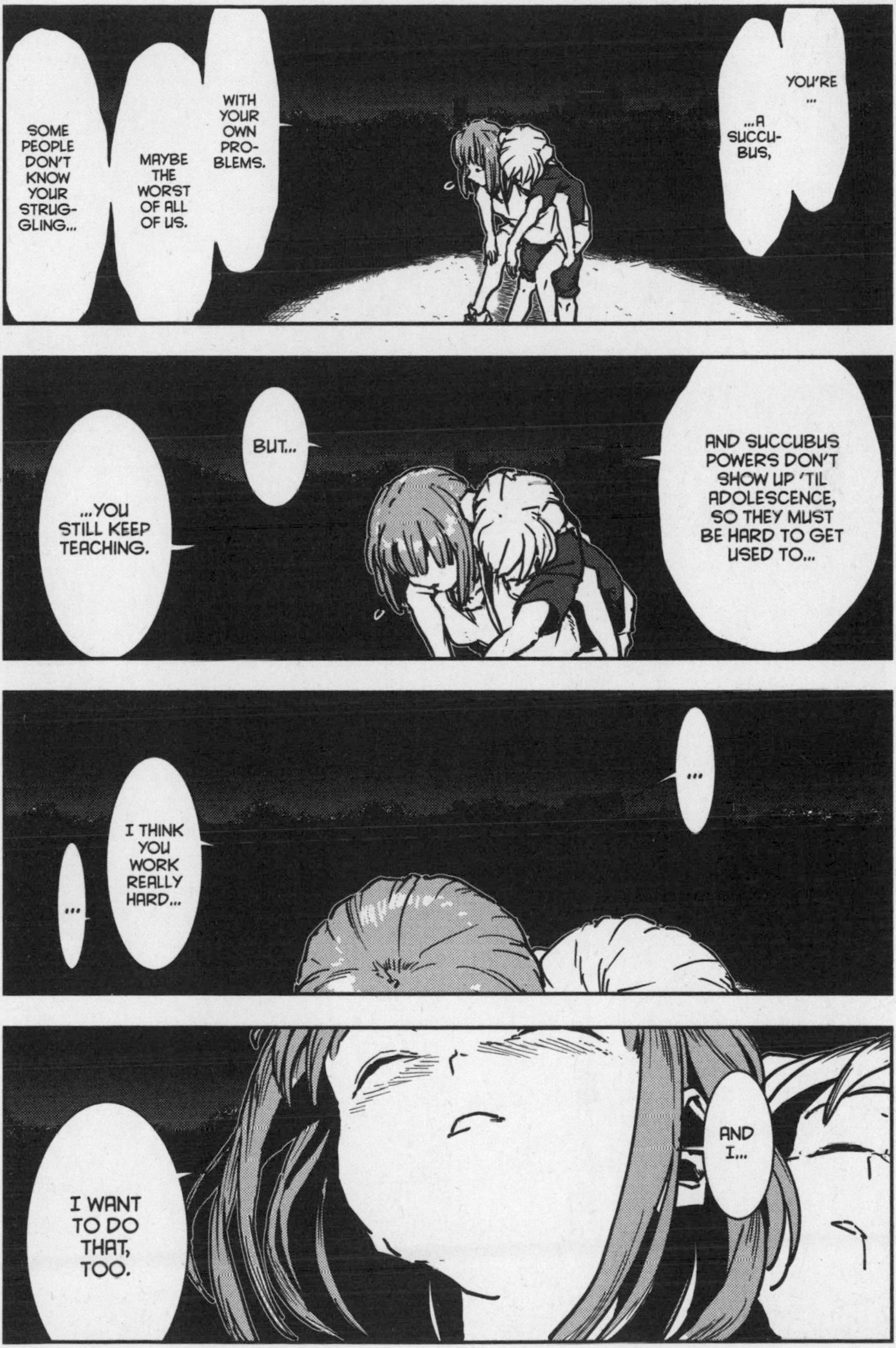
YOU'RE ...
...A SUCCU-BUS,
WITH YOUR OWN PRO-BLEMS.
MAYBE THE WORST OF ALL OF US.
SOME PEOPLE DON'T KNOW YOUR STRUG-GLING...
AND SUCCUBUS POWERS DON'T SHOW UP 'TIL ADOLESCENCE, SO THEY MUST BE HARD TO GET USED TO...
BUT...
...YOU STILL KEEP TEACHING.
...
I THINK YOU WORK REALLY HARD...
...
AND I...
I WANT TO DO THAT, TOO.

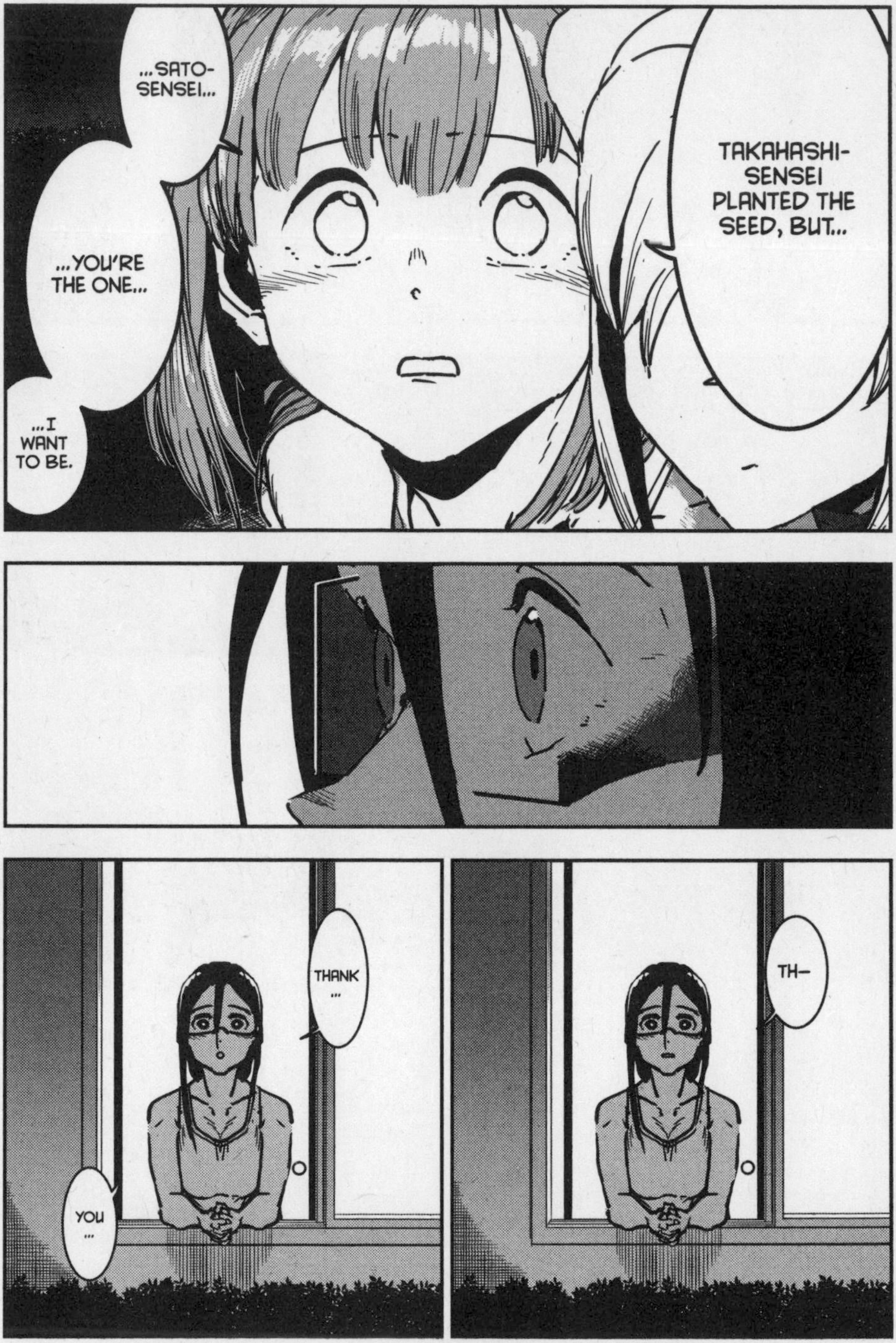
TAKAHASHI-SENSEI PLANTED THE SEED, BUT...
...SATO-SENSEI...
...YOU'RE THE ONE...
...I WANT TO BE.
TH—
THANK ...
YOU ...

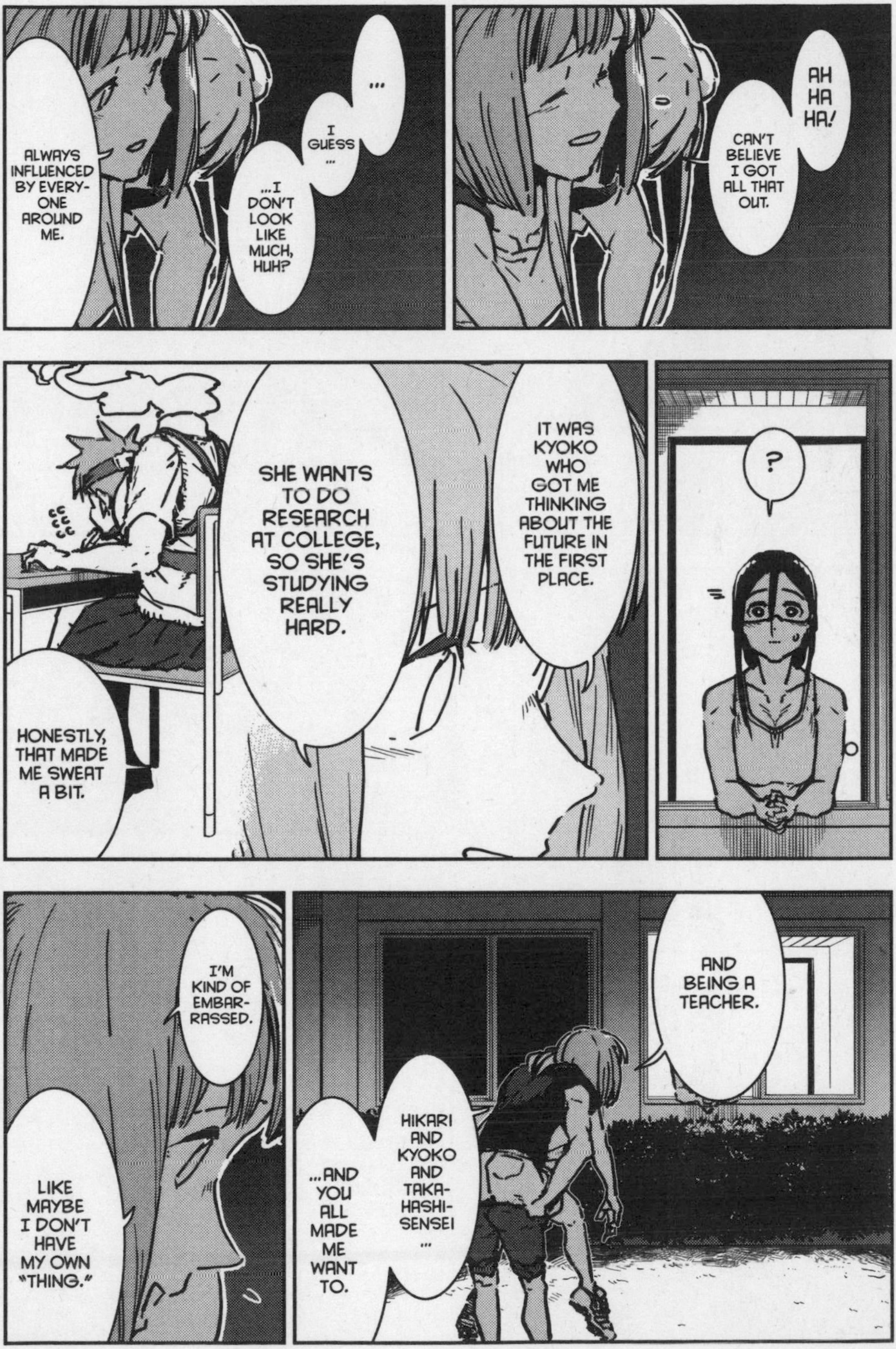
AH HA HA!
CAN'T BELIEVE I GOT ALL THAT OUT.
...
I GUESS ...
...I DON'T LOOK LIKE MUCH, HUH?
ALWAYS INFLUENCED BY EVERY-ONE AROUND ME.
?
IT WAS KYOKO WHO GOT ME THINKING ABOUT THE FUTURE IN THE FIRST PLACE.
SHE WANTS TO DO RESEARCH AT COLLEGE, SO SHE'S STUDYING REALLY HARD.
HONESTLY, THAT MADE ME SWEAT A BIT.
AND BEING A TEACHER.
HIKARI AND KYOKO AND TAKA-HASHI-SENSEI ...
...AND YOU ALL MADE ME WANT TO.
I'M KIND OF EMBAR-RASSED.
LIKE MAYBE I DON'T HAVE MY OWN "THING."

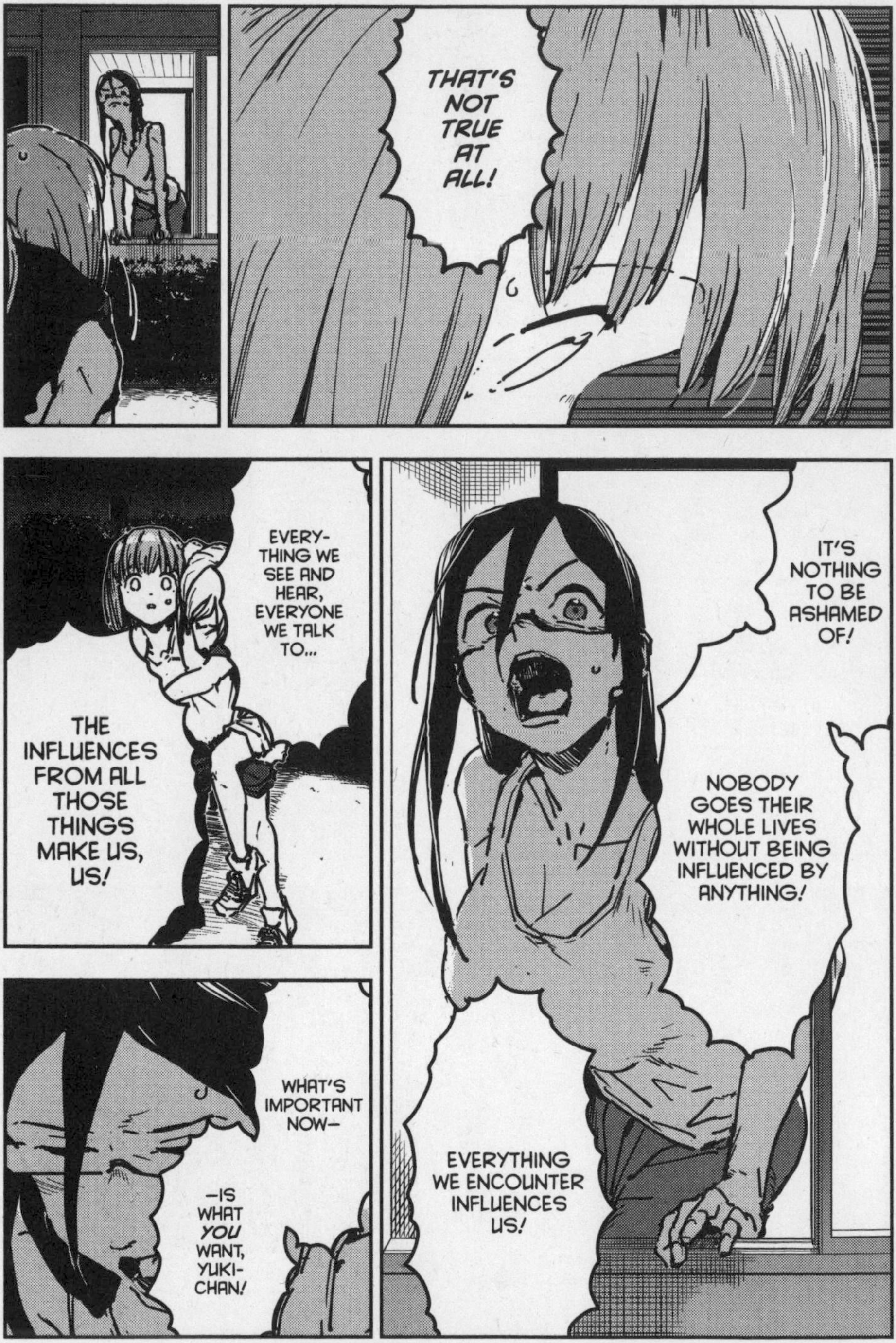
THAT'S NOT TRUE AT ALL!
IT'S NOTHING TO BE ASHAMED OF!
NOBODY GOES THEIR WHOLE LIVES WITHOUT BEING INFLUENCED BY ANYTHING!
EVERYTHING WE ENCOUNTER INFLUENCES US!
EVERY-THING WE SEE AND HEAR, EVERYONE WE TALK TO...
THE INFLUENCES FROM ALL THOSE THINGS MAKE US, US!
WHAT'S IMPORTANT NOW—
—IS WHAT *YOU* WANT, YUKI-CHAN!

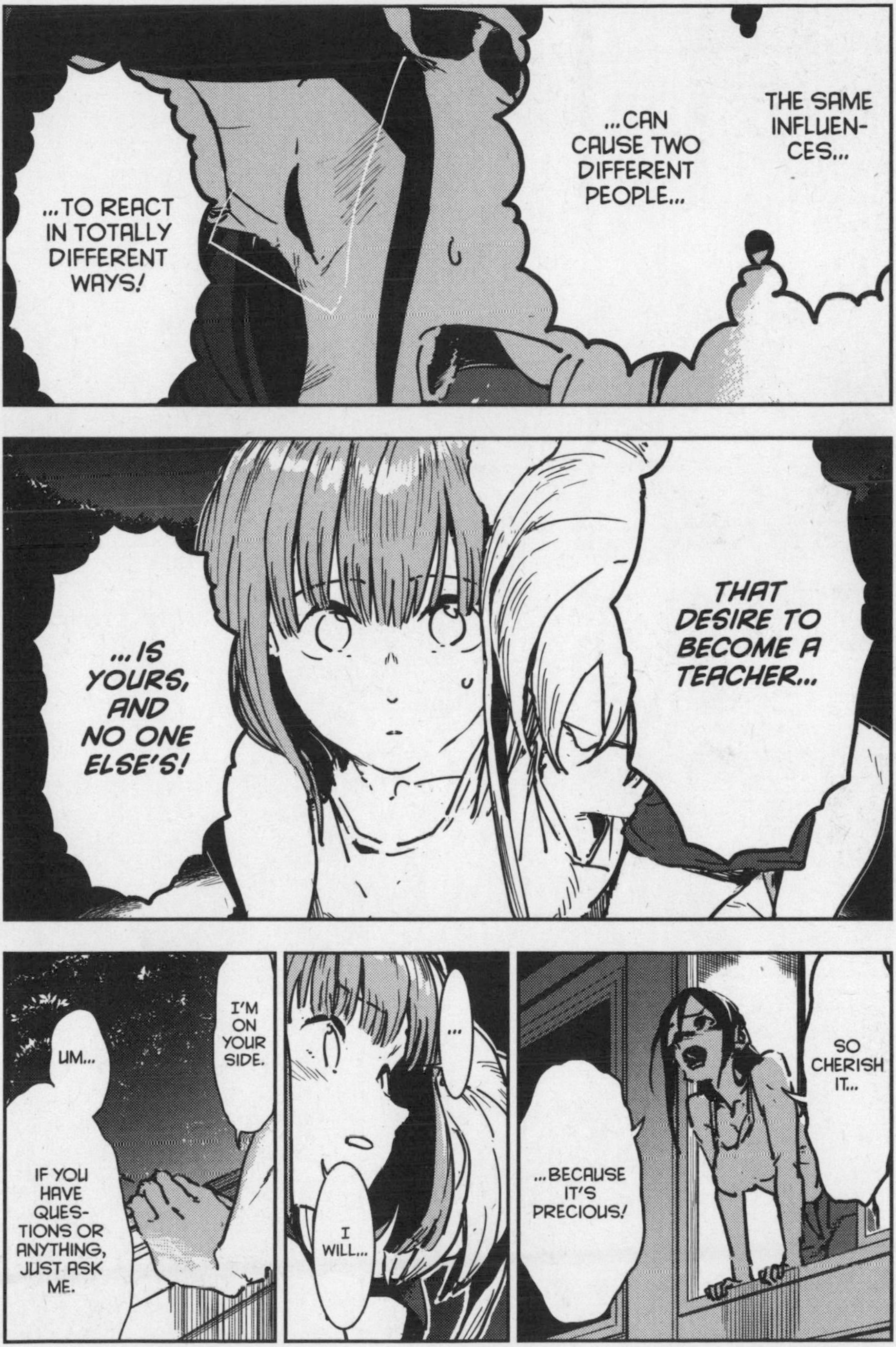
THE SAME INFLUEN-CES...
...CAN CAUSE TWO DIFFERENT PEOPLE...
...TO REACT IN TOTALLY DIFFERENT WAYS!
THAT DESIRE TO BECOME A TEACHER...
...IS YOURS, AND NO ONE ELSE'S!
SO CHERISH IT...
...BECAUSE IT'S PRECIOUS!
...
I WILL...
I'M ON YOUR SIDE.
UM...
IF YOU HAVE QUES-TIONS OR ANYTHING, JUST ASK ME.

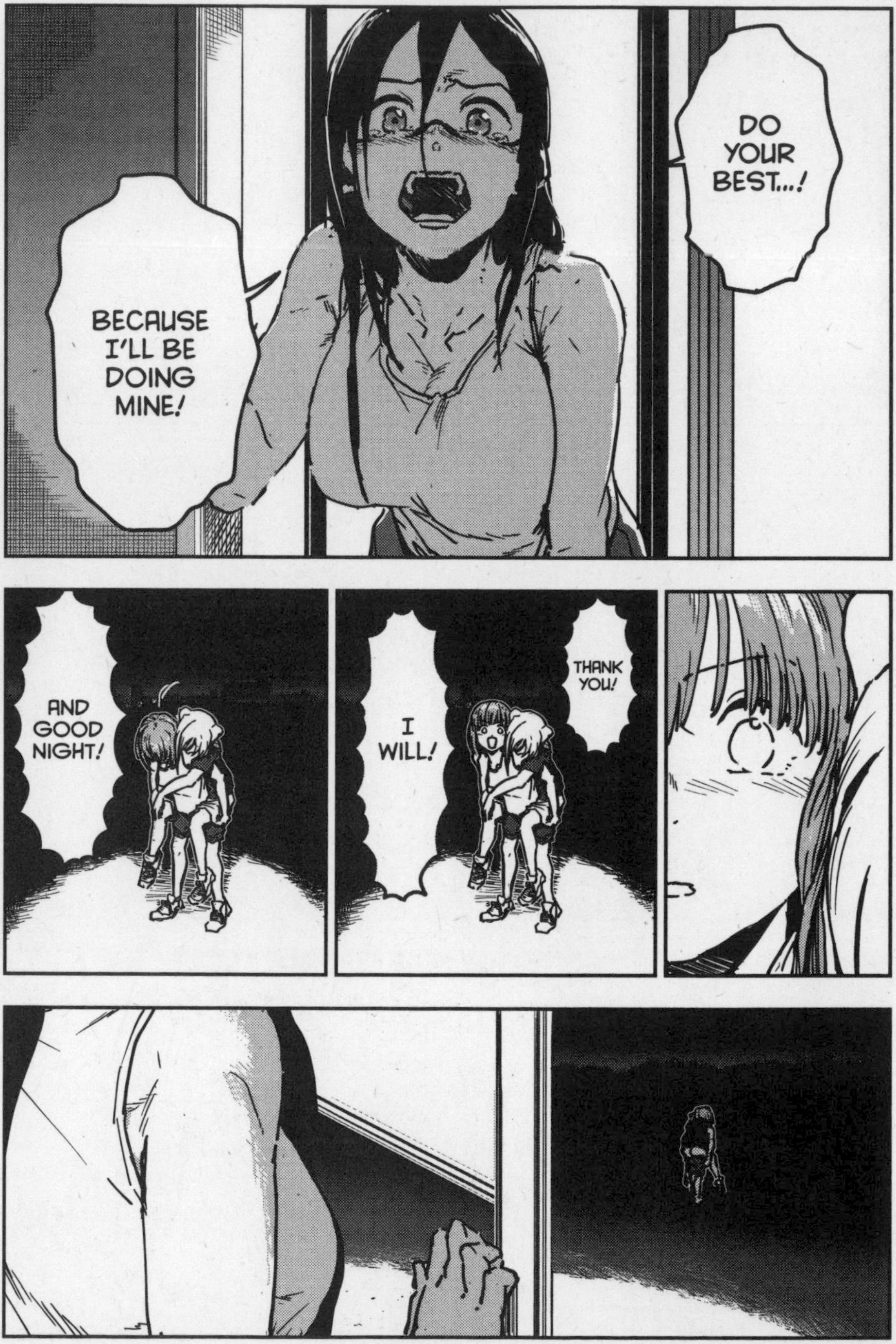
DO YOUR BEST...!
BECAUSE I'LL BE DOING MINE!
THANK YOU!
I WILL!
AND GOOD NIGHT!

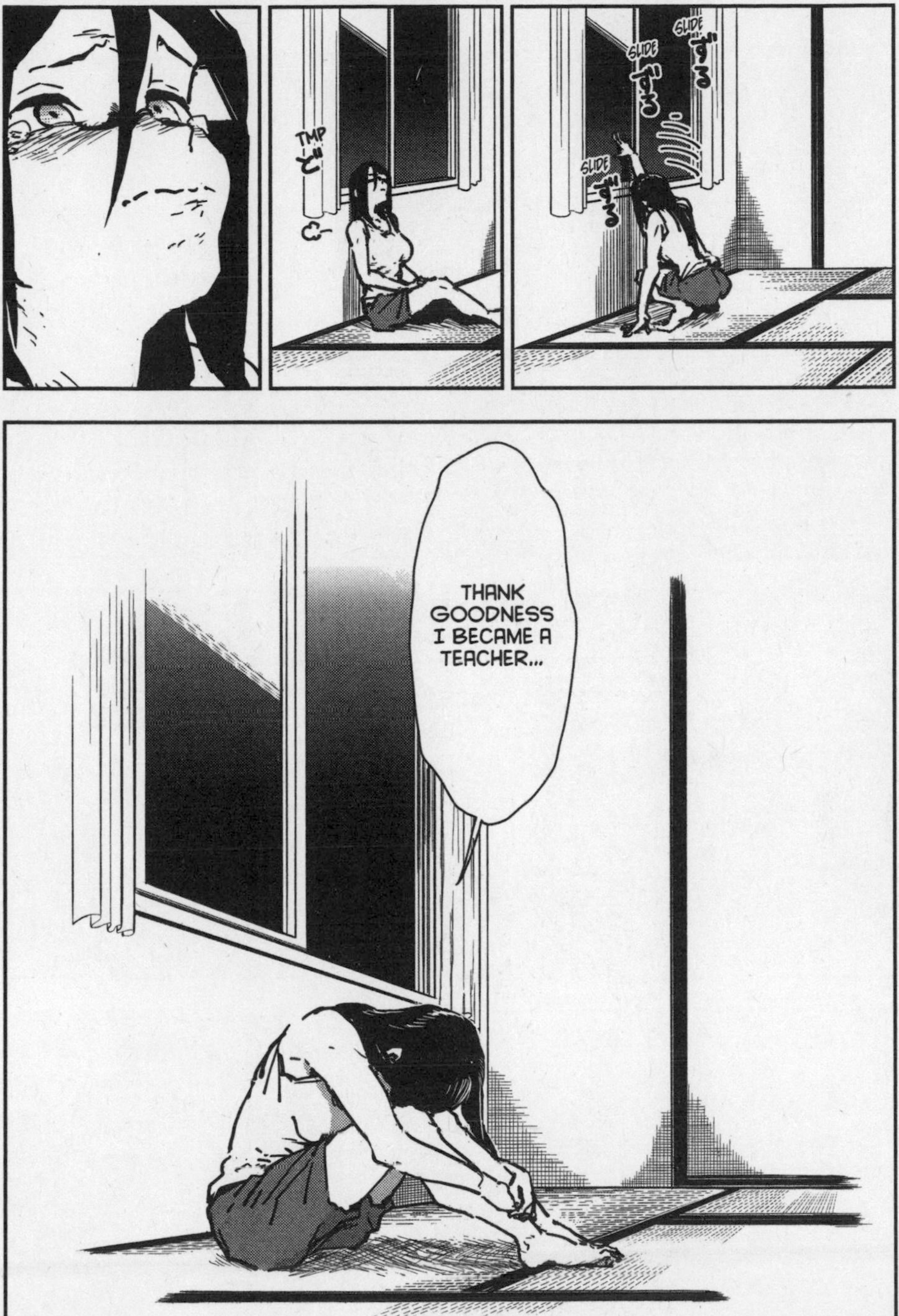
SLIDE ずる
SLIDE ずる
SLIDE ずる
TMP ど
THANK GOODNESS I BECAME A TEACHER...

VOLUME 6/END

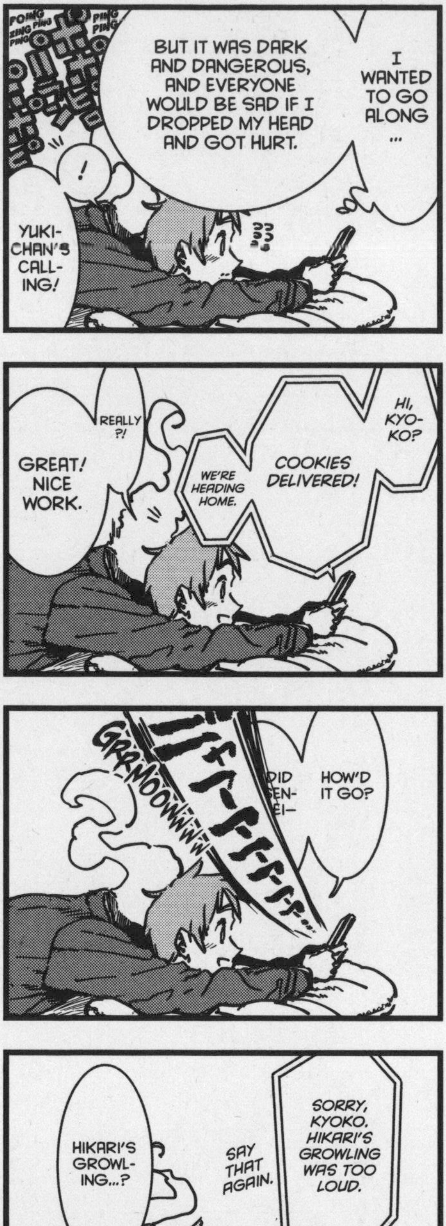
I WANTED TO GO ALONG ...
BUT IT WAS DARK AND DANGEROUS, AND EVERYONE WOULD BE SAD IF I DROPPED MY HEAD AND GOT HURT.
!
YUKI-CHAN'S CALL-ING!
HI, KYO-KO?
COOKIES DELIVERED!
WE'RE HEADING HOME.
REALLY ?!
GREAT! NICE WORK.
HOW'D IT GO?
DID SEN-
GRR-MOOWWWW
SORRY, KYOKO. HIKARI'S GROWLING WAS TOO LOUD.
SAY THAT AGAIN.
HIKARI'S GROWL-ING...?

INTERVIEWS WITH MONSTER GIRLS

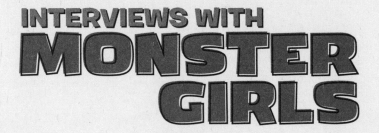

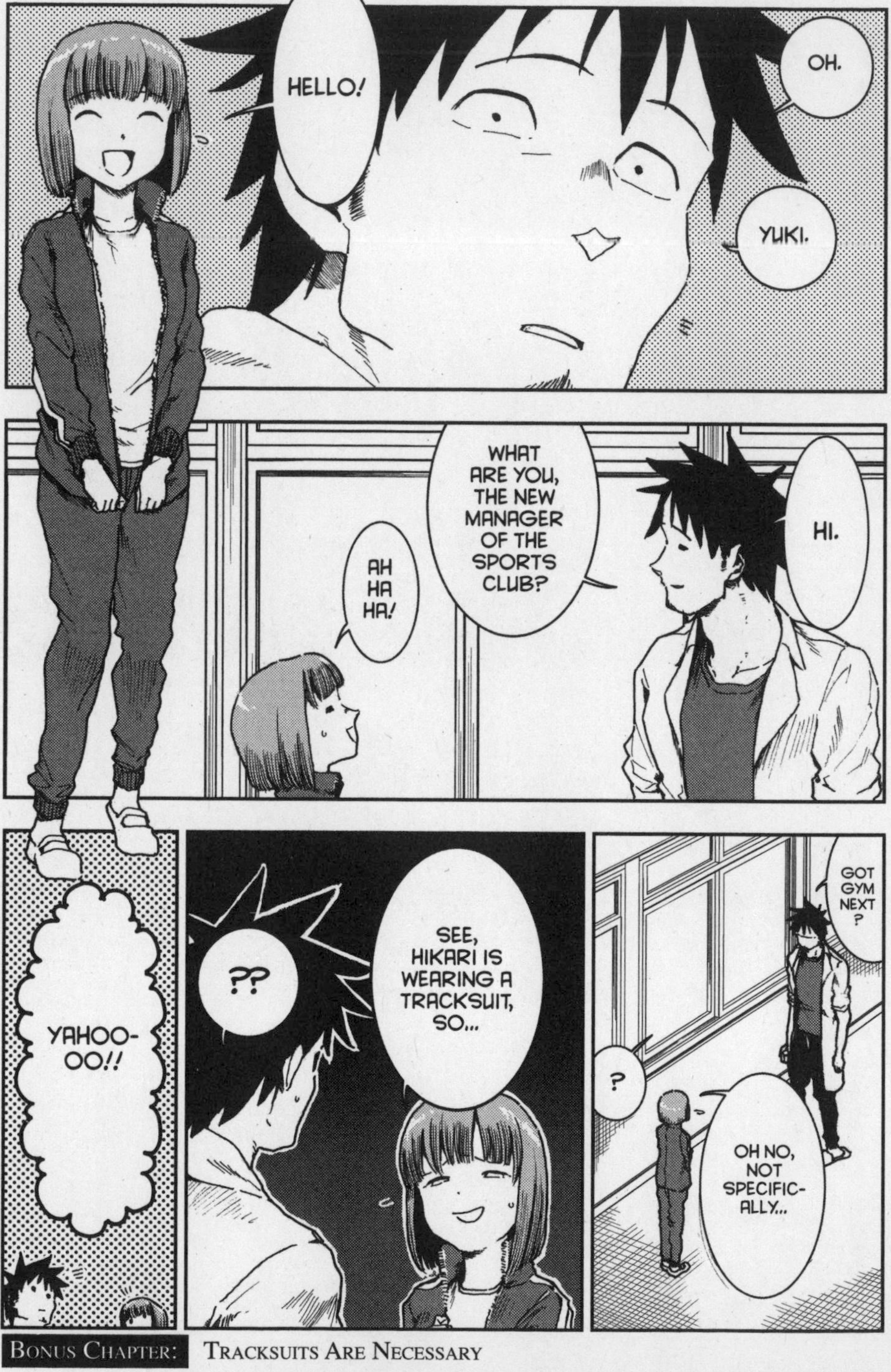
OH.
YUKI.
HELLO!
HI.
WHAT ARE YOU, THE NEW MANAGER OF THE SPORTS CLUB?
AH HA HA!
GOT GYM NEXT?
?
OH NO, NOT SPECIFIC-ALLY...
SEE, HIKARI IS WEARING A TRACKSUIT, SO...
??
YAHOO-OO!!

BONUS CHAPTER: TRACKSUITS ARE NECESSARY

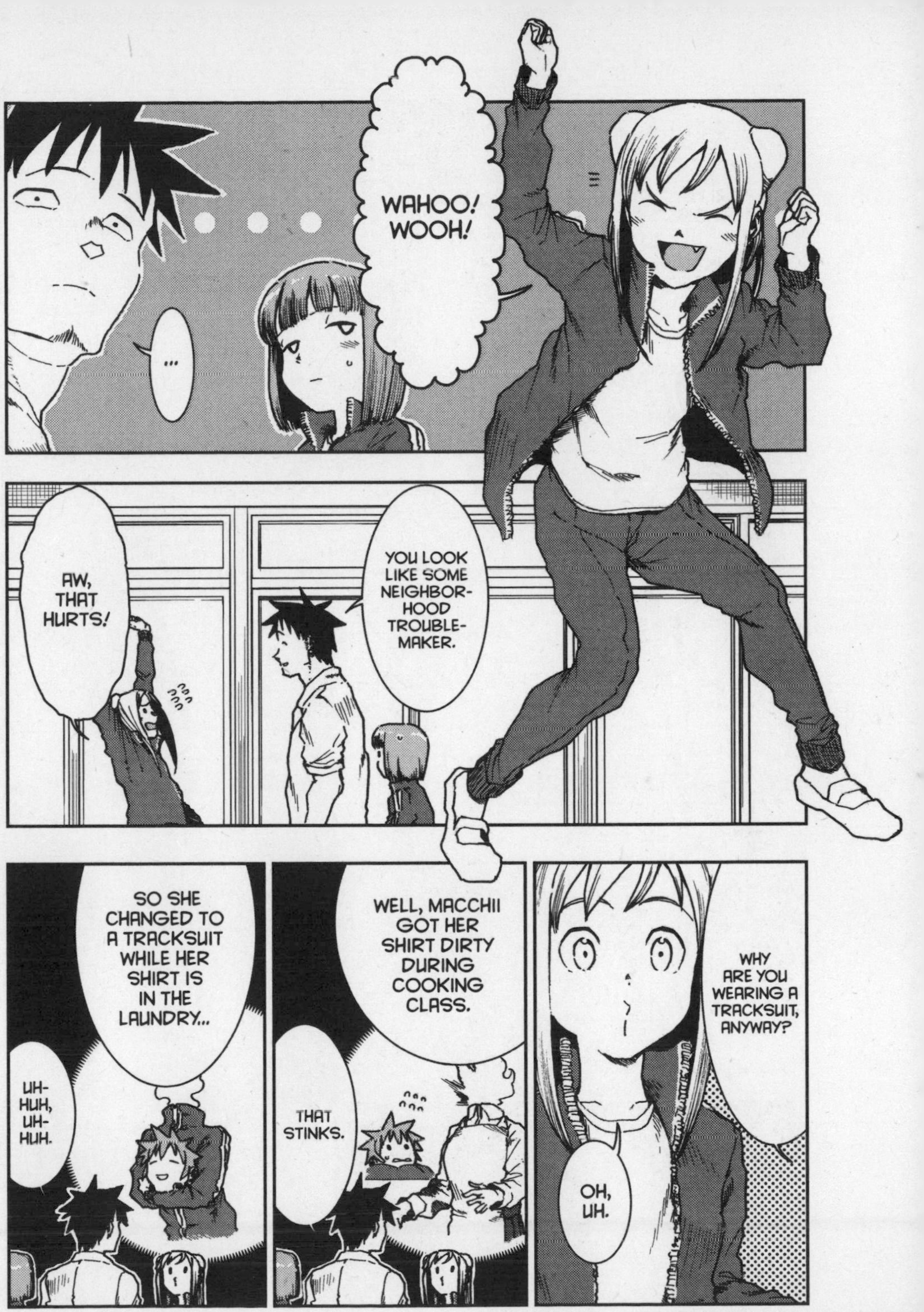
WAHOO! WOOH!
...
YOU LOOK LIKE SOME NEIGHBOR-HOOD TROUBLE-MAKER.
AW, THAT HURTS!
WHY ARE YOU WEARING A TRACKSUIT, ANYWAY?
OH, UH.
WELL, MACCHII GOT HER SHIRT DIRTY DURING COOKING CLASS.
THAT STINKS.
SO SHE CHANGED TO A TRACKSUIT WHILE HER SHIRT IS IN THE LAUNDRY...
UH-HUH, UH-HUH.

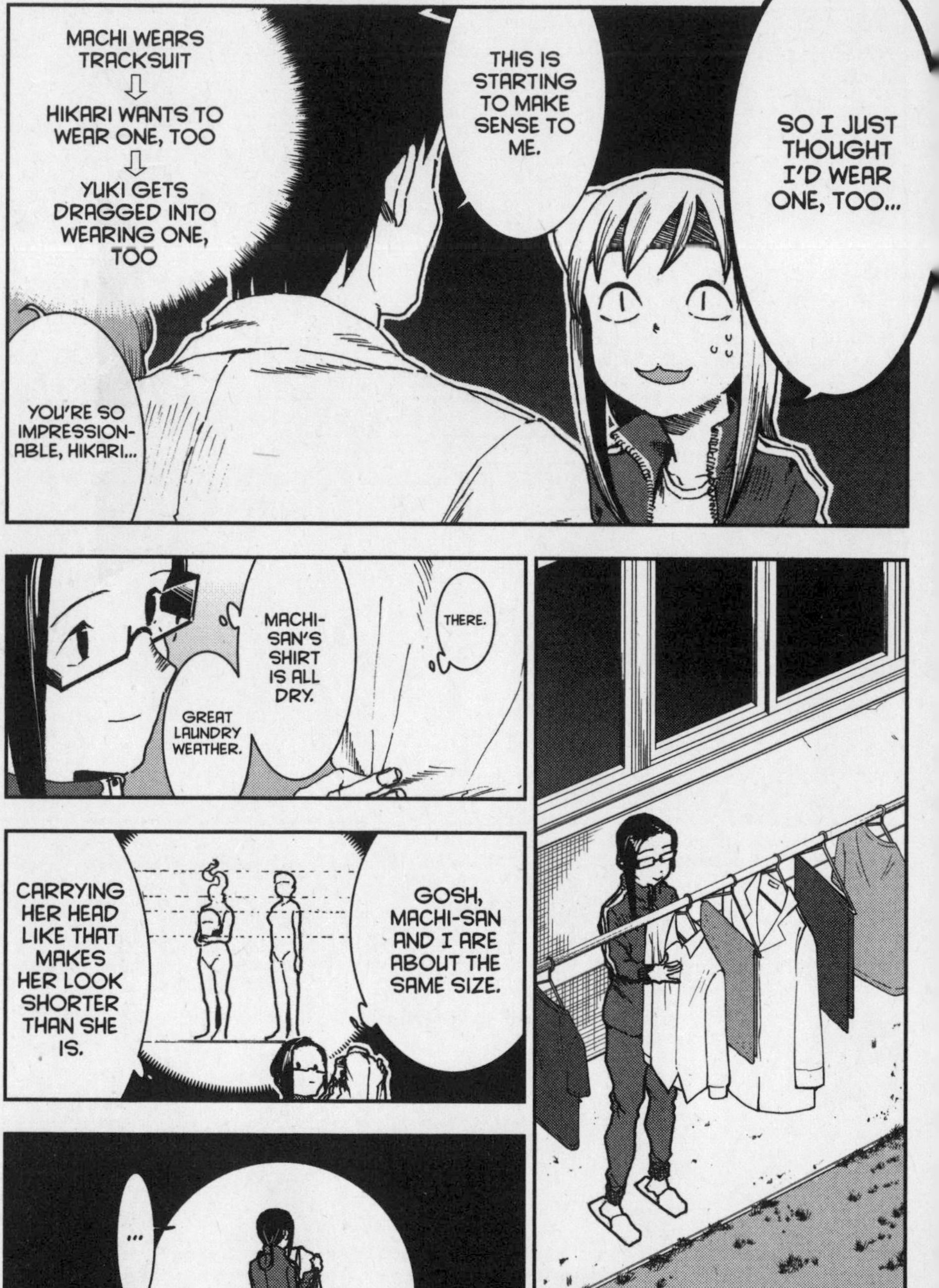
SO I JUST THOUGHT I'D WEAR ONE, TOO...
THIS IS STARTING TO MAKE SENSE TO ME.
MACHI WEARS TRACKSUIT ⇩ HIKARI WANTS TO WEAR ONE, TOO ⇩ YUKI GETS DRAGGED INTO WEARING ONE, TOO
YOU'RE SO IMPRESSIONABLE, HIKARI...
THERE.
MACHI-SAN'S SHIRT IS ALL DRY.
GREAT LAUNDRY WEATHER.
GOSH, MACHI-SAN AND I ARE ABOUT THE SAME SIZE.
CARRYING HER HEAD LIKE THAT MAKES HER LOOK SHORTER THAN SHE IS.
...

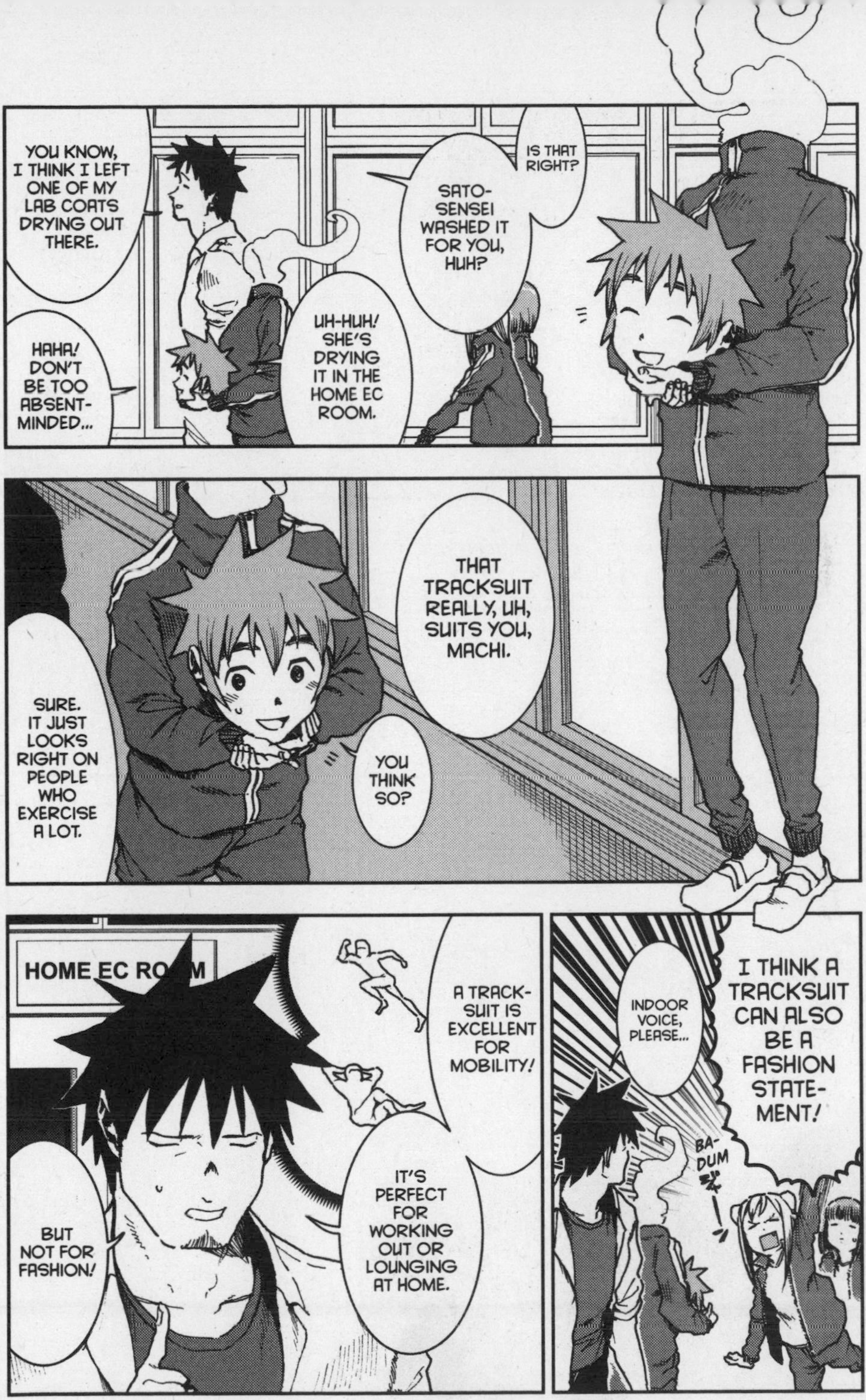

IS THAT RIGHT?
SATO-SENSEI WASHED IT FOR YOU, HUH?
UH-HUH! SHE'S DRYING IT IN THE HOME EC ROOM.
YOU KNOW, I THINK I LEFT ONE OF MY LAB COATS DRYING OUT THERE.
HAHA! DON'T BE TOO ABSENT-MINDED...
THAT TRACKSUIT REALLY, UH, SUITS YOU, MACHI.
YOU THINK SO?
SURE. IT JUST LOOKS RIGHT ON PEOPLE WHO EXERCISE A LOT.
I THINK A TRACKSUIT CAN ALSO BE A FASHION STATEMENT!
INDOOR VOICE, PLEASE...
BA-DUM
HOME EC ROOM
A TRACK-SUIT IS EXCELLENT FOR MOBILITY!
IT'S PERFECT FOR WORKING OUT OR LOUNGING AT HOME.
BUT NOT FOR FASHION!

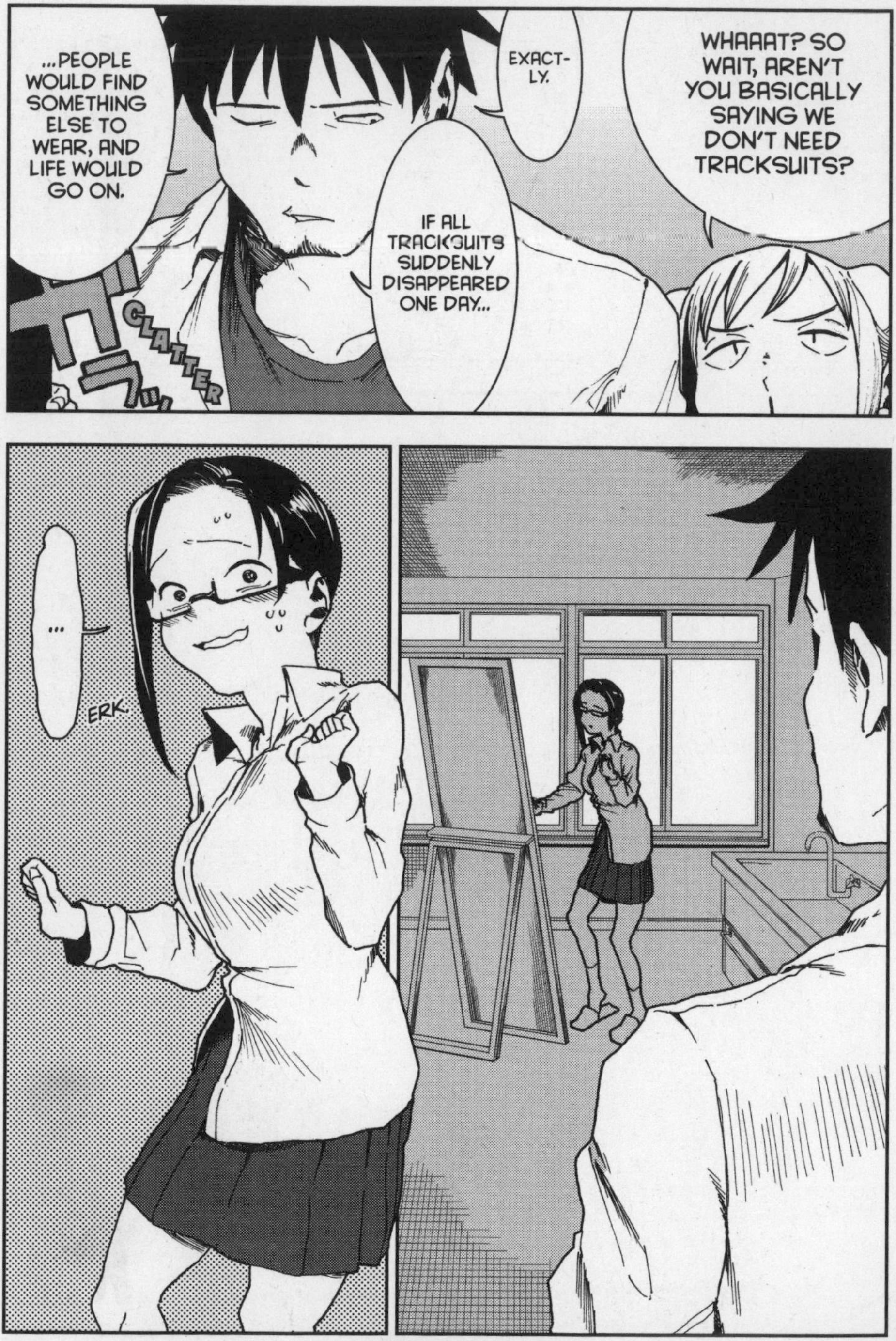
WHAAAT? SO WAIT, AREN'T YOU BASICALLY SAYING WE DON'T NEED TRACKSUITS?
EXACT-LY.
IF ALL TRACKSUITS SUDDENLY DISAPPEARED ONE DAY...
...PEOPLE WOULD FIND SOMETHING ELSE TO WEAR, AND LIFE WOULD GO ON.
CLATTER
...
ERK

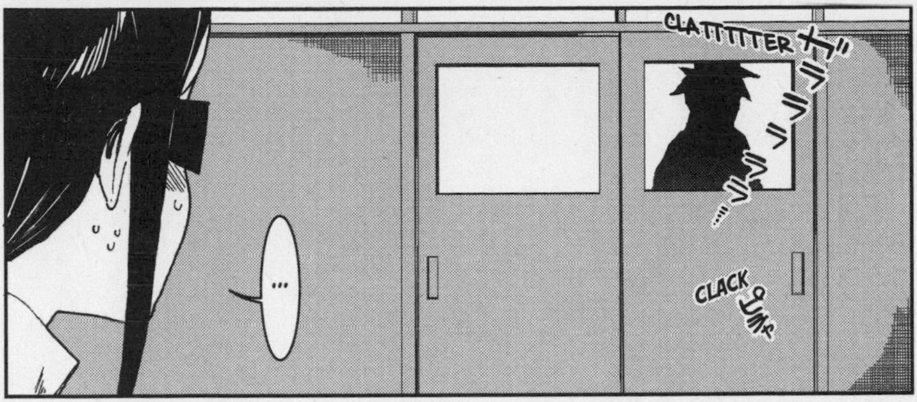
CLATTTTTER
CLACK
...

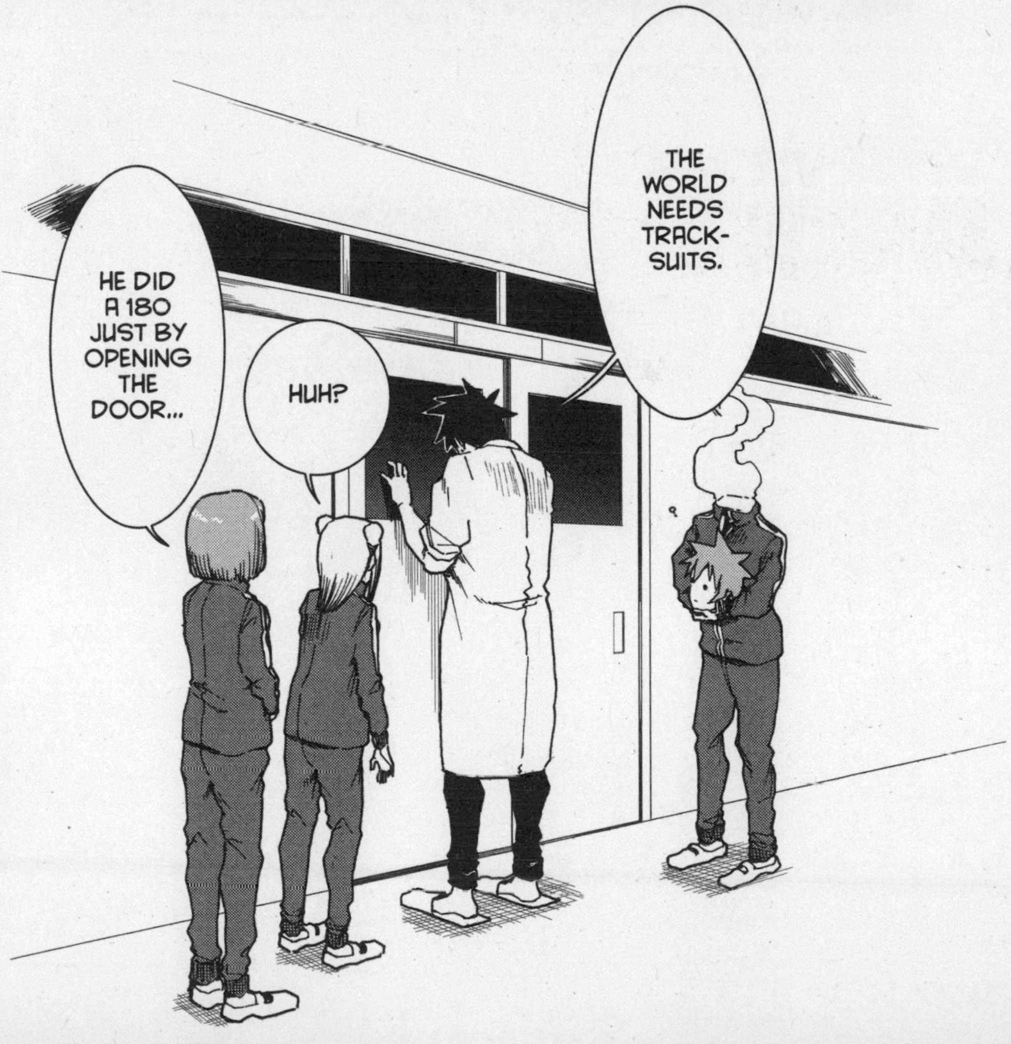
THE WORLD NEEDS TRACK-SUITS.
HUH?
HE DID A 180 JUST BY OPENING THE DOOR...

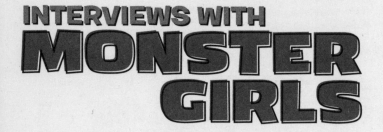

INTERVIEWS WITH MONSTER GIRLS

TRANSLATION NOTES

Tohoku, page 3
Tohoku is the northeastern region of Japan's main island of Honshu.

Six Mats, page 5
The floor space of Japanese rooms is commonly measured in *-jou*, or *tatami* mats. The chapter title actually refers to a *rokujouma* or "six-mat room"; six *jou* would be roughly nine square meters or about 96 square feet.

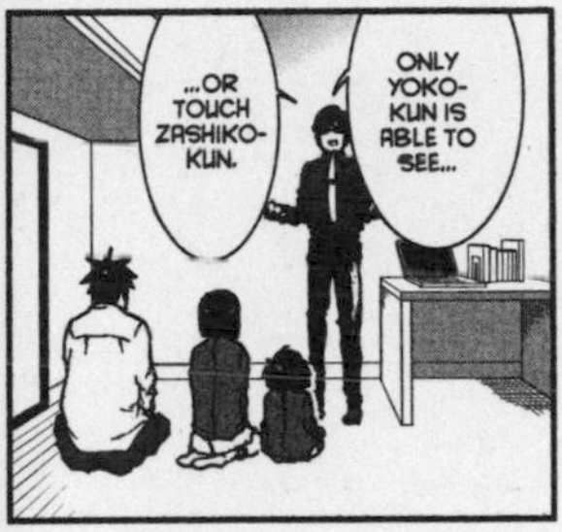
ONLY YOKO-KUN IS ABLE TO SEE...
...OR TOUCH ZASHIKO-KUN.

Yoko-kun and Zashiko-kun, page 14
Though the -kun suffix is mostly used for men, it is sometimes used to refer to women with whom the speaker works or knows in a professional context. Soma-sensei seems to use it universally.

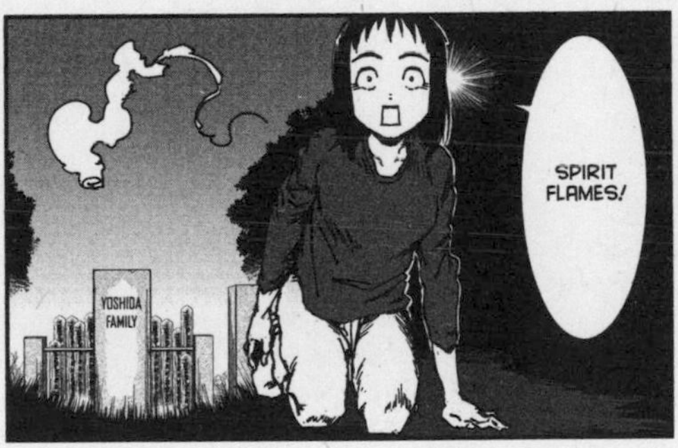
SPIRIT FLAMES!
YOSHIDA FAMILY

Spirit Flames, page 36
Hitodama (literally, "human souls") are bluish flames said to be the spirits of the dead. Don't confuse these with *kitsunebi*, or foxfire: small, blue lights carried by foxes in Japanese myth.

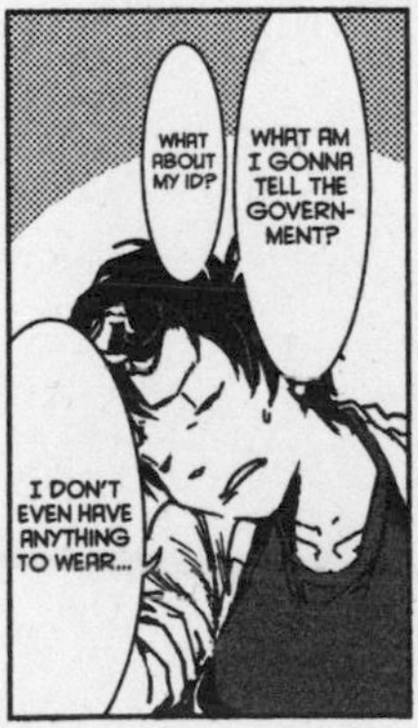
WHAT AM I GONNA TELL THE GOVERNMENT?
WHAT ABOUT MY ID?
I DON'T EVEN HAVE ANYTHING TO WEAR...

ID, page 52
In Japan, everyone has a *koseki*, or family register, which records details of births, deaths, marriages, and so on. In principle, it also specifies each family member's gender.

Izakaya, page 67
An *izakaya* is a traditional Japanese eating establishment. They serve soft and hard drinks, along with a variety of foods heavier than snacks but lighter than meals (think chicken wings).

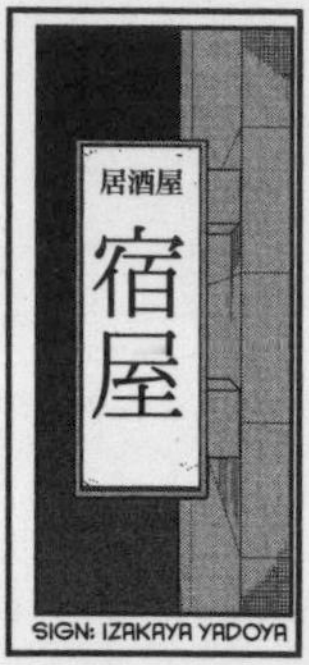
居酒屋
宿屋
SIGN: IZAKAYA YADOYA

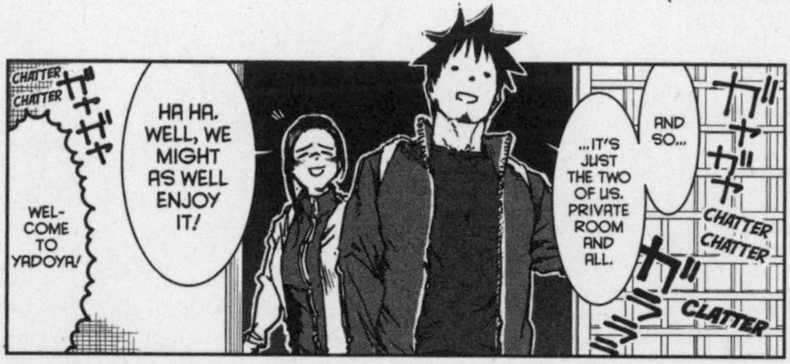
AND SO...
...IT'S JUST THE TWO OF US. PRIVATE ROOM AND ALL.
CHATTER CHATTER
CLATTER
HA HA. WELL, WE MIGHT AS WELL ENJOY IT!
CHATTER CHATTER
WEL-COME TO YADOYA!

Welcome, page 67
The staff in most Japanese shops, stores, and restaurants greet customers as they enter with some form of the phrase *irasshaimase!*, a polite expression roughly meaning, "come in!"

Private Room, page 67
Seating in an *izakaya* is usually in an open dining area, much like most restaurants. However, a handful of individual rooms are often available for parties, functions, or customers who want some privacy.

I Insist, page 67
Tetsuo invites Sakie to sit at the *kamiza*, literally meaning "the upper [or top] seat" but figuratively the place of honor, and is the seat farthest from the door. In general, the person of the highest social rank sits here—if a group of teachers were going out, for example, the most senior might take the *kamiza*, or the school principal if he were present. As both the older and more experienced colleague, Tetsuo arguably has the right to the *kamiza*, but he kindly offers it to Sakie instead.

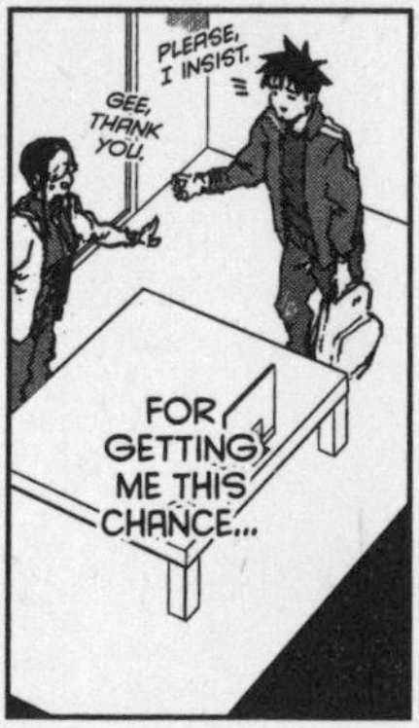
PLEASE, I INSIST.
GEE, THANK YOU.
FOR GETTING ME THIS CHANCE...

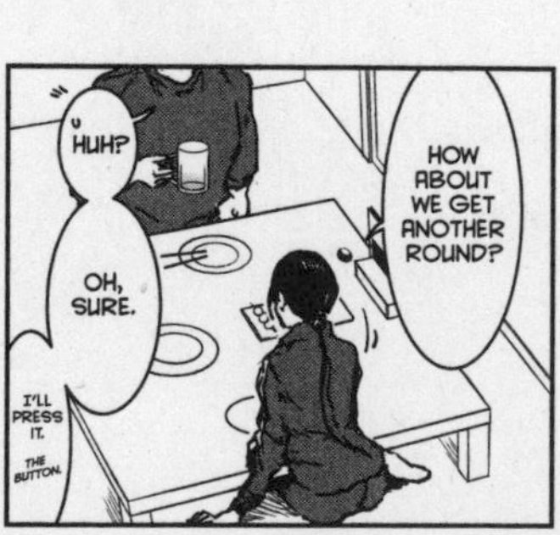
HOW ABOUT WE GET ANOTHER ROUND?
HUH?
OH, SURE.
I'LL PRESS IT.
THE BUTTON.

The Button, page 75
In many *izakaya* and similar restaurants, patrons press a chime button at the table to call a server.

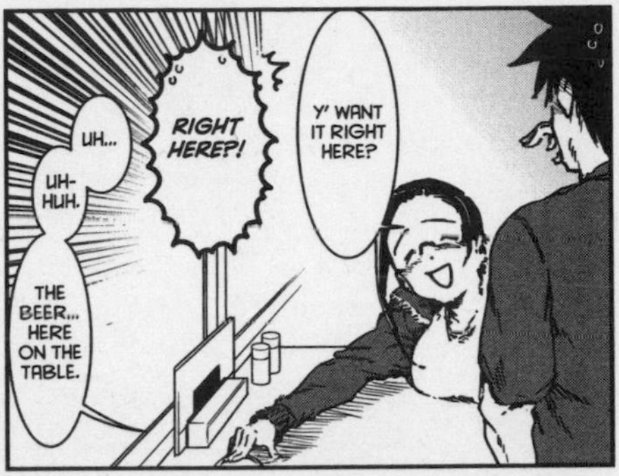
Y' WANT IT RIGHT HERE?
RIGHT HERE?!
UH...
UH-HUH.
THE BEER... HERE ON THE TABLE.

Right Here, page 76

In the Japanese, Sakie asks if Tetsuo is "okay with *nama*." *Nama* literally means "raw," and at a bar it means "draft beer" (*nama biiru*), which Sakie clarifies a couple of word balloons later. Tetsuo, however, most likely (if briefly) thinks she means *nama* in its slang sense of "unprotected sex."

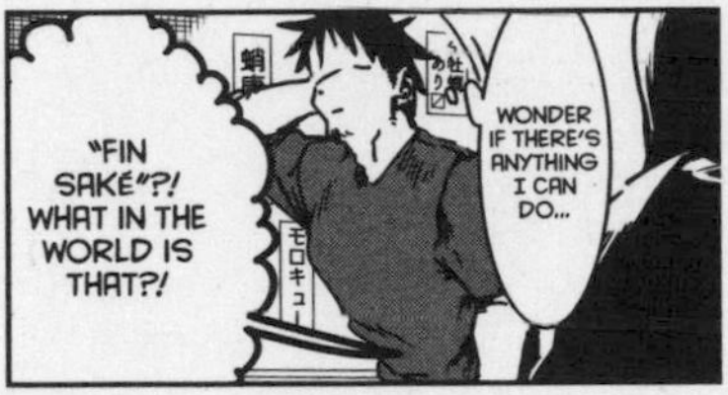
WONDER IF THERE'S ANYTHING I CAN DO...
"FIN SAKÉ"?! WHAT IN THE WORLD IS THAT?!

Fin Saké, page 79

Hire-zake is actually Japanese rice wine with the fin of a *fugu* (blowfish) steeping in it. The fin gives the wine a savory flavor.

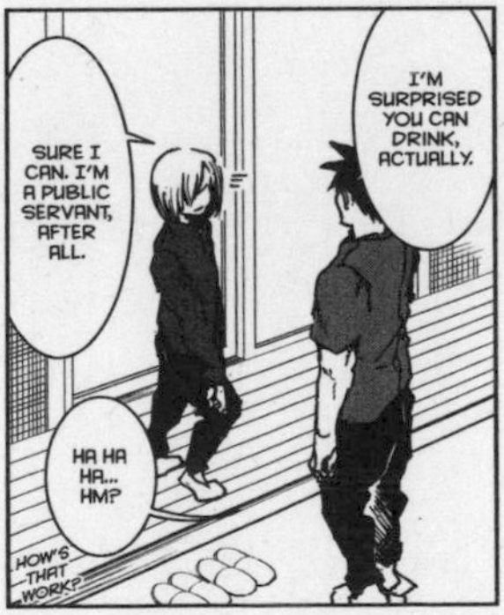
I'M SURPRISED YOU CAN DRINK, ACTUALLY.
SURE I CAN. I'M A PUBLIC SERVANT, AFTER ALL.
HA HA HA... HM?
HOW'S THAT WORK?

Surprised You Can Drink, page 85

The legal age for alcohol consumption in Japan is 20. Incidentally, notice how both characters are wearing indoor slippers provided by the *izakaya*, having left their shoes somewhere else (perhaps at the entrance to the restaurant). This is a common practice in many traditional restaurants and *izakaya*.

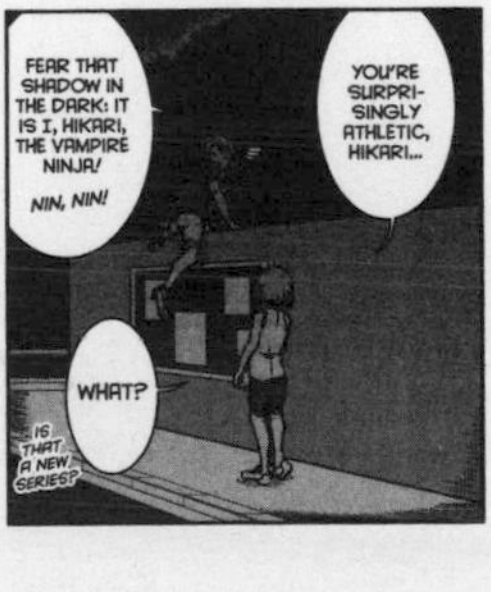
YOU'RE SURPRI-SINGLY ATHLETIC, HIKARI...
FEAR THAT SHADOW IN THE DARK: IT IS I, HIKARI, THE VAMPIRE NINJA!
NIN, NIN!
WHAT?
IS THAT A NEW SERIES?

Nin, Nin, page 115

Just a simple ninja-based sound gag.

INTERVIEWS WITH
MONSTER
GIRLS

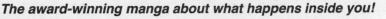
ANIME COMING SUMMER 2018

The award-winning manga about what happens inside you!

"Far more entertaining than it ought to be... What kid doesn't want to think that every time they sneeze, a torpedo shoots out their nose?"

—Anime News Network

Strep throat! Hay fever! Influenza! The world is a dangerous place for a red blood cell just trying to get her deliveries finished. Fortunately, she's not alone. She's got a whole human body's worth of cells ready to help out! The mysterious white blood cell, the buff and brash killer T cell, the nerdy neuron, even the cute little platelets—everyone's got to come together if they want to keep you healthy!

Cells at Work!

By Akane Shimizu

KODANSHA COMICS

Japan's most powerful spirit medium delves into the ghost world's greatest mysteries!

Story by Kyo Shirodaira, famed author of mystery fiction and creator of *Spiral*, *Blast of Tempest*, and *The Record of a Fallen Vampire*.

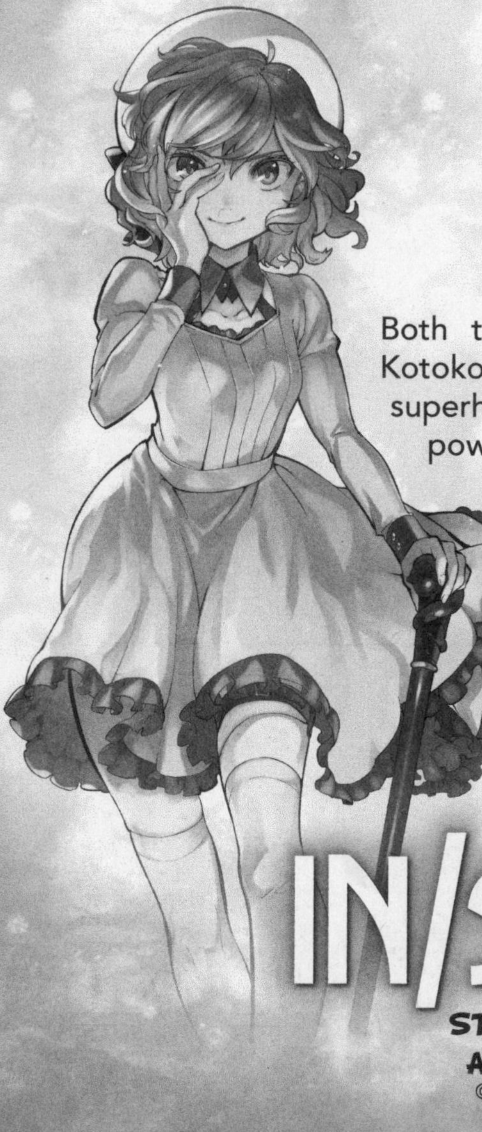

Both touched by spirits called yôkai, Kotoko and Kurô have gained unique superhuman powers. But to gain her powers Kotoko has given up an eye and a leg, and Kurô's personal life is in shambles. So when Kotoko suggests they team up to deal with renegades from the spirit world, Kurô doesn't have many other choices, but Kotoko might just have a few ulterior motives...

IN/SPECTRE

STORY BY KYO SHIRODAIRA
ART BY CHASHIBA KATASE

In love, there are
no save points.

ヲタクに恋は難しい

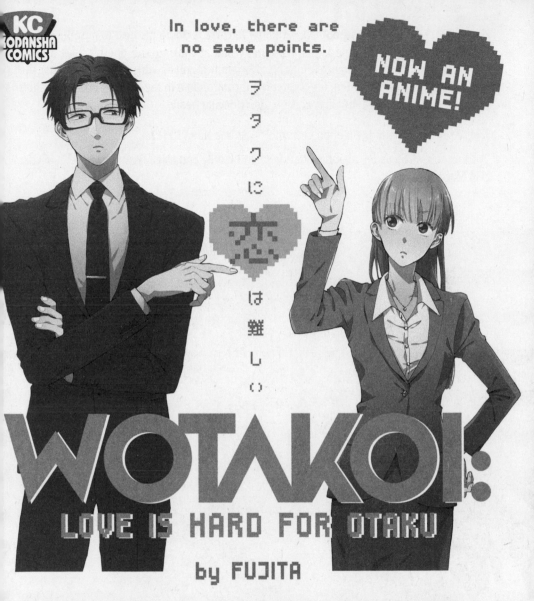

WOTAKOI:
LOVE IS HARD FOR OTAKU
by FUJITA

Narumi has had it rough: Every boyfriend she's had dumped her once they found out she was an otaku, so she's gone to great lengths to hide it. At her new job, she bumps into Hirotaka, her childhood friend and fellow otaku. When Hirotaka almost gets her secret outed at work, she comes up with a plan to keep him quiet. But he comes up with a counter-proposal: Why doesn't she just date him instead?

KC KODANSHA COMICS

Having lost his wife, high school teacher Kōhei Inuzuka is doing his best to raise his young daughter Tsumugi as a single father. He's pretty bad at cooking and doesn't have a huge appetite to begin with, but chance brings his little family together with one of his students, the lonely Kotori. The three of them are anything but comfortable in the kitchen, but the healing power of home cooking might just work on their grieving hearts.

"This season's number-one feel-good anime!" —Anime News Network

"A beautifully-drawn story about comfort food and family and grief. Recommended." —Otaku USA Magazine

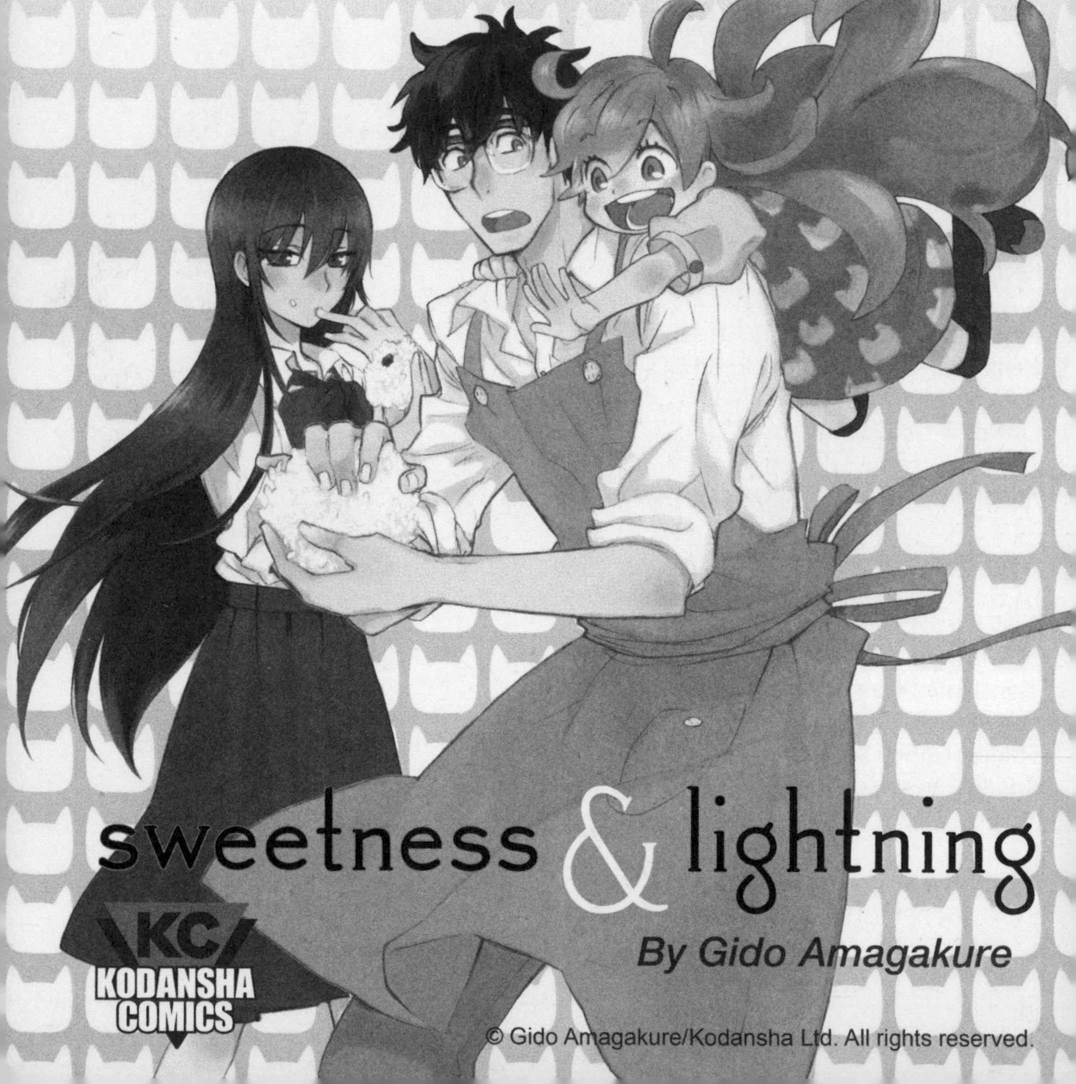
sweetness & lightning
KC
KODANSHA COMICS
By Gido Amagakure

Interviews with Monster Girls volume 6 is a work of fiction. Names, characters, places, and incidents are the products of the author's imagination or are used fictitiously. Any resemblance to actual events, locales, or persons, living or dead, is entirely coincidental.

A Kodansha Comics Trade Paperback Original.

Interviews with Monster Girls volume 6 copyright © 2018 Petos
English translation copyright © 2018 Petos

Published in the United States by Kodansha Comics, an imprint of Kodansha USA Publishing, LLC, New York.

Publication rights for this English edition arranged through Kodansha Ltd., Tokyo.

First published in Japan in 2018 by Kodansha Ltd., Tokyo, as *Demi-chan wa Kataritai*, volume 6.

ISBN 978-1-63236-487-6

Printed in the United States of America.

www.kodanshacomics.com

9 8 7 6 5 4 3 2 1

Translation: Kevin Steinbach
Lettering: Paige Pumphrey
Editing: Lauren Scanlan
Kodansha Comics edition cover design: Phil Balsman